45 Strategies
That Support Young
Dual Language Learners

45 Strategies That Support Young Dual Language Learners

by

Shauna L. Tominey, Ph.D.
Assistant Professor of Practice
Parenting Education Specialist
Oregon State University
Corvallis, Oregon

and

Elisabeth C. O'Bryon, Ph.D.
Co-founder and Head of Research
Family Engagement Lab
Oakland, California

PAUL H. BROOKES PUBLISHING CO.

Baltimore • London • Sydney

Paul H. Brookes Publishing Co.
Post Office Box 10624
Baltimore, Maryland 21285-0624
USA

www.brookespublishing.com

Copyright © 2018 by Paul H. Brookes Publishing Co., Inc.
All rights reserved.

"Paul H. Brookes Publishing Co." is a registered trademark of
Paul H. Brookes Publishing Co., Inc.

Typeset by Progressive Publishing Services, York, Pennsylvania.
Manufactured in the United States of America by Sheridan Books, Chelsea, Michigan.

All examples in this book are composites. Any similarity to actual individuals or circumstances is coincidental, and no implications should be inferred.

Purchasers of *45 Strategies That Support Young Dual Language Learners* are granted permission to download, print, and photocopy the forms in the text for educational purposes. These forms may not be reproduced to generate revenue for any program or individual. Photocopies may only be made from an original book. *Unauthorized use beyond this privilege may be prosecutable under federal law.* You will see the copyright protection notice at the bottom of each photocopiable page.

Library of Congress Cataloging-in-Publication Data

Names: Tominey, Shauna, author. | O'Bryon, Elisabeth C., author.
Title: 45 strategies that support young dual language learners / by Shauna L.
 Tominey, Ph.D. and Elisabeth C. O'Bryon, Ph.D.
Other titles: Forty-five strategies that support young dual language learners
Description: Baltimore, Maryland: Paul H. Brookes Publishing, [2017] |
 Includes bibliographical references and index.
Identifiers: LCCN 2017020186 (print) | LCCN 2017039442 (ebook) | ISBN
 9781681252513 (pdf) | ISBN 9781681252506 (epub) | ISBN 9781681250434
 (paperback)
Subjects: LCSH: Bilingualism in children. | Education, Bilingual. | Early
 childhood education. | Multicultural education. | BISAC: EDUCATION /
 Bilingual Education. | EDUCATION / Multicultural Education. | EDUCATION /
 Preschool & Kindergarten.
Classification: LCC LC3723 (ebook) | LCC LC3723 .T66 2018 (print) | DDC
 370.117—dc23
LC record available at https://lccn.loc.gov/2017020186

British Library Cataloguing in Publication data are available from the British Library.

2021 2020 2019 2018 2017

10   9   8   7   6   5   4   3   2   1

Contents

About the Downloads..ix

About the Authors..xi

Foreword   *Guadalupe Díaz*..xiii

Note to the Reader...xv

Acknowledgments...xvii

1. **Introduction to Dual Language Learners**..1

2. **Getting Started: Foundations for Supporting Dual Language Learners**...9
    Strategy 1: Get Comfortable with Key Terms and Definitions................................12
    Strategy 2: Expand Your Knowledge of Dual Language Learners and Their Families..13
    Strategy 3: Understand the Benefits of Being a Dual Language Learner...............17
    Strategy 4: Support Development of the Home Language and English.................19
    Strategy 5: Implement Culturally Responsive Teaching Practices........................20

3. **Setting Up Your Classroom to Support Dual Language Learners**..27
    Strategy 6: Get to Know the Children in Your Class and Their Families...............29
    Strategy 7: Establish a Welcoming Learning Environment..................................30
    Strategy 8: Organize the Classroom to Support Success......................................33
    Strategy 9: Embed Best Practices...35
    Appendix 3.1 Vocabulary Word Lists..42
    Appendix 3.2 Sample Parent Questionnaire in English..50
    Appendix 3.3 Sample Parent Questionnaire in Spanish.......................................51

4. **Fostering a Classroom Community of Diverse Learners**.....................53
    Strategy 10: Set the Foundation for Warm and Trusting Relationships................55
    Strategy 11: Anticipate Children's Challenges and Needs....................................57
    Strategy 12: Create a Classroom Community..61
    Strategy 13: Frame Diversity as a Strength..62
    Appendix 4.1 Identifying Student Needs..72

5. **Using Classroom Management Practices That Support Diverse Learners**..73
    Strategy 14: Narrate Children's Actions to Promote Self-Regulation and Language Development..75
    Strategy 15: Apply Best Practices to Classroom Management.............................76

Strategy 16: Plan and Support Transitions...78
Strategy 17: Be a Positive Role Model for Behavior Standards.................................79
Strategy 18: Keep a Sense of Humor and Be Flexible...80

6. Supporting Social and Emotional Learning for Dual Language Learners 87
Strategy 19: Create an Emotionally Supportive Classroom....................................89
Strategy 20: Recognize and Scaffold Children's Social and Emotional Needs...92
Strategy 21: Teach Social and Emotional Skills..93
Strategy 22: Support Social and Emotional Development in English and in Each Child's Home Language 95
Strategy 23: Involve Families in Children's Social and Emotional Learning 96
Strategy 24: Use a Growth Mindset to Teach Social and Emotional Skills 97
Appendix 6.1 Vocabulary Word List 104

7. Enhancing Early Academic Skills for Dual Language Learners 105
Strategy 25: Make Learning Activities Accessible to Diverse Learners......................107
Strategy 26: Embed Best Practices into Read-Alouds 108
Strategy 27: Embed Best Practices into Math and Science Activities........................110
Strategy 28: Draw Connections Between Activities and Children's Home Language and Culture 112
Strategy 29: Engage Families in Children's Learning 113
Appendix 7.1 Vocabulary Word Lists 123
Appendix 7.2 Books for the Dual Language Learner Classroom...............................126

8 Engaging Dual Language Learners Through Music and Movement...129
Strategy 30: Learn About Culture Through Music and Movement..............................131
Strategy 31: Invite Children and Families to Share Music with the Classroom..............132
Strategy 32: Share Classroom Music with Families 133
Strategy 33: Build Children's Vocabulary and Early Literacy Skills Through Music..134
Appendix 8.1 Music Vocabulary 141
Appendix 8.2 Children's Songs in English and Spanish......................................142

9 Engaging Families from Diverse Backgrounds............................145
Strategy 34: Help Children Prepare for the Transition to School...........................148
Strategy 35: Promote Regular Communication with Families 149
Strategy 36: Provide Families with Ways to be Engaged in School 150
Strategy 37: Approach Challenging Conversations with Empathy and Understanding 153
Strategy 38: Ask Families For Feedback 154

10 Continuing to Grow Through Professional Development....................159
Strategy 39: Develop Cultural Awareness and Adopt Self-Reflective Practices 160
Strategy 40: Expand Your Multicultural Knowledge 162
Strategy 41: Participate in Professional Development Activities..........................163
Strategy 42: Learn How to Effectively Conduct Assessments 164

Strategy 43: Involve Families in Decisions Related to Assessments 167
Strategy 44: Understand Mandated Reporting Laws and Regulations...................... 168
Strategy 45: Think of Yourself as a Lifelong Learner 169

Glossary..177

Quiz Answer Key 181

Multicultural Library List 189

References 191

Index.. 197

About the Downloads

Purchasers of this book may download, print, and/or photocopy the blank forms in this book for educational use. These materials are included with the print book and are also available at http://www.brookespublishing.com/tominey/materials for both print and e-book buyers.

About the Authors

Shauna Tominey, Ph.D., is an assistant professor of practice and parenting education specialist at Oregon State University. She previously served as Director of Early Childhood Programming and Teacher Education at the Yale Center for Emotional Intelligence. She brings her previous experiences as an early childhood educator and parenting educator to her research, which focuses on the development of programs that promote social and emotional skills for children and adults. Shauna holds undergraduate degrees in music and psychology from the University of Washington, an M.S. in family studies and human services from Kansas State University, and a Ph.D. in human development and family sciences from Oregon State University.

Elisabeth O'Bryon, Ph.D., is a co-founder and Head of Research at Family Engagement Lab, a nonprofit that helps schools ignite the power of families to support learning. Previously, she was Director of Research and Evaluation at GreatSchools. Elisabeth holds an undergraduate degree in Psychology from Hamilton College and a Ph.D. in psychology, with a specialization in school psychology, from the University of Rhode Island. She received postdoctoral training at the Yale Center for Emotional Intelligence. Her research has focused on how to promote the educational success of students identified as English language learners, as well as ways to support home–school partnerships with culturally and linguistically diverse families.

Foreword

Engaging and supporting dual language learners (DLLs) and their families has become a critical component of being a teacher. As a parent, a researcher, a DLL and a teacher, I am all too familiar with the excitement and challenges of engaging and supporting DLLs: As a parent, I experienced the hesitation of coming into the classroom to ask questions. As a researcher, I continuously explore the challenges faced by DLLs and their families and strive to find ways to better understand and inform their learning needs. As a DLL, I remember the confusion and fear of being in a classroom where I could not understand what others said. Finally, as a former teacher, I can still remember the DLLs in my classroom and the multiple times I was unsuccessful at addressing their academic and social needs. I also remember feeling the need to connect with families but hesitating out of fear of unknowingly offending them. The issues we face in supporting DLLs and their families extend beyond language and involve reflecting on our own beliefs and culture, recognizing our own bias, and understanding beliefs and cultures different from our own.

This book provides an introduction to engaging and supporting DLLs and their families in a way that goes beyond simply addressing children's language needs. Tominey and O'Bryon take a comprehensive, strengths-based approach to supporting dual language learners by providing 45 effective strategies that acknowledge the assets dual language learners and families bring into classrooms and that address the challenges families experience in navigating an unfamiliar school system.

These 45 strategies address a range of issues faced by teachers that can be used regardless of what languages are spoken by the DLLs in the classroom. For each of the recommended strategies, a real-world example is provided that illustrates the daily experiences of children, teachers, and their parents. Tominey and O'Bryon offer guidance for implementing the strategies and explain the benefits that dual language learners and their families receive. For example, throughout the book, readers are reminded not to take the "tourist approach" by limiting acknowledgement of DLLs and their families to holidays, artifacts, and celebrations. This recommendation provides a foundation for engaging DLLs and their families and reminds readers of the importance of continuously embracing and recognizing the assets that these families bring to the classroom. Additionally, Tominey and O'Bryon provide readers with strategies to connect with families to understand the challenges they face navigating the classroom and community. This book serves as a key resource in the educator's tool box for engaging dual language learners and their families as part of a continuous effort to improve professional development.

The authors outline effective strategies and the resources to implement these strategies to address the academic, social, and emotional learning needs of DLLs. In addition, Tominey and O'Bryon acknowledge that while there will be some missteps as educators learn how best to support DLLs and their families, it's important to forgive one's self and move forward. As the authors emphasize, effectively engaging dual language learners should include a continuous process of reflecting on successes or missteps. Being able to learn from both can help enhance educators' efforts to engage DLLs and encourage their families to feel welcome in the classroom.

Guadalupe Díaz, Ph.D.
University of California, Irvine

Note to the Reader

Thank you for taking an important step toward expanding your strategies for supporting DLLs by reading this book. We are so excited to share ideas and resources that we hope will add to your toolbox for supporting children and families.

Each of us came to this book from a different set of experiences. Elisabeth grew up in a multicultural family and attended a Spanish immersion school, experiencing first-hand the benefits and challenges of being a DLL herself. Shauna also grew up in a multicultural family and heard many different languages spoken during her childhood, including Mandarin and Taiwanese. She valued the exposure to a range of cultural traditions and values but also witnessed the challenges that can occur when communication barriers exist.

These early experiences shaped each of our professional careers, and in 2012 we met at the Yale Center for Emotional Intelligence. Together, we worked on a team developing a social-emotional learning program called Preschool RULER. One of the challenges the team faced was that many teachers struggled to implement the intervention with children who did not speak English. Our team provided Spanish translations for many of the intervention materials, but we quickly realized that this was not enough. Many teachers shared that they wanted additional support and training on strategies for supporting DLLs. Teachers also shared that it was challenging to engage families, especially those from diverse cultural and linguistic backgrounds. It was from these shared experiences that we decided to write this book.

Our goal in writing this book is to share practical strategies for supporting DLLs that can be used in early childhood learning settings, whether center-based or home-based, by administrators or teachers at any stage in their education or career. In this book, you will find 45 strategies for supporting DLLs and their families in early childhood learning settings. These strategies are divided across 10 chapters. Each chapter includes a set of reflection questions, which can be used to discuss the content of the book in group settings or to reflect individually on your own experiences and teaching practices. You can also check your learning by taking the end-of-chapter quizzes (which start in Chapter 2) and learn more about each chapter's topics by exploring the lists of additional resources provided.

We hope you will put strategies into action in your own classroom by using the classroom activities found at the end of chapters 3–8. Each activity emphasizes ways to include best practices for supporting DLLs as well as culturally responsive practices, which emphasize the importance of adapting best practices to meet the needs of children and families from diverse backgrounds. And finally, be sure to check out the appendices, which include rich supplemental information such as sample parent questionnaires in English and Spanish and vocabulary word lists. Chapter quizzes, reflection questions, activities, resources, and appendices are included in the book and are also available for download in printable formats.

Whether you are an early childhood education student, educator, administrator, or faculty member preparing the next generation of educators, we hope that you enjoy this book and learn new ideas and strategies to help children and families thrive.

Acknowledgments

With thanks to my family for surrounding me with a wonderfully diverse community and helping me to learn the value of celebrating others from all walks of life. I would also like to thank the children, families, and educators who inspire me on a daily basis through their commitment to supporting one another. And finally, I want to thank my co-author, Elisabeth, whose enthusiasm and teamwork made this book a pleasure to write.   —S.T.

I would like to thank the educators, mental health professionals, children, and families who I have learned from and who inspire my work and ongoing commitment to improving educational systems for diverse families. And a special thank you to Shauna, a wonderful collaborator who was a joy to work with on this book.   —E.O.

We would both like to thank Sharon Shapses and Svea Olsen for their careful review of this book and the thoughtful feedback they provided.

To my family for their never-ending support and love. —S.T.

To my husband, Tristan, for his unwavering encouragement and positivity. —E.O.

Introduction to Dual Language Learners

Isabella's family recently immigrated to the United States from Mexico. She just turned 4 years old and is starting school in an early childhood center. One day, as snack time is ending, she turns to her teacher and says, "Quiero leche." What happens next depends on her teacher.

Isabella is one of a steadily growing number of children attending preschool in the United States who are **dual language learners** (DLLs)—children who are learning more than one language at the same time. Being a DLL is an asset to children! Speaking more than one language fluently provides children with many benefits. For example, children who are bilingual have stronger social and emotional skills (including social competence and self-regulation) than their monolingual peers (Bialystok & Martin, 2004; Halle et al., 2014). Being a DLL also comes with cultural benefits for children, including exposure to multiple languages and the values of multiple cultures. It is important to note that exposure to multiple languages and cultures is enriching and beneficial for all children in a classroom, not just for DLLs. Children who learn alongside peers from diverse backgrounds have invaluable opportunities to learn about and appreciate different perspectives.

It is not uncommon for early childhood educators to have a child in their class who speaks a language that they themselves do not speak.

Many early childhood classrooms include children who are DLLs, and it is not uncommon for early childhood educators to have a child in their class who speaks a language that they themselves do not speak.

In the United States, DLLs are often thought of as Spanish speakers, but that is not always the case. Although an estimated 85% of DLLs enrolled in Head Start speak Spanish as a primary language, more than 140 languages are represented in early childhood classrooms (Office of Head Start, 2008). Many early childhood classrooms include children who speak a variety of languages (Child Trends, 2014). With research suggesting that children who are dual language learners are at risk for falling behind academically if they are not effectively supported (Guerrero et al., 2013; McBride, 2008), knowing how to promote the success of DLLs is essential for early childhood educators to ensure that all children have the opportunity to thrive. *Support,* in the context of this book, refers to those efforts to promote success. Effectively supporting DLLs, however, can be challenging for early childhood educators who are not equipped with tools for effectively teaching all learners. The goal of this book is to equip educators with a set of tools and strategies for meeting the needs of diverse students to facilitate and encourage positive outcomes for all children in their classrooms.

The importance of supporting DLLs has gained attention in research as well as policy. The U.S. Department of Health and Human Services and U.S. Department of Education issued a policy statement focused on supporting the development of DLLs in early childhood programs. A link to this policy statement as well as links to related resources are presented in the resources section at the end of this chapter.

> *Knowing how to promote the success of DLLs is essential ... to ensure that all children have the opportunity to thrive.*

Developing a toolbox of strategies for effectively teaching and engaging DLLs as well as supporting families from culturally and linguistically diverse backgrounds is critical to creating an effective classroom learning environment and helping *all* children to succeed socially and academically in school and beyond.

Let's see what happens when we put Isabella in three different scenarios with teachers who have a range of skill levels and strategies for working with DLLs.

SCENARIO 1: MRS. SIMPSON

Mrs. Simpson is a monolingual English speaker and has few tools and strategies for effectively teaching DLLs.

Isabella: *"Quiero leche."*

Mrs. Simpson: *"I can't understand what you are saying. Let's go sit down on the rug with the other children. It's group time."*

Isabella: *"Quiero leche,"* Isabella repeats as she points to the milk pitcher on the table.

Mrs. Simpson feels flustered because she is not sure what Isabella needs. She repeats, *"Why don't we sit down on the rug for group time. See what the other children are doing? I need you to sit on the rug now, too."*

Isabella is still thirsty and feels disappointed that she was not able to communicate what she needed but follows Mrs. Simpson to the rug and sits down with the other children. Isabella feels sad that Mrs. Simpson could not understand her and decides that it is better not to ask her for things in the future. Mrs. Simpson leaves the interaction feeling discouraged, knowing that she was not able to meet Isabella's needs in the moment but unsure of what else she could have done.

SCENARIO 2: MRS. LOPEZ

Mrs. Lopez speaks both English and Spanish and has many tools and strategies for effectively teaching DLLs.

Isabella: *"Quiero leche."*

Mrs. Lopez: *"¿Quieres leche? You would like milk? Of course! Let's practice saying that together in English, too!"*

Mrs. Lopez helps Isabella pour a glass of milk and then leads children at the table in practicing saying both words: *leche* and *milk*. Isabella smiles at her new teacher as she drinks her milk. She feels supported and connected with the other children as they practice saying words together in both English and Spanish. Mrs. Lopez feels a sense of accomplishment. She watches Isabella smile with pride as she teaches her classmates words in Spanish while also eagerly learning new words from them in English.

SCENARIO 3: MR. JONES

Mr. Jones is a monolingual English speaker but has many tools and strategies for effectively teaching DLLs.

Isabella: *"Quiero leche."*

Mr. Jones: *"Hmm...can you show me? Is this what you want?"* Mr. Jones points to the pitcher of water and then to the pitcher of milk.

Isabella: *"Quiero leche."* This time Isabella points to the milk pitcher on the table.

Mr. Jones: *"Milk! Leche—is that milk? Can you say milk? Let's practice together. Milk. Let's teach all of our friends that leche is the Spanish word for milk—this is another way we can say milk in our classroom."*

Mr. Jones creates a label with a picture of a gallon of milk that reads "milk/leche" and adds it to the picture of foods near the lunch table. Isabella does not always understand what Mr. Jones is saying, but she can tell he is doing his best to understand when she tries to tell him something. She enjoys teaching him new words in Spanish and learning new English words from him and her classmates. Mr. Jones takes pride in the fact that he considers himself to be a learner—just like the children in his class. He continually looks for new ways to support children who are DLLs by seeking out professional development opportunities, consulting with his colleagues, building close relationships with families, and reflecting on his own daily trial-and-error process. Sometimes the strategies he tries work out well, like in this example. Sometimes they don't. Even when they don't, he uses the opportunity to reflect on what went well and what did not so that he can try a new approach next time.

Many strategies do not depend on a language or ethnicity match between teacher and child.

Each of these three teachers managed the interaction with Isabella in the best way that he or she knew how with the skills he or she had. As you have seen, each interaction led to a different outcome for Isabella. As an educator, it can feel overwhelming to support children when you do not share their home language. Feeling discouraged, as Mrs. Simpson did, is understandable and not uncommon for a teacher who has not yet learned strategies to effectively support children who are dual language learners. Consider Mr. Jones's experience, however. Even without knowing more than a few words in Spanish, Mr. Jones was able to use strategies that helped Isabella feel supported. In addition, Mr. Jones involved other children in the class in the conversation, helping them learn words in Spanish as well as strategies that could help them build relationships with diverse peers (e.g., demonstrating interest in learning words in another language, modeling empathy).

As Mr. Jones demonstrated, there are many strategies for supporting DLLs that educators can use to facilitate learning. These strategies can also be used to build classroom relationships among peers and teach valuable skills related to getting along with others. Having a range of strategies is critical for teachers whether or not they have a language match with a child, as Mrs. Lopez did with Isabella. Although Mrs. Lopez is able to communicate with Isabella in Spanish, she can expand the support she offers Isabella by promoting her English language development as well.

Learning skills to promote language development in English as well as in each child's home language is one part of the puzzle for effectively supporting DLLs (National Association for the Education of Young Children [NAEYC], 2009b; Nemeth, 2012). It is not the only piece of the puzzle, however. Many DLLs are also learning about and adapting to a new culture. Making sure that these children receive maximum benefit from early childhood learning settings involves using culturally responsive teaching practices to respect and support children in their home language as well as their home culture (NAEYC, 2009b). By valuing children's home culture, educators can help children remain connected to their families and communities, which promotes positive development (NAEYC, 2009b). **Cultural responsiveness** is defined as having skills associated with supporting children and families from diverse linguistic and cultural backgrounds (NAEYC, 2015). Culturally responsive practices involve gaining knowledge of and an appreciation for different cultural perspectives, values, and beliefs (Han & Thomas, 2010). Having a range of tools and strategies to integrate culturally responsive practices into early childhood classrooms can help prepare educators to feel successful in their interactions with children and families from diverse backgrounds.

Imagine that Isabella's family culture encourages children not to ask for anything from adults but instead to appreciate what they are given. The scenario at the snack table could have turned out very differently. Isabella might not have felt comfortable asking for *leche* and instead would have sat quietly at the table with her head down, hoping that her teacher would pour milk for her. Unless they had some understanding of her family culture, Mrs. Simpson, Mr. Jones, and Mrs. Lopez all might have encouraged Isabella to sit down at group time in English or Spanish without having any idea that she had a need that was not being met.

THE 45 STRATEGIES

Whether your experiences with DLLs are more like those of Mrs. Simpson, Mrs. Lopez, or Mr. Jones, we hope that this book will be helpful in expanding your toolbox of **developmentally appropriate strategies** to improve outcomes for children and families from diverse backgrounds. In this book, we provide 45 strategies to help you expand your knowledge of research and best practices related to children who are DLLs and their families, with an emphasis on culturally responsive practices. The strategies included in this book are accompanied by specific application suggestions for putting each strategy into practice in your own early childhood center, classroom, or home learning environment. Strategies are divided as follows across the subsequent chapters:

Chapter 2: Getting Started: Foundations for Supporting Dual Language Learners

- Strategy 1: Get Comfortable with Key Terms and Definitions
- Strategy 2: Expand Your Knowledge of Dual Language Learners and Their Families
- Strategy 3: Understand the Benefits of Being a Dual Language Learner
- Strategy 4: Support Development of the Home Language and English
- Strategy 5: Implement Culturally Responsive Teaching Practices

Chapter 3: Setting Up Your Classroom to Support Dual Language Learners

- Strategy 6: Get to Know the Children in Your Class and Their Families
- Strategy 7: Establish a Welcoming Learning Environment

- Strategy 8: Organize the Classroom to Support Success
- Strategy 9: Embed Best Practices

Chapter 4: Fostering a Classroom Community of Diverse Learners

- Strategy 10: Set the Foundation for Warm and Trusting Relationships
- Strategy 11: Anticipate Children's Challenges and Needs
- Strategy 12: Create a Classroom Community
- Strategy 13: Frame Diversity as a Strength

Chapter 5: Using Classroom Management Practices That Support Diverse Learners

- Strategy 14: Narrate Children's Actions to Promote Self-Regulation and Language Development
- Strategy 15: Apply Best Practices to Classroom Management
- Strategy 16: Plan and Support Transitions
- Strategy 17: Be a Positive Role Model for Behavior Standards
- Strategy 18: Keep a Sense of Humor and Be Flexible

Chapter 6: Supporting Social and Emotional Learning for Dual Language Learners

- Strategy 19: Create an Emotionally Supportive Classroom
- Strategy 20: Recognize and Scaffold Children's Social and Emotional Needs
- Strategy 21: Teach Social and Emotional Skills
- Strategy 22: Support Social and Emotional Development in English and in Each Child's Home Language
- Strategy 23: Involve Families in Children's Social and Emotional Learning
- Strategy 24: Use a Growth Mindset to Teach Social and Emotional Skills

Chapter 7: Enhancing Early Academic Skills for Dual Language Learners

- Strategy 25: Make Learning Activities Accessible to Diverse Learners
- Strategy 26: Embed Best Practices into Read-Alouds
- Strategy 27: Embed Best Practices into Math and Science Activities
- Strategy 28: Draw Connections Between Activities and Children's Home Language and Culture
- Strategy 29: Engage Families in Children's Learning

Chapter 8: Supporting Dual Language Learners Through Music and Movement

- Strategy 30: Learn About Culture Through Music and Movement
- Strategy 31: Invite Children and Families to Share Music with the Classroom

- Strategy 32: Share Classroom Music with Families
- Strategy 33: Build Children's Vocabulary and Early Literacy Skills Through Music

Chapter 9: Engaging Families from Diverse Backgrounds
- Strategy 34: Help Children Prepare for the Transition to School
- Strategy 35: Promote Regular Communication with Families
- Strategy 36: Provide Families with Ways to Be Engaged in School
- Strategy 37: Approach Challenging Conversations with Empathy and Understanding
- Strategy 38: Ask Families for Feedback

Chapter 10: Continuing to Grow Through Professional Development
- Strategy 39: Develop Cultural Awareness and Adopt Self-Reflective Practices
- Strategy 40: Expand Your Multicultural Knowledge
- Strategy 41: Participate in Professional Development Activities
- Strategy 42: Learn How to Effectively Conduct Assessments
- Strategy 43: Involve Families in Decisions Related to Assessments
- Strategy 44: Understand Mandated Reporting Laws and Regulations
- Strategy 45: Think of Yourself as a Lifelong Learner

At the end of each chapter, we provide reflection questions and a brief quiz to check your learning. Many chapters also include resources that you can use in your classroom (e.g., games and activities, vocabulary lists in English and Spanish) as well as recommendations for books and web-based resources where you can learn more about the chapter topic. Many of the resources we provide focus on supporting DLLs who are Spanish speakers; however, the strategies presented throughout this book are applicable to DLLs who speak any language.

We hope that you will find the research and practical activities in this book useful and easy to integrate into your current teaching practices. We also hope that by the end of the book, you will have a new appreciation for the joys and benefits that linguistically and culturally diverse children and families bring to all our lives and will feel more confident in the skills and strategies you have to effectively engage all learners.

> *Many of the resources we provide focus on supporting DLLs who are Spanish speakers; however, the strategies are applicable to DLLs who speak any language.*

Chapter 1: Reflection Questions

1. What type of education or professional development opportunities have you participated in that focused on dual language learners?

2. What skills and strengths do you use to support children who are dual language learners?

3. What strategies are you already using in your classroom that support diverse learners?

4. What is one thing you hope to gain by reading this book?

Chapter 1: Additional Resources

WEB-BASED RESOURCES:

Dual Language Learner Toolkit
Head Start, Early Childhood Learning and Knowledge Center (ECLKC)
Year: 2016
Web site: https://eclkc.ohs.acf.hhs.gov/hslc/tta-system/cultural-linguistic/Dual%20Language%20Learners/toolkit

Policy Statement on Supporting the Development of Children Who Are Dual Language Learners in Early Childhood Programs
U.S. Department of Health and Human Services, U.S. Department of Education
Year: 2016
Web site: https://www.acf.hhs.gov/sites/default/files/ecd/dll_policy_statement_final.pdf

② Getting Started: Foundations for Supporting Dual Language Learners

Ms. Ming is an early childhood educator and is fluent in both English and Mandarin. At the child development center where she is a teacher, she is often asked to serve as a translator to help other teachers communicate with children and families who speak Mandarin. She also serves as a **cultural broker,** helping colleagues learn about Chinese traditions and cultural values that might affect family engagement at school. Ms. Ming helps Asian parents within the program connect with one another as well as with cultural groups and resources in the community.

STRATEGIES

1. Get Comfortable with Key Terms and Definitions
2. Expand Your Knowledge of Dual Language Learners and Their Families
3. Understand the Benefits of Being a Dual Language Learner
4. Support Development of the Home Language and English
5. Implement Culturally Responsive Teaching Practices

Although speaking Mandarin helps her to reinforce learning concepts in both English and Mandarin for the children in her class who speak Mandarin, Ms. Ming does not have the language fluency abilities to support all of the children who are dual language learners in her class, especially those who speak other languages such as Spanish or Arabic. She also recognizes that many of the children who speak a variety of other languages in her class come from different cultural backgrounds and that supporting them effectively may require additional knowledge of culturally responsive practices.

Although Ms. Ming feels confident in her ability to support many of the students in her class, she realizes that "good teaching" is not good enough. She continuously seeks out professional development opportunities to expand her knowledge of best practices to support diverse learners and their families. Ms. Ming has found many resources on good teaching practices in general, but she often wishes there were more resources specifically addressing culturally responsive teaching practices to help her better support families from all cultures.

> *Effectively supporting DLLs requires more than just "good teaching."*

As Ms. Ming has come to realize, effectively supporting DLLs requires more than just good teaching and a language match between a teacher and child (Castro, Páez, Dickinson, & Frede, 2011; De Jong & Harper, 2005). Professional development opportunities focused specifically on supporting DLLs, however, can be hard to find. Unfortunately, many early childhood educators report that they receive little training or education on working with children and families from diverse linguistic and cultural backgrounds (Zepeda, Castro, & Cronin, 2011)—which is one of the reasons we wrote this book! Having exposure to the culture and home language of children in your classroom can certainly help, but it is not realistic to expect that early childhood educators will have had exposure to all of the cultures and languages represented in their classrooms. It's important to learn about the languages and cultures represented by the children in your classroom and their families to understand and effectively meet the needs of learners from diverse backgrounds.

> *It's important to learn about the languages and cultures represented by the children in your classroom and their families to understand and effectively meet the needs of learners from diverse backgrounds.*

There are many skills that can be practiced and developed to help diverse learners thrive. Learning how to enhance children's language and vocabulary development is one important skill (Ackerman & Tazi, 2015). Having a rich vocabulary can help children understand and interpret the world around them, express their feelings and needs, form positive relationships, and benefit from learning opportunities. Children who are DLLs are learning the vocabulary of two (or more) languages. Many studies show that DLLs have smaller vocabularies in early childhood in each individual language they speak in comparison with their monolingual peers (August, Carlo, Dressler, & Snow, 2005; Hoff et al., 2012). Having a limited English language vocabulary may put children at risk for missing out on learning opportunities and limiting their social interactions in the classroom. With effective and supportive teaching, however, the combined vocabulary that DLLs have may be greater than their peers.

In addition to supporting DLLs in their language development (see Chapter 3, Strategy 9 for more information on this topic), it is also important for educators to have a strong understanding of cultural responsiveness so that all children have the same access to high-quality educational experiences regardless of their language abilities or home culture. Practicing cultural responsiveness includes many steps:

- Reflecting on your own personal beliefs and values and on how your home culture affects your teaching
- Expanding your knowledge of other cultures and the way culture may affect children's development and their family's engagement in school
- Developing multicultural skills that help you consider your own biases and support children and families in the way they want and need to be supported
- Using multiculturally responsive teaching practices in your classroom (Han & Thomas, 2010)

Whenever she hears the families of children in her classroom talk about the importance of their child's education, Ms. Ming always thinks about her own family. From a young age, her parents stressed to her that going to school was her most important job. Her parents did not just talk about the importance of education; they supported her through their actions in countless ways. Her parents made sure she did her homework every night; they worked multiple jobs to ensure she had the books and supplies she needed, and they encouraged her to participate in extracurricular enrichment activities.

One thing her parents did not do was question decisions made by her teachers. In her home culture, teachers are revered, and disagreeing with a teacher is seen as disrespectful. The first time one of the families in Ms. Ming's classroom questioned one of her curriculum decisions, Ms. Ming was taken aback. She could not believe that a parent would show disrespect in this way. To Ms. Ming, it clearly showed a lack of value for their child's education. Even though she did not mean to, she found herself avoiding the parent and treating the child differently in the classroom. This bothered her, but she was not sure what else to do.

In this example, considering the situation with a culturally responsive lens might help Ms. Ming reframe the situation from the parents' perspective. Even though Ms. Ming's home culture did not condone questioning teachers, the opposite may be true in this particular family's home culture. Discussing and even debating a teacher's decisions may be seen as a sign of interest and engagement in their child's education.

Practicing and developing cultural responsiveness is an ongoing process and one that requires reflectiveness.

Practicing cultural responsiveness can help Ms. Ming reflect on her own beliefs and values (i.e., "Parents should value their child's education; one of the ways they do this is by being respectful of their child's teacher"), how these values affect her relationship with families and children (i.e., "Families who question their child's teacher are disrespectful and should be avoided"), and, ultimately, how she reflects on this information to make culturally responsive decisions (i.e., "Some families may show respect in different ways than mine did, and perhaps this is one of those times; maybe I should set up a time to talk with the family about their concerns as well as how we can better communicate with each other"). Practicing and developing cultural responsiveness is an ongoing process and one that requires reflectiveness.

In this chapter, we present five strategies to help you get started with expanding your knowledge of DLLs and their families as well as learn how to best support children and families from diverse backgrounds using culturally responsive practices. The five strategies covered in this chapter are these:

- Strategy 1: Get Comfortable with Key Terms and Definitions
- Strategy 2: Expand Your Knowledge of Dual Language Learners and Their Families
- Strategy 3: Understand the Benefits of Being a Dual Language Learner
- Strategy 4: Support Development of the Home Language and English
- Strategy 5: Implement Culturally Responsive Teaching Practices

STRATEGY 1: Get Comfortable with Key Terms and Definitions

Young children who are learning a second language are often also learning their first language at the same time. There are many different terms used to describe children who have exposure to more than one language, including *bilingual, English language learners,* and *dual language learners*. Understanding how these terms are similar to or different from one another and why you might choose one term over another is an important place to begin. Here are a few terms and definitions that are commonly used when talking about children and their language learning abilities.

- **Monolingual:** A monolingual child speaks one language or is learning to speak only one language. Sometimes throughout this book we will talk about children who are monolingual English speakers, meaning children who only speak English.

- **Bilingual learner:** Children who are bilingual speak two languages equally well and fluently. Research is showing that there are many positive outcomes for children who are bilingual and have mastered more than one language, including stronger self-regulation skills and better relationships with peers in comparison with children who are monolingual (Halle, Hair, Wandner, McNamara, & Chien, 2012; Han, 2010).

- **English language learner:** This term refers to a child who is learning English for the purpose of his or her education. Most often, English language learners are children who speak another language at home (e.g., Spanish, Chinese, Creole) but who are receiving their formal education in English. English language learners have also been referred to as children who are "English as a second language students" or "limited English proficient students" (National Council of Teachers of English, 2008). There is growing concern that using terms like "limited English proficient students" encourages a deficit-focused lens—one through which children could be viewed as having a deficiency for not speaking English or as being behind or lesser than their English-speaking peers. Terms such as *English language learner* or *DLL* recognize that students are growing and learning a skill, rather than focusing on the presence of a skill deficit.

- **Dual language learner:** A dual language learner is a child who is learning two languages at the same time or learning a second language while mastering his or her first language (Office of Head Start, 2008). Some definitions of dual language learners specify that they are children who are in dual language programs and receiving instructional support in two languages. For example, a child who is receiving bilingual education at school where lessons are taught in two different languages (e.g., English and Spanish; English and French) is a dual language learner.

In this book, we primarily use the term *dual language learner (DLL)* because during the early childhood years, young children who speak a language other than English in the United States are often learning their home language as well. Unless you are teaching in a bilingual program, the children in your care may not technically be in a dual language learning program; however, we believe that referring to children who are learning more than one language as dual language learners recognizes the importance of learning in both English and the home language. We also believe this term emphasizes that learning more than one language is an asset to children, not a deficit.

Apply Strategy 1

- Think about the terms that are used in your early childhood education setting, whether you are in a school-, center-, or home-based program. Which term do you prefer to use and why? Has reading this strategy strengthened your decision to use that term or led to a shift in which term you prefer to use? Choosing the terms you use intentionally can have an effect on how you think about the children in your classroom and their families and, as a result, how well you are able to support them. Using a term that emphasizes learning more than one language as a strength may help you highlight that strength for the children in your classroom and their families as well as in the conversations you have with your colleagues.

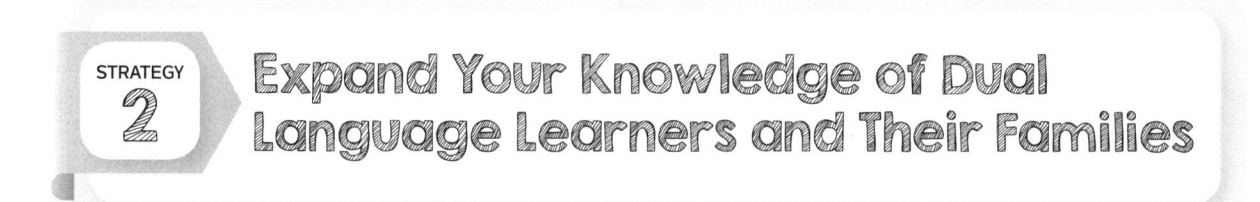

STRATEGY 2: Expand Your Knowledge of Dual Language Learners and Their Families

This strategy encourages teachers to take time to acknowledge just how diverse the group of children labeled as dual language learners can be. Consider the following children:

- Lena is 4 years old. She has been raised in Norway, speaking Norwegian at home and learning both Norwegian and English at school. She is fluent in Norwegian and knows many English words. Her family recently moved to the United States and she will be attending an English-speaking preschool. Both of her parents have lived in the United States before and are very familiar with the culture.

- Miguel is 2 and a half years old. He was born in the United States. His mother speaks English to him at home. His grandmother, who cares for him during the day, speaks Spanish to him. He is about to start child care for the first time. His teacher, Ms. Zarate, speaks both Spanish and English.

- Luciano is being raised in the United States in an Italian-speaking family and neighborhood. He is 3 years old and about to start preschool for the first time with many of his Italian-speaking friends in a classroom where the teacher speaks only English. Luciano knows very few English words.
- Aya's family recently immigrated to the United States from Syria. Neither Aya nor her family members know how to speak English. They know very little about American culture or the country to which they have just moved. Up to this point, Aya's childhood has been filled with turmoil. She has experienced significant trauma and she spent the last year of her life living in a refugee camp.

Although these are just a few examples of children who can be considered DLLs, even within this small group the diversity is evident. For DLLs, diversity exists in the languages children speak, their proficiency in each language, the way they are learning language (simultaneously or sequentially), their family and cultural background (including their family's English-speaking abilities and approach to acculturation), their socioeconomic background, and much more. The following section includes research and statistics to help expand your knowledge of the diversity within the population of children in the United States who are considered to be DLLs. It explains how acknowledging and understanding this diversity can help you implement practices to improve outcomes for children and families from diverse backgrounds.

Who Are Dual Language Learners in the United States?

The number of DLLs is rapidly increasing in the U.S. preschool and school-age population (National Clearinghouse for English Language Acquisition, 2011). From 1994 to 2010, the overall population of children enrolled in pre-K through 12th grade programs grew by 4.44%; in that same time period, the percentage of children who were DLLs enrolled in pre-K through 12th grade programs grew by 63.54% (National Clearinghouse for English Language Acquisition). Many DLLs are born in the United States into families who primarily speak a language other than English at home. Other DLLs move to the United States after birth, in early childhood, or later as immigrants or refugees. A child's family history has a profound effect on the type of support a child needs.

> *A child's family history has a profound effect on the type of support a child needs.*

Diversity in Language

In 2014, approximately 30% of children enrolled in Head Start came from families that spoke a language other than English at home, representing more than 140 other languages (Office of Head Start, 2008). Other than English, Spanish is the most common primary home language and is spoken in nearly 25% of American households (Office of Head Start). Following Spanish, the top five most common languages spoken by DLLs in the 2013–2014 school year were Arabic, Chinese, Vietnamese, Haitian/Haitian Creole, and Somali (Office of English Language Acquisition, 2015).

Diversity in Language Learning

Children learn language in different ways and may have different needs depending on whether they are learning two languages simultaneously or sequentially, how old they are, and their individual differences (e.g., temperament, personality, and level of comfort with risk-taking behaviors) (Tabors, 2008). The timing, exposure and experience, and quantity and quality of language support can also affect the rate at which children develop English skills (Wisconsin Center for Education Research, 2014). For example, there are fewer language demands on infants and toddlers than on older children, so learning a second language from a very young age may be easier than starting a second language at a later age. In summary, there are many circumstances and experiences that contribute to the range of linguistic skills exhibited by DLLs in early childhood classrooms.

Some DLLs are learning two or more languages simultaneously. For example, consider Celina, who is growing up in a home with her mother and grandmother. Her grandmother only speaks Spanish with Celina, and her mother speaks primarily English. Celina grows up hearing both languages from birth and is learning the two languages simultaneously. In other words, she is learning two languages at the same time. What this means for Celina is that she is discovering what language is in the context of these two languages. In both English and Spanish, Celina is learning about the following aspects of language:

- **Phonology:** the sounds of a language. Celina is simultaneously learning about the letters that represent sounds unique to the Spanish language (/ñ/, /rr/), the sounds unique to the English language, and the many letters and sounds that the two languages have in common.

- **Vocabulary:** the words included in each language. Celina is learning different sets of vocabulary for each of the languages she is learning to speak. In English, she learns that the word *cat* represents the family pet and that in Spanish they call him *gato*. Some words that name the same thing are extremely different (*dog* and *perro*), whereas others are very similar (*elephant* and *elefante*). Words like *elephant* (English) and *elefante* (Spanish) that sound similar across different languages are called **cognates**.

- **Grammar:** how words are put together to make sentences. Celina is learning that the way sentences are made can differ across these two languages. For example, she learns that in English, she should say "My gray cat," but in Spanish, she should reverse the order of noun and adjective and say "Mi gato gris."

- **Discourse:** how sentences are put together to create stories and dialogues. Celina loves to listen to the stories her grandmother shares with her from her own childhood. From these stories, Celina is learning how to describe the world her grandmother lived in when growing up in Mexico. She is learning critical thinking skills and problem-solving skills as well as the words she needs to describe her own experiences with the world in Spanish and in English.

- **Pragmatics:** the rules related to how people use language and have conversations. From her mother, Celina learns that talking about her feelings in English is okay, and she openly tells her mother when she is excited or sad. She has an extensive English vocabulary to talk about feelings. From her grandmother, however, she receives the message that she should "be strong" and keep her feelings to herself and so learns a very limited vocabulary of feeling words in Spanish. These rules may be cultural and apply to others who share her family's cultural background or they may be generational (beliefs prevalent for her grandmother's generation but not with younger generations), or based on individual differences.

Although each of these components of language learning might be a little different in each language and culture, Celina is learning about all of these aspects of English and Spanish at the same time. Research shows that for children like Celina who are learning two languages at once, the size of her vocabulary in either language is likely smaller than the vocabulary size of her monolingual peers, but her combined vocabulary is likely greater (Hoff, 2006; Hoff et al., 2012).

Other DLLs may learn two or more languages sequentially or successively. **Simultaneous language development** refers to learning two or more languages at the same time. **Sequential language development** means learning one language and then adding another. Imagine Henri, who was raised with his family in France. Henri's family moved to the United States when he was well on his way to becoming fluent in French at age 4. He then started learning English when he entered an English-speaking preschool. Although Henri will continue to develop his French language skills for several more years, he is significantly farther along in French than he is in English. Because of this, Henri is considered to be learning two languages sequentially (one after the other) (Bialystok, 2001). Henri first learned about phonology, vocabulary, grammar, discourse, and pragmatics, all in French. When he came to the United States and started learning English, he already had an understanding of what language was and how to use words to label objects, people, and events as well as how to put words together in sentences and more. Now Henri is learning each of the components of language all over again in English.

When Henri first entered preschool, he tried communicating with his teachers and classmates in French. Even though no one seemed to understand him, he continued to try for several weeks. After feeling as if he was not making much progress communicating in French, he entered a nonverbal period where he observed, listened, and tried to communicate in other ways. A period of nonverbal communication is commonly observed in children who are dual language learners (Tabors & Snow, 2001). With support from both his teachers at school and his parents at home, Henri began to use telegraphic speech using English words and phrases (e.g., "Henri play?") and finally moved on to productive speech (e.g., "Can I play too?").

Family and Cultural Diversity and Poverty

In addition to language-use differences, there are many other differences in children's families and life contexts. As previously mentioned, a large number of DLLs speak Spanish as a primary language and come from Latino or Hispanic descent. Data on children living in non-English-language households reveal that two-thirds of DLLs (16 million in 2013) live in Spanish-speaking households. Other Indo-European language households represent the next largest group (e.g., French, German, Russian, Hindi), then Asian or Pacific Island language households (Child Trends, 2014).

According to the U.S. Census Bureau (2011), 32.3% of children from Hispanic families live in poverty, which is higher than the national average of children living in poverty (21.6%). Living in poverty has many potential effects on children. For example, children who live in poverty are more likely than their peers to experience academic difficulties as well as emotional and behavioral challenges. They are also more likely to be exposed to parent mental health issues and stress, have an increased risk for experiencing learning disabilities and developmental delays, and have exposure to more dangerous neighborhood situations as well as risk of diminished physical health (e.g., malnutrition, food shortages, lead exposure) (Brooks-Gunn & Duncan, 1997; Dearing, Berry, & Zaslow, 2006).

Studies have shown that DLLs who are living in poverty are less likely to experience home literacy environments and parenting practices that are rich in language and literacy supports (Boyce, Gillam, Innocenti, Cook, & Ortiz, 2013). Because of the high number of children who are DLLs living in poverty, research on the impact of being a DLL cannot always be untangled from the impacts of poverty (e.g., Wanless, McClelland, Tominey, & Acock, 2011).

For educators, it's helpful to know that the families of DLLs may experience myriad risk factors, including a number of factors linked to poverty (e.g., stress) as well as ethnic and racial discrimination and acculturative stress (e.g., the social and psychological struggles related to adjusting to a new culture).

Apply Strategy 2

- Take time to reflect on your beliefs about DLLs—who they are and what skills they may bring with them to the classroom. After reading this strategy, has your understanding of who DLLs are changed? In what way? How will this knowledge affect the approach you take to supporting DLLs in your classroom?

- Get to know each child in your class as a unique individual. Although labels are often easy to apply to help us put children into a group that can be identified as having a unique or special quality (e.g., the group of children who are dual language learners), in doing so one may also be mentally grouping these children together in a way that ignores their unique differences and needs. Getting to know children as individuals and getting to know their families can help you identify the best ways to support them.

- Learn more about DLLs, including who they are, what strengths they have, and what challenges they might experience. As we highlight in this chapter, the population of children who are considered to be DLLs is extremely diverse. Children come from a range of linguistic, cultural, and socioeconomic backgrounds. They are learning language in different ways (simultaneously versus sequentially) and they exhibit individual differences and distinct learning needs. Taking a "one size fits all" approach toward them and their families neglects to take this diversity into account. Expanding your toolbox of teaching strategies that honor each learner as an individual can help DLLs to thrive.

STRATEGY 3: Understand the Benefits of Being a Dual Language Learner

There are many benefits to being a DLL. Children who are DLLs are able to speak more than one language and may be exposed to more than one set of cultural beliefs and values. They may be more empathic and compassionate toward others and be more open to other cultures (Tochon, 2009). Research finds that children who are dual language learners are rated as having equal or higher social competence than their peers (Halle et al., 2014). Research also shows that children who are dual language learners, particularly children who are bilingual, have stronger self-regulation skills than their monolingual peers (Bialystok & Martin, 2004; Morales, Calvo, & Bialystok, 2013). Think about the skills it takes to be able to switch back and forth between two or more languages. Children need to be able to remember the vocabulary that comes with each language. They need to be able to group these vocabulary words with the appropriate language and use them at the appropriate time and place. Different languages use different grammatical rules, and children need to be able to navigate these differences, switch back and forth between languages, and more. It is no wonder that being bilingual leads to stronger self-regulation—children are practicing these skills continually!

Having children who are DLLs in your classroom can also benefit the other children in your class. It exposes all children in your classroom to a range of languages, cultures, beliefs, and values. Helping children view diversity as a strength teaches children important messages about the world they live in. With the help of educators, children can learn to appreciate similarities and differences between themselves and their classmates as well as how to talk about these similarities and differences in a way that shows genuine interest, curiosity, and understanding. Interactions such as these help children approach the society around them with interest, empathy, and compassion. Positive exposure to diversity can also help children develop a stronger understanding of their own family values and culture, establish their own identity, and build their self-esteem.

> *Having a classroom that includes children from diverse linguistic and cultural backgrounds exposes all children . . . to a range of languages, cultures, beliefs, and values.*

> *With the help of educators, children can learn to appreciate similarities and differences between themselves and their classmates as well as how to talk about these similarities and differences in a way that shows genuine interest, curiosity, and understanding.*

Apply Strategy 3

- Create a handout or bulletin board to share at your center and with families about the benefits of being a DLL and of having diverse classrooms. "The Importance of Home Language" series found in Head Start's Early Childhood Learning and Knowledge Center provides free downloadable and printable handouts on this topic and others that you can share or display for families in English, Spanish, Arabic, Chinese, Brazilian Portuguese, Haitian Creole, and Russian. A link to this web site is provided in the Additional Resources section in Chapter 9.

- Talk with families about the benefits of sharing their home language and culture with their child and with your classroom (Goldenberg, Hicks, & Lit, 2013). Many parents incorrectly believe that promoting their home language may hurt their child's English language development and thus their education (Fránquiz, Salazar, & DeNicolo, 2011). Let all families know that you view their home language and culture as a strength that enhances your classroom community and that incorporating their home language is important for their child's learning. Families may feel self-conscious about the aspects of their language or culture that make them stand out from others. Communicating to families that you and your program believe their language and culture are valuable to their child's learning and showing them that you are doing your best to incorporate multiple languages and cultures into the classroom will support the development of a positive relationship with each child's family and encourage their involvement at school.

- Use language that reflects a **strengths-based approach** when talking about the diversity within your classroom to all children and families. For example, celebrate diversity by inviting family members to share unique cultural traditions with you and your class. This models to all families, whether they come from the dominant culture or a nondominant culture, that you value their family language and culture and the language and culture of all children in the classroom. Setting this example may help other families adopt this same mindset toward the classroom and program community.

STRATEGY 4: Support Development of the Home Language and English

Embedding children's home language into learning activities can help support vocabulary development in English as well as a child's home language. Incorporating each child's home language into the classroom is one of the ways that educators can ensure that DLLs receive the same quality education and care as their monolingual peers (Ackerman & Tazi, 2015). Research overwhelmingly shows that children who receive support in their home language, specifically children who are in bilingual classrooms or transitional classrooms, experience positive gains, not only in their home language but also in English, as well as significant growth in early achievement skills (Burchinal, Field, López, Howes, & Pianta, 2012; Durán, Roseth, & Hoffman, 2010; Farver, Lonigan, & Eppe, 2009; Rolstad, Mahoney, & Glass, 2005). It is not always possible for a program to provide bilingual instruction in English and each child's home language, but there are many ways that educators can support vocabulary development and incorporate children's home language into classroom practices and activities.

> *Children who receive support in their home language ... experience positive gains, not only in their home language but also in English, as well as significant growth in early achievement skills.*

Incorporating a child's home language into instruction can support a DLL's ability to learn new content, as they do not have to simultaneously struggle to learn new vocabulary while learning other skills (Nemeth, 2012). In the strategies we share in subsequent chapters, we provide suggestions for how to incorporate children's home languages and promote vocabulary development in a home language and English. Studies have shown that children who are DLLs who have slow vocabulary development are less likely than their peers to score at grade level on literacy tasks. Supporting vocabulary development in English and a child's home language may help reduce the likelihood of these achievement gaps (August et al., 2005).

Apply Strategy 4

- Support children's language development by narrating children's behaviors and interactions throughout the day. Providing a verbal narration of what you observe helps expose children to phonology, vocabulary, grammar, discourse, and pragmatics of language. For example, you might say, "I see the way you are marching with your knees up high over to the slide." In addition, narrating the choices you make and that you see children making throughout the day can help promote vocabulary as well as the development of problem-solving skills and critical thinking abilities, leading to stronger self-regulation (McClelland & Tominey, 2015). An example of this would be saying, "I am going to walk far around the swing set like this so that I do not get hurt," or "I see you are putting your coat on so that you will be warm when we go outside."

- As you narrate for children, incorporate words from children's home languages whenever possible ("I see you are putting your coat on—*tu chaqueta*"). Repeat key words and phrases and pair words with pictures or visual aids. For your narration to be most effective for DLLs, it is important to connect the words you are saying with concrete actions or objects as well as words in their home language so that children can understand the meaning of new words to develop their vocabulary. Using gestures, body language, and facial expressions that correspond with what you are saying is another way to help bring your words to life for children with varying levels of language abilities and for children who are DLLs.

STRATEGY 5: Implement Culturally Responsive Teaching Practices

Using culturally responsive practices is another part of effectively supporting children who are DLLs. Cultural responsiveness involves relating to and learning from individuals in your own culture as well as from other cultures. At the heart of cultural responsiveness is understanding and empathy (McAllister & Irvine, 2002). The Golden Rule is a well-known encouragement for people to treat others as they themselves would like to be treated. Although the Golden Rule is a nice reminder to think of others and model kindness, a common interpretation of this rule fails to take into account that individuals may not all want to be treated the same way and that what is meaningful to one individual may not have the same meaning to another. Taking a culturally responsive approach encourages an individual to treat others in the way *he or she* would like to be treated (sometimes known as the Platinum Rule), recognizing that this may be different from the way *the individual* would like to be treated.

Effectively supporting children and families in the way they would like and need to be supported requires getting to know them, their individual personalities, and their family beliefs and values. It also involves a high level of self-reflectiveness and a perspective that views parents and families as experts of their own home culture and values (Souto-Manning & Mitchell, 2010). Using a culturally responsive lens also means seeking out information from families and using their guidance to support their child's growth and development in a way that respects and values their home language and culture (NAEYC, 2009b).

Taking a culturally responsive approach encourages an individual to treat others in the way he or she would like to be treated.

Apply Strategy 5

- Get to know the children in your class and their families. Learn about each family's values and beliefs related to their child's development and education as well as how they would like to be engaged in school. Send home surveys to families asking them to share their perspective on being involved in school. Consider asking families directly about ways they would like to be involved or how you can best communicate with them, e.g., during pick-up or drop-off time, during a home visit, or at a parent–teacher conference. Families can help you get to know children's academic and social needs as well as how their family culture might affect their child's interactions at school. The strategies in

Chapter 9 are dedicated to applying cultural responsiveness to engaging families from diverse backgrounds.

- Be flexible and willing to make adaptations in the classroom to support the individual and cultural needs of children and families when possible. As you increase your multicultural knowledge and learn about the needs of children in your class and their families, issues may arise that make you reflect on and even change your teaching practices. For example, you may discover that praising some children out loud (e.g., "Samantha, you are being so careful and putting the blocks away in just the right spot") helps them feel proud of their actions and that, as a result, these children seek out ways to continue receiving praise. For other children, however, receiving recognition may be something that is not done in their home and may leave them feeling uncomfortable, embarrassed, or singled out. In this case, pointing out a child's actions could actually result in a child trying to avoid situations in which he or she might be noticed (e.g., a child who no longer participates in cleaning up the blocks) (Weinstein, Tomlinson-Clarke, & Curran, 2004). As a result, you might adapt how you let certain children know when they are doing well, such as by giving them a smile or letting them know privately.

- Realize that making accommodations for every cultural belief may not be possible, and you may instead develop a process of **mutual accommodation**. Mutual accommodation involves determining when a teacher can best accommodate a child or family versus when the teacher expects them to accommodate the needs of a classroom or school (Weinstein et al., 2004). For example, a family may share with you that they spoon-feed their 4-year-old child at home and ask if you would be willing to do the same at school. Given that the child does not have special needs that require this accommodation, this may not be a request that can be met in the classroom. Communicating openly with families about when accommodations can be made and when they cannot and why (e.g., "One of the goals of the classroom is to help prepare children with the self-help skills and independence they will need to thrive in preschool and kindergarten.") can help foster positive communication between school and home.

- Plan many different types of learning activities focused on the same key words and concepts as part of your typical classroom day to support the needs of children from diverse backgrounds. Children need multiple and repeated exposures to new words and concepts to be able to learn new information effectively. Best practices for supporting DLLs and diverse learners in general focus on using a wide range of methods to support children's learning. Often, the schedule or routine in early childhood settings is already set up to facilitate experiential learning through large- and small-group activities, learning centers, individual play and exploration, dramatic play, outdoor play, music and movement, and more. Intentionally embedding children's home languages as well as culturally responsive practices into each type of activity can help ensure that diverse learners are being supported throughout the day.

- Integrate discussions and activities into the classroom day on a regular basis that help children explore culture—their own culture and the culture of others (Souto-Manning & Mitchell, 2010). Making multicultural experiences part of the daily curriculum (rather than focusing on cultural differences only when talking about holidays, for example) is an important way to help children understand the role of culture in society around them and will help them develop their own skills to appreciate the similarities and differences between themselves and their classmates.

- Realize that you will likely make missteps along the way when working with children and families from diverse linguistic and cultural backgrounds. Missteps might include making an incorrect assumption about a child or family (e.g., assuming a parent is not interested in getting to know you because he or she does not enter the classroom, when in reality, the parent does not know if it is proper or respectful to do so) or not thinking to send resources home in languages other than English. Whatever missteps arise, be forgiving of yourself. Acknowledge your mistake and offer a genuine apology when necessary. Express interest in better understanding the perspective and feelings of each family and child in order to best support them in the way they would like and need to be supported.

CHAPTER CONCLUSIONS

The population of children who are DLLs and their families is an extremely diverse group. Recognizing this diversity, as well as recognizing the benefits that having a diverse classroom of students can have for all learners, is foundational to helping all children and families thrive. Considering the diversity that exists culturally and linguistically within early childhood learning settings is an important step toward practicing cultural responsiveness and creating a learning environment to meet the needs of children from all backgrounds.

Chapter 2: Check Your Learning

1. Good teaching is all that is required to effectively support dual language learners.
   a) True
   b) False

2. Which of the following is true about children who are dual language learners? Select all that apply.
   a) They are likely to have a smaller vocabulary in each language they speak in comparison to their peers.
   b) Their combined vocabulary across languages is often greater than that of their monolingual peers.
   c) They have a smaller vocabulary than their peers, even when accounting for combined vocabulary across languages.
   d) None of the above

3. Practicing cultural responsiveness involves which of the following activities?
   a) Reflecting on your personal beliefs and values and their impact on your teaching
   b) Expanding your knowledge of other cultures and the potential impact of culture on children's development and family engagement
   c) Developing multicultural skills that help you consider your own biases related to supporting diverse learners and their families
   d) All of the above

4. Which of the following terms applies a strength-based approach when describing children who are learning more than one language?
   a) Dual language learner
   b) English language learner
   c) Limited English proficient student
   d) All of the above

5. For a child to be considered a dual language learner in the United States, he or she must be born in another country and come to the United States as an immigrant or refugee.
   a) True
   b) False

6. After English, what is the next most common primary home language in the United States?
   a) Arabic
   b) Chinese
   c) Spanish
   d) Creole

7. A child who is struggling to put words in the right order—for example, saying "my ball red" instead of "my red ball"—is still learning which of the following?
   a) Phonology
   b) Pragmatics
   c) Discourse
   d) Grammar

8. According to the U.S. Census Bureau, which of the following is true?
   a) The percentage of children in Hispanic families living in poverty is higher than the national average of children living in poverty.
   b) The percentage of children in Hispanic families living in poverty is lower than the national average of children living in poverty.
   c) The percentage of children in Hispanic families living in poverty is the same as the national average of children living in poverty.
   d) None of the above

9. Which of the following are positive benefits of being bilingual?
   a) Increased self-regulation
   b) Greater empathy and openness to other cultures
   c) High levels of social competence
   d) All of the above

10. Taking an English-only approach at school and at home is considered best practice for supporting dual language learners.
    a) True
    b) False

For answers to this chapter quiz, please refer to the Answer Key on page 181.

Chapter 2: Reflection Questions

1. Which terms are used in your early childhood program to describe children who are learning more than one language? What terms do you prefer to use and why?

   _____
   _____
   _____
   _____

2. Were any of the statistics related to dual language learners surprising to you? Which ones? Why?

   _____
   _____
   _____
   _____

3. In what ways are you already incorporating children's home languages into activities and routines in your classroom?

   _____
   _____
   _____
   _____

4. What is one specific way you can communicate to families that their home language and culture are valued in your classroom and program?

   _____
   _____
   _____
   _____

Chapter 2: Additional Resources

BOOKS:

Basics of Supporting Dual Language Learners
Author: Karen N. Nemeth
Year: 2012
Publisher: National Association for the Education of Young Children

Getting it RIGHT for Young Children from Diverse Backgrounds (2nd edition)
Author: Linda M. Espinosa
Year: 2014
Publisher: Pearson

The New Voices ~ Nuevas Voces: Guide to Cultural and Linguistic Diversity in Early Childhood
Authors: Dina C. Castro, Betsy Ayankoya, Christina Kasprzak
Year: 2011
Publisher: Paul H. Brookes Publishing Co.

One Child, Two Languages: A Guide for Early Childhood Educators of Children Learning English as a Second Language (2nd edition)
Author: Patton O. Tabors
Year: 2008
Publisher: Paul H. Brookes Publishing Co.

Say What You See for Parents and Teachers
Author: Sandra R. Blackard
Year: 2012
Publisher: Language of Listening

Skilled Dialogue: Strategies for Responding to Cultural Diversity in Early Childhood (2nd edition)
Authors: Isaura Barrera, Lucinda Kramer, T. Dianne Macpherson
Year: 2012
Publisher: Paul H. Brookes Publishing Co.

WEB-BASED RESOURCES:

Child Trends Databank: Dual Language Learners
Year: 2014
Web site: http://www.childtrends.org/?indicators=dual-language-learners

Cultural and Linguistic Responsiveness
Head Start, Early Childhood Learning and Knowledge Center (ECLKC)
Web site: http://eclkc.ohs.acf.hhs.gov/hslc/tta-system/cultural-linguistic

(continued)

Chapter 2 Additional Resources (continued)

Dual Language Learners in the Early Years: Getting Ready to Succeed in School
Authors: Keira Gebbie Ballantyne, Alicia R. Sanderman, Nicole McLaughlin; National Clearinghouse for English Language Acquisition
Year: 2008
Web site: https://ncela.ed.gov/files/uploads/3/DLLs__in_the_Early_Years.pdf

The Early Years: Dual Language Learners
Wisconsin Center for Education Research; WIDA
Year: 2014
Web site: https://www.wida.us/resources/focus/WIDA_Focus_on_Early_Years.pdf

English Language Learners: A Policy Research Brief Produced by the National Council of Teachers of English
Year: 2008
Web site: http://www.ncte.org/library/NCTEFiles/Resources/PolicyResearch/ELLResearchBrief.pdf

Key Demographics and Practice Recommendations for Young English Learners
National Clearinghouse for English Language Acquisition
Year: 2011
Web site: http://www.ncela.us/files/uploads/9/EarlyChildhoodShortReport.pdf

PreK–3rd: Challenging Common Myths About Dual Language Learners
Year: 2013
Author: Linda M. Espinosa
Web site: http://fcd-us.org/sites/default/files/Challenging%20Common%20Myths%20Update.pdf

Supporting Cultural Competence: Accreditation of Programs for Young Children Cross-Cutting Theme in Program Standards
National Association for the Education of Young Children
Year: 2012
Web site: https://www.naeyc.org/academy/files/academy/file/TrendBriefsSupportingCulturalCompetence.pdf

3 Setting Up Your Classroom to Support Dual Language Learners

Mirtau felt nervous taking her son Emil to preschool. Although he was learning English more quickly than she was, she worried about how he would be treated in his new school. Their family had recently moved to a predominantly white suburban neighborhood, and she wondered how others would view his dark skin. She also worried about how their family values and culture might isolate them from his teachers or other families in the program. On the first day of school, she held her breath as they walked through the doors, but breathed a sigh of relief when they reached Emil's classroom. On the door was a sign that said, "Good Morning!" in English and the other languages represented in the classroom, including their home language, Creole ("Bonjou!"). Looking around the room, she saw posters and books on display depicting children from many different backgrounds and in several different languages. Her son's teacher, Ms. Miles, had clearly thought intentionally about helping children and families feel welcome in her classroom. These gestures helped set up a positive relationship between Emil's family and his school from their very first day.

STRATEGIES

6. Get to Know the Children in Your Class and Their Families
7. Establish a Welcoming Learning Environment
8. Organize the Classroom to Support Success
9. Embed Best Practices

APPENDICES

3.1 Vocabulary Word Lists
3.2 Sample Parent Questionnaire in English
3.3 Sample Parent Questionnaire in Spanish

There are many things educators can do to help prepare a center, a classroom, or home-based setting to feel welcoming to children and families from diverse backgrounds and to support their growth and development throughout the year. The physical layout of the classroom and the classroom environment is one of the first things children and families will see when arriving at school. Carefully choosing and creating display materials that reflect the linguistic and cultural diversity represented in your program can have a profound impact on how well connected families feel with the program and classroom.

Intentionally setting up the classroom to support diverse learners is a good way to help families feel welcome and an important part of providing high-quality early childhood education. NAEYC has specific recommendations included in its accreditation criteria for ways that educators can set up the classroom environment to promote an appreciation for diversity. Head Start includes similar recommendations in its program standards. Links to the NAEYC and Head Start criteria are included at the resources provided at the end of this chapter.

It is important to assess how well early childhood programs are promoting an appreciation for diversity in the classroom, and researchers have developed measures to do so. Although these measures are used primarily for research purposes, their existence indicates the field's recognition of an appreciation for diversity as an important aspect of early childhood education. The Early Childhood Environment Rating Scale–Revised Edition (ECERS-R) is an example of a measure that assesses the quality of an early childhood environment by looking at a combination of many different items, including specific items related to "promoting acceptance of diversity" (Harms, Clifford, & Cryer, 2014). The Four Curricular Subscales Extension to the Early Childhood Environment Rating Scale (ECERS-E) includes a specific set of diversity questions that emphasize planning for children's individual learning needs as well as having an awareness of the importance of gender equity and racial equality (Sylva, Siraj-Blatchford, & Taggart, 2003).

> *Carefully choosing and creating display materials that reflect the linguistic and cultural diversity represented in your program can have a profound impact on how well connected families feel with the program and classroom.*

There are many ways that diversity can be acknowledged and appreciated as you set up your classroom to support diverse learners. In this chapter, we provide practical strategies that can be put into practice in your classroom environment before the school year starts or any time during the year. The strategies presented in this chapter are as follows:

- Strategy 6: Get to Know the Children in Your Class and Their Families
- Strategy 7: Establish a Welcoming Learning Environment
- Strategy 8: Organize the Classroom to Support Success
- Strategy 9: Embed Best Practices

STRATEGY 6: Get to Know the Children in Your Class and Their Families

To best meet the needs of the children in your class and their families, it is important to get to know them! There are many ways educators can learn about the children and families before the school year even begins as well as throughout the year. Getting to know children and families will help you to provide support for them in the ways that they want and need, providing you with information critical to setting up your classroom and using culturally responsive practices.

> *Getting to know children and families will help you to provide support for them in the ways that they want and need.*

Apply Strategy 6

- Take time to learn about the children in your class and their families before the school year begins. Many educators and program leaders find it helpful to send surveys to families as part of the school enrollment process or prior to a child starting school. **Family surveys** are questionnaires that are administered to parents or caregivers for various purposes. These surveys can be a wonderful way to begin getting to know the children in your class and their families. Using a culturally responsive lens, you might consider asking families about children's previous child care experiences, if they have any concerns about starting school, children's likes and dislikes, languages spoken at home, how parents would like to receive information, how families would like to be involved in school, and other questions that help you get to know their child as well as the family's expectations and values related to school. This information can be used to help inform the way you approach families and what activities you plan for their children at school. For example, information such as children's favorite food can be used to plan snack or meal choices (if possible) and to introduce other children in the class to new and different foods.

- We provide a list of sample questions in Appendices 3.2 and 3.3 in English and Spanish that you can use to create your own survey. When creating your own survey, be sure to provide space for families to write answers. It is important to be mindful that families may have varying levels of literacy in English as well as their home language. A survey may not be the best way to communicate with some families; a phone or in-person meeting, if possible, might be preferred. Ask families how they prefer to share and receive information (e.g., paper survey, e-mail survey, phone call, in-person conversation) and involve an interpreter or translator if necessary.

- For families who speak a language other than English, send home a vocabulary list of words and phrases that children are likely to hear frequently at the beginning of the school year. A vocabulary word list is provided for you to use in Appendix 3.1. Ask parents to fill out the appendix's list of words and phrases in their home language and return it to you if they are able to do so. Seek help from speakers of other languages represented in your classroom to translate key words and phrases and to provide audio recordings of pronunciations for these words. Asking families to help with these translations rather than using a computer program helps ensure accuracy and that the words you use are those that the child is accustomed to hearing. Involving families in this way also shows them that you value the use of their home language in your classroom and that you are interested in involving them in their child's learning. This is an activity that you may only have to do with a few families to gather vocabulary words in each of the key languages represented in your classroom.

- Reach out to community leaders or cultural brokers who can share cultural and linguistic information that may help you to build connections with families from diverse backgrounds. Cultural brokers are individuals who serve as a "bridge" between people or groups from different cultures. Look for organizations in the community that offer services or resources for families from specific cultural backgrounds. For instance, many communities have organizations that provide services (e.g., translation services, connections to community resources, English as a second language classes) for immigrant and refugee families from a range of countries.

- If time allows, consider meeting families in person prior to the start of the school year. Conduct short home visits to meet each of the children and families in their home environment, if they are comfortable participating. Schedule short periods of time for families to visit the classroom individually or in groups so that you can meet them and provide them with an opportunity to get acclimated to the classroom before school begins. Home visits or classroom visits can also be held in the middle of the school year to help a new child feel more comfortable during this transition.

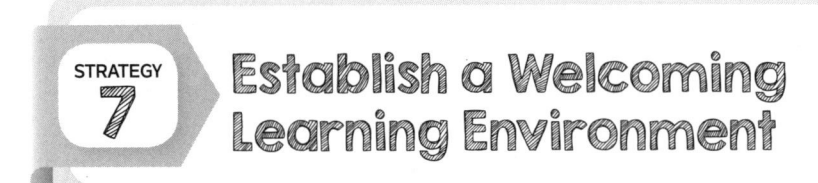

STRATEGY 7: Establish a Welcoming Learning Environment

There are many things early childhood educators can do to help children and families feel welcome inside and outside of the classroom. For families who are arriving at school at the beginning of the year or starting new in the middle of the year, make sure signs for classrooms are clearly marked so that family members know where to take their child during the first days of school. Consider having program staff available to greet parents at the school door during the first week to welcome them and help guide them to their child's classroom.

Apply Strategy 7

- Create a welcome bulletin board, collage, poster, or display near the entrance of your classroom and at the entrance of your program or center. Embedding each of the languages represented in your classroom may help put families at ease as soon as they arrive. In addition to the word *welcome,* consider creating a collage of words with the heading "How we want your child to feel at school." Include feelings such as happy, excited, peaceful, safe, and curious. You can even add a space where families can add words in English and their home language that represent how they would like their children to feel at school. In this simple way, you can show parents that how they would like their child to feel at school matters to you. This may help encourage parents to be engaged in thinking about their child's school experience right from the start.

- Create a community bulletin board for families where multicultural events and resources can be displayed and shared. Point the board out to families and invite them to contribute to it if they have resources to share. To keep the board current, remove signs for events that have passed and ask staff members to contribute items to the board if possible.

- Set a peaceful tone through music. Maintain a multicultural music library for use throughout the day in the classroom and, during arrival and drop-off periods, play inviting and soothing music that represents a wide range of languages and cultures. You can ask parents to share CDs with the class or to make recommendations for music that is special or meaningful to their family.

- Choose and display materials around your classroom that show children and families from diverse cultural and linguistic backgrounds and especially images depicting backgrounds similar to those of the children in your class (Magruder, Hayslip, Espinosa, & Matera, 2013). Be sure to choose a range of images that represent diversity in age, gender, race, language, and culture in nonstereotypical ways (NAEYC, 2015). Examples of nonstereotypical images might include boys and girls participating in a range of activities (e.g., both boys and girls playing house or dressing up as doctors), many different family forms (not just mother- and father-headed families, but also single parents, grandparent-headed families, and same-sex parents-headed families), and individuals from a range of racial and ethnic backgrounds participating in daily activities.

- Seeing images of people, cultures, and places that feel familiar to them may help children and families feel at ease. Displaying multicultural images and books communicates to families that cultural diversity is valued in the classroom. Display materials also play an important role in the lives of children from the dominant culture who are in your classroom. As young children learn about the world around them, they are often interested in people and things that are new and different from what they know. Children who are entering school for the first time may already have extensive exposure to different cultures or they may have little or no exposure to cultures aside from their own. Many studies show that even before they can talk, young children look longer at things that are unfamiliar to them (e.g., Turk-Browne, Scholl, & Chun, 2008). What we might call staring (and discourage children from doing) is actually a natural part of the learning process, as most children have a genuine curiosity about the world around them. Displaying multicultural images around the classroom helps make these images more familiar and comfortable to children and reinforces the message that diversity is a valued part of the classroom community. Having books and materials available and on display in multiple languages also sends the message to families that their home language and culture is valued at school. Make these books available for parents to read with children when they visit the classroom or to borrow to read at home.

Displaying multicultural images and books communicates to families that cultural diversity is valued in the classroom.

- Label objects around the classroom in English, Spanish, and other languages represented in your classroom. Labeling objects around the classroom helps all children begin to associate print language with spoken language. Putting labels in several languages on the different classroom areas (block area, bathroom) and commonly used objects (chair, door) not only supports the development of children's emergent literacy skills but also engages families in that learning process by acknowledging the importance of their home language in school—and may even help families learn new words in English. In addition to putting words on labels, include a picture of the item so that it is clear what object is connected to the word. These labels can be used throughout the day as a reminder for you to incorporate words in other languages as well as to support children's vocabulary development and classroom management practices, as we discuss in Chapter 5. Vocabulary lists of items and areas commonly found around the classroom are included in Appendix 3.1 in English and Spanish.

- Create a visual classroom schedule that is labeled with each of the key activities that you have planned for the class each day (e.g., Morning Meeting, Free Play, Snack). Include key words in English and Spanish or other languages represented in your classroom and pair these words with pictures. Display the classroom schedule in a place where children can see it so that you can refer to it throughout the day and so that families can see it during drop-off or pick-up. Consider creating a child-friendly version of the classroom schedule that you can print and share with children to color or draw on during an extension activity. Encourage children to take it home and share it with their family. Ask children to identify someone they will share the schedule with at home and practice talking through each of the different activities together in small groups.

- Create a quiet space in your classroom where individual children or small groups of children can take a break if they need to. Some teachers call this area the **quiet corner,** "calm corner," or "cozy corner." The quiet corner can provide children with an opportunity to calm down when experiencing intense emotions, have quiet time when feeling overwhelmed, or seek out one-on-one time with an adult or classmate. Some classrooms have a built-in alcove that serves nicely as the quiet corner. If your classroom does not, you might consider creating a space in the way you arrange your classroom furniture or bookshelves to create a cozy nook. Another option is to use a large refrigerator- or oven-sized cardboard box placed on one side of the room or in one corner of the room to serve as a quiet space that an individual child or a small number of children can fit in. Fill your quiet corner with soft items, such as pillows or stuffed animals. You might also post images of faces depicting different feelings in the area to support conversations about emotions or pictures of children with their families.

- Remember that diversity doesn't only refer to differences in culture and language. Diversity also includes differences in age, gender, abilities/disabilities, learning styles, family forms, and more. As you strive to establish a welcoming classroom environment, make sure that your approach embraces the many different forms diversity may take. Consider the following example:

Amina liked seeing the diversity in pictures and artwork displayed in her daughter's preschool classroom. There were pictures from around the world and pictures showing children and adults in many different types of dress, in many different locations, and with many different abilities and disabilities. There were also pictures depicting different types of families, including multigenerational families, single-parent families, and adopted families. Although these images communicated to her that diversity was valued in their classroom community, there was one picture that made her uncomfortable. One of the pictures showed two fathers with a newborn. In her home country and culture, same-sex couples were seen as deviant and harmful to society. She did not understand why her daughter's teacher, Ms. Phipps, would display such an image to young children, so she decided to ask during her parent–teacher conference. In as nonjudgmental a way as possible, Ms. Phipps explained that in the United States, same-sex marriages are legal. She also shared that there were same-sex parents of children in the classroom community and she had displayed the picture to make sure they felt welcome, just as she had done for families from different cultural backgrounds. Although this came as a surprise to Amina, she understood Ms. Phipps's desire to help everyone feel welcome. Over the year, Amina watched other parents at family events, trying to identify the same-sex parents of a child in the class. Through her observations, she came to realize that they were very caring and attentive parents, just like the other parents in the class. The images of diverse families that Ms. Phipps had on display were having the effect she had hoped for. Not only were children seeing many different family forms as acceptable, but parents were as well.

STRATEGY 8: Organize the Classroom to Support Success

Give careful thought to the organization of the classroom, including the organization of the classroom daily schedule as well as the organization of the physical layout of the classroom. Having a clear and consistent daily schedule can help DLLs learn classroom rules and routines more quickly through regular repetition than a classroom with a schedule that varies from day to day. In addition, classroom schedules that consider children's energy levels and physiological needs throughout the day (e.g., high-energy activities mid-morning, routine snacks and bathroom tries) can ensure that children are comfortable and thus ready to participate and learn. Finally, classroom environments that are set up to support children's movement and access to materials can help DLLs navigate the day successfully. When children can see items or objects that they need, they can use multiple modes of communication to make use of them.

Apply Strategy 8

- Devise a classroom daily schedule that meets children's changing needs across the day. Think about children's energy levels at different times of day, and plan activities to match those energy levels. For example, planning a music and movement activity right before group or circle time might help children release energy in a way that helps them prepare to pay attention for a sVhort lesson. Planning outdoor time directly after rest time when children are still waking up and feeling groggy, however, might not be the most effective way to help them expel their energy on the playground. Strategies like these are important for DLLs as well as all children in a classroom. When children's physiological needs are being met, they will be better prepared to learn.

- Look around your classroom to make sure that children have access to the materials they need in various areas in the room. Are art materials (e.g., paints, brushes, scissors, paper) organized according to color, size, and purpose? Are smocks placed where children can reach them near the easel? Is there a place where children can choose books to read near the reading area or library? Setting up the classroom in a way that allows children access to the materials they need can facilitate children's independence and minimize frustration. For DLLs, easy access to materials can help them find what they need themselves or communicate those needs through gestures. A classroom that is organized in a way that supports movement and flow by allowing children access to what they need can help support smooth transitions throughout the day. Having materials readily accessible can also help children better show you what they need throughout the day through indicating or pointing. This may be especially important for children who are DLLs as they learn vocabulary associated with the classroom.

- Consider materials that you may *not* want children to have easy access to. For example, during the first few weeks of school, move scissors out of reach until children have had an opportunity to practice cutting during teacher-led activities to make sure children are able to do so safely. In addition, consider where areas in the room are in relation to one another. Placing the quiet or cozy corner near the block area—an area that is often noisy—may not be conducive to using the area as it is intended. Setting up the quiet or cozy corner near the library or reading area instead may be a better arrangement. Having blocks on the shelves around the area that also serves as the circle time rug may be distracting for children during group activities. Look for ways to remove this distraction by turning the shelf around or covering the block area.

- Place picture labels around the classroom that show the number of children allowed in each area during independent play and small group times. On each label include the number symbol (e.g., 3, 4) as well as a visual image depicting the number using stick figures or another shape to represent children. Visual supports like these can be used to help guide children through choosing activities and eventually enable them to determine for themselves if there is enough space in each particular area of the classroom. These visual supports can be especially helpful for children who are DLLs as a way to help make classroom rules easy to understand.

- Identify areas in the classroom that tend to be problematic at different times of day. For example, if you observe that the block area is particularly challenging during independent exploration or free play, limit the number of children allowed in that area or make sure a teacher is stationed in that area to prevent conflicts and support problem solving. The role that educators play to guide children through interactions and challenging situations is critical, as educators can narrate what they see and offer words to children to help support them through interactions if they do not have the vocabulary themselves.

STRATEGY 9: Embed Best Practices

As you plan lessons in preparation for a new school year, it is especially important to consider the needs of diverse groups of children. There are many different factors that might affect each child's ability to benefit from social interactions and learning experiences, including a child's language ability, age, and developmental stage. Getting to know the children in your classroom will give you a better sense of their learning needs as well as ways you can support individual children and the class as a whole. The following practices help support effective lesson planning for children from diverse backgrounds at the beginning of the school year and throughout the year. They are **best practices for supporting DLLs**—practices whose usefulness has been supported by research.

Apply Strategy 9

- At the beginning of the year, when planning small- or large-group activities, plan activities that are short so that children can get used to group learning activities and develop their ability to pay attention and focus.

- To effectively support children who are DLLs and who have diverse learning needs, focus on small-group activities rather than large-group activities, especially at the beginning of the year. Pairing small groups of children with individual teachers will help you to get to know individual children better and help the children to get to know each other. If there are one or more teachers in the classroom who speak the home languages of DLLs, pair them in a group together so that they can receive instruction in their home language as well as in English during activities.

- Focus on activities that help children get to know you and their classmates. For example, play games and sing songs that help children learn one another's names as well as the names of their teachers. Learning the names of the adults and children around them can help children feel comfortable in a new learning environment.

- Plan learning center activities that require minimal effort to set up and clean up during the first weeks of school. Being able to give as much of your full attention as possible to the children will help you manage transitions more smoothly throughout the day.

- Focus early lessons on helping children learn key words and phrases that will help them navigate the school day, including words that help them express their needs and feelings and interact effectively with other children. Focusing lessons on teaching children advanced vocabulary words (such as the names of dinosaurs) may be better saved for later in the school year once children have mastered basic words that will be most relevant to them. Vocabulary lists in English and Spanish are provided in Appendix 3.1.

- At the beginning of the year, choose themes that are relevant to children that can be extended throughout the day into many different types of learning experiences. For example, themes that are relevant at the beginning of the school year might include "I am special," "making new friends," and "fall/autumn season." Focusing on themes relevant in children's everyday life will provide an opportunity to teach vocabulary that children may need during typical interactions. As the year continues and you learn more about the children in your classroom, consider adopting an emergent curriculum approach and choosing themes based on the interests of children in your class. Pay attention to the conversations that children have as well as the books, activities, materials, or toys that they seem most interested in. For example, if your dramatic play area is set up as a doctor's office but children are using the stethoscope with animals, consider transitioning to a veterinarian theme. If children feel connected to and excited about your classroom themes, they will be more likely to engage in learning activities associated with the theme.

CHAPTER CONCLUSIONS

There are many things early childhood educators can do before school begins to help support children who are DLLs. Although setting up your classroom with these strategies at the beginning of the school year may be especially helpful, we hope that the strategies presented in this chapter can also be useful at any point during the school year. Remember that the first few days, weeks, and even months of school will be an important period of adjustment for the children in your classroom and their families and that flexibility and understanding is key. As you get to know the children that will be in your class and their families, use knowledge of culture to guide you in the supports you offer them but avoid making assumptions about children and families based on race, ethnicity, culture, or language. Take the time to get to know each child and family individually so that you can start the school year meeting the needs of each in the way they would like.

> *Take the time to get to know each child and family individually so that you can start the school year meeting the needs of each in the way they would like.*

Chapter 3: Check Your Learning

1. The National Association for the Education of Young Children provides specific recommendations for using the classroom environment to promote _____.
   a) An understanding of compassion
   b) An awareness of self and others
   c) An appreciation for diversity
   d) A and b only

2. Name the strategies presented in this chapter that educators can use to get to know children and families before the school year begins. Select all that apply.
   a) Conduct a home visit.
   b) Send family surveys.
   c) Engage community organizations or cultural brokers.
   d) Invite them to visit the classroom.

3. The Early Childhood Environment Rating Scale–Revised Edition (ECERS-R) and the Four Curricular Subscales Extension to the Early Childhood Environment Rating Scale (ECERS-E) are assessments designed to measure the quality of an early childhood environment. However, neither assessment measures criteria related to diversity, including race and gender.
   a) True
   b) False

4. Labeling objects in the classroom in English, Spanish, and other classroom languages will _____.
   a) Discourage associations between print language and spoken language
   b) Help children learn how to say *milk* and *block* in multiple languages
   c) Communicate the importance of children's home languages
   d) Stall the development of new vocabulary words

5. How can a quiet or calm corner be used to benefit dual language learners (DLLs)?
   a) By providing children with a space to calm down when overwhelmed
   b) By punishing children through putting them into "time out"
   c) By designating a place where children can seek one-on-one time with a teacher or peer
   d) A and c only

6. Why is it important to consider children's energy levels, access to materials, and classroom layout when creating an activity schedule?
   _____
   _____
   _____
   _____

7. Group lessons planned at the beginning of the year should be short so that children can get used to group learning activities and develop the ability to focus.
   a) True
   b) False

8. _____ is foundational to creating an effective learning environment for all children, including DLLs.
   a) Celebrating the children most likely to succeed
   b) Building relationships with families and children
   c) Engaging in dialogue about language and culture
   d) Engaging in dialogue about home–school connections

9. At the beginning of the school year, it is better to limit access to materials that children need to complete activities so that children have to ask a teacher if they need something.
   a) True
   b) False

10. At the beginning of the year, planning more _____ group activities rather than _____ group activities may help teachers to get to know children better and allow opportunities to provide individualized support.
    a) Low energy . . . high energy
    b) High energy . . . low energy
    c) Large . . . small
    d) Small . . . large

For answers to this chapter quiz, please refer to the Answer Key on page 182.

Chapter 3 — Reflection Questions

1. How would you like children and families to feel when they enter your classroom for the first time?

   _____
   _____
   _____
   _____

2. How do you think children and families might be feeling at the start of the school year? How might the feelings of dual language learners and their families be similar to or different from those of other families?

   _____
   _____
   _____
   _____

3. What are your favorite strategies for helping families from diverse backgrounds feel welcome at the beginning of the year?

   _____
   _____
   _____
   _____

4. What materials do you have for display or use in your classroom that can help children to develop an appreciation for diversity? What additional materials might be helpful?

   _____
   _____
   _____
   _____

Chapter 3: Classroom Activities

ACTIVITY 1: Calm Basket

MATERIALS: Basket or box, an assortment of materials that might help a child feel calm or calm down (e.g., stuffed animal, blanket, book), images of actions that might help a child feel calm or calm down (e.g., hugging a teacher)

INSTRUCTIONS: In the quiet corner of your classroom, place a box or basket with an assortment of materials intended to help children feel calm or calm down after experiencing intense feelings. Along with these items, include images of things that children can do to help them feel calm or calm down. Help children learn to look through the basket when they need support calming down and identifying something that might help them feel better or that they would like to try.

SKILL DEVELOPMENT: Using the items in the calm basket is one way that educators can help children manage their emotions. The concrete nature of the calm basket may make it easier for children to learn to find a strategy on their own once they have learned how to use the basket and have strategies that they identify as being helpful to them.

APPLYING CULTURALLY RESPONSIVE PRACTICES TO THIS ACTIVITY: Recognize that children might need different strategies to help them feel calm and safe. Providing a calm basket of choices can help children identify a strategy that best fits their needs. Use information from families to help determine items that should be included in the calm basket to support the diverse needs of the children in your classroom. Label each item in English, Spanish, or other languages represented in your classroom.

ACTIVITY 2: Family Pictures

MATERIALS: Family photos, photo album, art supplies to decorate pages (optional)

INSTRUCTIONS: At the beginning of the school year, ask families to send a family picture to school that can be included in the classroom family photo book. Use the family photo book in a number of ways, including at drop-off if children are feeling sad about separating from their family members, for sharing at circle time, and to help build relationships between children and one another and you.

SKILL DEVELOPMENT: Provide children with the opportunity to practice oral language skills through sharing their family picture with their classmates at circle time. Ask children to share about members of their family and what their family likes to do together. Family photos can also be used to help children practice and develop social and emotional skills. For example, looking at photos together with a teacher or friend can help children regulate unpleasant feelings they may experience when separating from family members at the beginning of the day or if they are missing family members throughout the day.

APPLYING CULTURALLY RESPONSIVE PRACTICES TO THIS ACTIVITY: Highlight and celebrate the diversity in your classroom when sharing family photos as a class. The children in your class may have many different people in their families as well as different family sizes. Point out this diversity with children in an objective manner (e.g., "Some of the families in our class have two people. Some have three, four, or even more people"; "Some of our classmates live with a grandparent. Some live with their mom, their dad, their aunt, or other family members"). Discussing similarities and differences across families in an objective way communicates to children that families can take many different forms and that all family forms are valued. Help support dual language learners (DLLs) in their ability to share information about their families along with the other children in the class. Ask children to name each person in their photo if they are able

(continued)

Chapter 3 Classroom Activities (continued)

to and ask questions that help them practice family-related words in English and in their home language (e.g., "Is that your grandmother? Abuela? Let's all try saying those words: *grandmother, abuela*"). DLLs may be able to participate in discussions about their family in different ways depending on their level of English language development. For example, dual language learners may be able to point at different family members when asked (e.g., "Show me your brother") or they may be able to provide more in-depth responses to questions about their families as their vocabulary develops (e.g., "What do you and your family like to do together?").

Chapter 3: Additional Resources

BOOK:

Many Languages, Building Connections: Supporting Infants and Toddlers Who Are Dual Language Learners
Author: Karen Nemeth
Year: 2012
Publisher: Gryphon House

WEB-BASED RESOURCES:

50 Multicultural Books Every Child Should Know
Cooperative Children's Book Center, School of Education, University of Wisconsin-Madison
Compiled by: Kathleen T. Horning, Carling Febry, Merri T. Lindgren, Megan Schliesman
Web site: https://ccbc.education.wisc.edu/books/detailListBooks.asp?idBookLists=42

Centering Your Classroom: Setting the Stage for Engaged Learners
Young Children on the Web
Author: Gayle M. Stuber
Year: 2007
Web site: https://www.naeyc.org/files/yc/file/200707/OfPrimaryInterest.pdf

Serving Head Start's Diverse Children and Families: What Is the Law? What Are the Regulations?
Office of Head Start, National Center on Cultural and Linguistic Responsiveness
Web site: http://eclkc.ohs.acf.hhs.gov/hslc/tta-system/cultural-linguistic/fcp/docs/serving-head-starts-diverse-families-laws-regs.pdf

How to Choose the Best Multicultural Books
Authors: Luther B. Clegg, Etta Miller, Bill Vanderhoof, Gonzalo Ramirez, Peggy K. Ford
Scholastic
Web site: http://www.scholastic.com/teachers/article/how-choose-best-multicultural-books

NAEYC Early Childhood Program Standards and Accreditation Criteria and Guidance for Assessment
National Association for the Education of Young Children
Year: 2015
Web site: http://www.naeyc.org/files/academy/file/AllCriteriaDocument.pdf

Welcome Children and Families to Your Classroom
National Association for the Education of Young Children
Teaching Young Children
Year: 2009
Web site: http://www.naeyc.org/tyc/article/welcome-children-and-families-to-your-classroom

Appendix 3.1

Vocabulary Word Lists

Common Words and Phrases for the Beginning of the Year		
English	Spanish	Other Language
hello	hola	
goodbye	adiós	
please	por favor	
thank you	gracias	
friend	la amiga/el amigo	
eat/snack/lunch	comer/la merienda/el almuerzo	
milk	la leche	
water	el agua	
circle time	hora de actividades en círculo	
nap time	hora de la siesta	
story time	hora de escuchar cuentos	
book/to read	el libro/leer	
time to go outside	hora de salir	
time to go inside	hora de entrar	
Do you want a hug?	¿Quieres un abrazo?	
My name is…/His or her name is…	Mi nombre es…/Su nombre es…	
Do you want to play?	¿Quieres jugar?	
Mom/Dad will be back after school.	Mamá/Papá regresará cuando termine la escuela.	
I don't like that.	No me gusta eso.	
I like that.	Me gusta eso.	
yes	sí	
no	no	
Do you need to go to the bathroom?	¿Necesitas ir al baño?	
I don't understand.	No entiendo.	
Can you show me?	¿Puedes mostrarme?	

(continued)

Appendix 3.1 Vocabulary Word Lists *(continued)*

Words to Label Items in Your Classroom		
English	Spanish	Other Language
door	la puerta	
window	la ventana	
cubby	el casillero	
table	la mesa	
chair	la silla	
floor	el piso	
water fountain	la fuente para beber agua	
bathroom	el baño	
crayons	los crayones	
markers	los marcadores	
paper	el papel	
scissors	las tijeras	
pencils	los lápices	
clock	el reloj	
blocks	los bloques	
dolls	las muñecas	
cars	los autos/coches	
trucks	los camiones	
kitchen	la cocina	
mirror	el espejo	
sink	el lavamanos	

Prosocial Phrases		
English	Spanish	Other Language
please	por favor	
thank you	gracias	
Want to play?	¿Quieres jugar?	
Can I play too?	¿Puedo jugar yo también?	
My name is . . .	Mi nombre es . . .	

(continued)

Appendix 3.1 Vocabulary Word Lists (continued)

English	Spanish	Other Language
What's your name?	¿Cómo te llamas?	
Let's take turns!	¡Vamos a tomar turnos!	
your turn	tu turno	
my turn	mi turno	
Can you help me?	¿Puedes ayudarme?	
Can I help you?	¿Puedo ayudarte?	
I'm sorry.	Lo siento.	
Are you okay?	¿Estás bien?	
I don't like it when you do that.	No me gusta cuando haces eso.	
Please stop.	Por favor, deja de hacer eso.	

Classroom Items

English	Spanish	Other Language
backpack	la mochila	
cubby	el casillero	
books	los libros	
blocks	los bloques	
pen	el bolígrafo	
pencil	el lápiz	
markers	los marcadores	
table	la mesa	
scissors	las tijeras	
glue	el pegamento	
chair	la silla	
teacher	el maestro/la maestra	
friends	los amigos/las amigas	
clock	el reloj	

(continued)

45 Strategies That Support Young Dual Language Learners by Shauna L. Tominey and Elisabeth C. O'Bryon.
Copyright © 2018 Paul H. Brookes Publishing Co., Inc. All rights reserved.

Appendix 3.1 Vocabulary Word Lists (continued)

On the Playground

English	Spanish	Other Language
swings	el columpio	
slide	el tobogán	
monkey bars	las barras	
climbing structure	la estructura para trepar	
sandbox	la caja de arena	
teeter totter	subibaja/balancín	
run	correr	
play	jugar	
jump	saltar/brincar	

Clothes

English	Spanish	Other Language
shirt	la camisa	
pants	los pantalones	
dress	el vestido	
skirt	la falda	
coat/jacket	el abrigo/la chaqueta	
gloves	los guantes	
hat	el gorro	
shoes	los zapatos	
socks	los calcetines	

Food

English	Spanish	Other Language
apple	la manzana	
orange	la naranja	
banana	la banana/el plátano	
bread	el pan	
cereal	el cereal	

(continued)

Appendix 3.1 Vocabulary Word Lists (continued)

English	Spanish	Other Language
beans	los frijoles	
corn	el maíz	
rice	el arroz	
ice cream	el helado	

Colors

English	Spanish	Other Language
red	rojo/a	
orange	naranja	
yellow	amarillo/a	
green	verde	
blue	azul	
purple	morado/a	
brown	marrón	
black	negro/a	
white	blanco/a	
gray	gris	
rainbow	el arco iris	
colors	los colores	

Weather and Seasons

English	Spanish	Other Language
sun	el sol	
rain	la lluvia	
snow	la nieve	
clouds	las nubes	
fog	la niebla	
winter	el invierno	
spring	la primavera	
fall	el otoño	
summer	el verano	

(continued)

Appendix 3.1 Vocabulary Word Lists (continued)

Animals		
English	Spanish	Other Language
dog	el perro	
cat	el gato	
cow	la vaca	
horse	el caballo	
goat	la cabra	
sheep	la oveja	
chicken	el pollo	
bird	el pájaro	
bug	el insecto	
butterfly	la mariposa	
fish	el pez	
shark	el tiburón	
tiger	el tigre	
elephant	el elefante	
lion	el león	
zebra	la cebra	
giraffe	la jirafa	
fox	el zorro	

Days of the Week		
English	Spanish	Other Language
Sunday	domingo	
Monday	lunes	
Tuesday	martes	
Wednesday	miércoles	
Thursday	jueves	
Friday	viernes	
Saturday	sábado	

(continued)

Appendix 3.1 Vocabulary Word Lists (continued)

Months of the Year		
English	Spanish	Other Language
January	enero	
February	febrero	
March	marzo	
April	abril	
May	mayo	
June	junio	
July	julio	
August	agosto	
September	septiembre	
October	octubre	
November	noviembre	
December	diciembre	

People		
English	Spanish	Other Language
mother	la madre/mamá	
father	el padre/papá	
brother	el hermano	
sister	la hermana	
cousin	el primo/la prima	
grandmother	la abuela	
grandfather	el abuelo	
aunt	la tía	
uncle	el tío	
friend	el amigo/la amiga	
neighbor	el vecino/la vecina	
nanny	el niñero/la niñera	
teacher	el maestro/la maestra	

(continued)

Appendix 3.1 Vocabulary Word Lists *(continued)*

Parts of the Body		
English	Spanish	Other Language
head	la cabeza	
shoulders	los hombros	
arms	los brazos	
hands	las manos	
legs	las piernas	
foot	los pies	
eyes	los ojos	
ears	las orejas	
mouth	la boca	
nose	la nariz	
elbows	los codos	
knees	las rodillas	
hair	el cabello	

Verbs		
English	Spanish	Other Language
walk	caminar	
run	correr	
jump	saltar/brincar	
dance	bailar	
stomp	pisar fuerte	
tiptoe	andar en puntas de pie	
eat	comer	
play	jugar	
sleep	dormir	
share	compartir/repartir	
write	escribir	
draw	dibujar	

Appendix 3.2

Sample Parent Questionnaire in English

Dear Family,

Welcome! We are excited to welcome you and your child to our classroom. Please help us learn about your child as we prepare for a new school year.

- Has your child attended preschool before?

- What language (or languages) does your family speak at home?

- What language is your child most comfortable speaking?

- Who is in your family?

- What are your child's favorite toys and activities?

- What are your child's favorite foods?

- How does your child let you know that he or she is hungry?

- How does your child let you know when he or she needs to go to the bathroom?

- What words do you use at home to talk about going to the bathroom?

- Does your child have any fears?

- What do you usually do to help your child calm down when he or she is upset?

- Does your child take naps? If so, for how long?

- Is there anything that helps your child fall asleep?

- What are your favorite family activities?

- What is the best way for us to share information with you?

We look forward to meeting you and your family! If you have any questions, please contact

_____.

Appendix 3.3

Sample Parent Questionnaire in Spanish

Estimadas familia,

¡Bienvenidos a _____! Estamos muy contentos de darle la bienvenida a usted y a su hijo/a a nuestro aula. Por favor, ayúdenos a reunir más información acerca de su hijo/a mientras nos preparamos para el nuevo año escolar.

- ¿Su hijo/a ha asistido antes a la escuela preescolar?

- ¿Qué idioma (o idiomas) hablan usted y su familia en la casa?

- ¿En qué idioma prefiere hablar su hijo/a?

- ¿Quiénes integran su familia?

- ¿Cuáles son los juguetes y las actividades que su hijo/a prefiere?

- ¿Cuáles son las comidas favoritas de su hijo/a?

- ¿De qué manera le hace saber su hijo/a que tiene hambre?

- ¿De qué manera le hace saber su hijo/a que tiene que ir al baño?

- ¿Qué palabras usa usted en su casa para hablar de ir al baño?

- ¿Su hijo/a tiene miedo de algo?

- ¿Qué hace usted para calmar a su hijo/a cuando se siente mal?

- ¿Toma siestas su hijo/a? Si es así, ¿por cuánto tiempo?

- ¿Hay algo que ayuda a su hijo/a a dormir?

- ¿Cuáles son las actividades favoritas de la familia?

- ¿Cuál es la mejor manera de compartir información con usted?

¡Esperamos conocerle y a su familia! Si tiene alguna pregunta, haga el favor de contactarnos:

_____.

4 Fostering a Classroom Community of Diverse Learners

It is the middle of the school year and Claudia and her family have just moved to a new town. Her parents enrolled her in a preschool for the first time. Claudia was born in the United States but grew up in a Portuguese-speaking neighborhood. She hears English on television and in the community, so she knows a few English words, but she is most comfortable speaking Portuguese at home. When she goes to her preschool classroom for the first time, she does not know what to expect and feels overwhelmed by all there is to see—a new environment, new faces, a new routine—all in a language that she is only just beginning to learn. Claudia's teacher, Ms. Adele, hopes that Claudia will feel comfortable and safe in her classroom, but she knows it may take time to get to that point. During Claudia's first few weeks of school, Ms. Adele's primary focus is on helping children get to know Claudia and helping Claudia get to know other children in the class while she is adjusting to a new place and routine.

STRATEGIES

10 Set the Foundation for Warm and Trusting Relationships

11 Anticipate Children's Challenges and Needs

12 Create a Classroom Community

13 Frame Diversity as a Strength

APPENDIX

4.1 Identifying Student Needs

Starting a new school or starting school for the first time can be overwhelming for children whether they are dual language learners like Claudia or fluent English speakers. Typical challenges children might experience at the beginning of a new school year include the following:

- Separation anxiety
- Getting used to a new environment
- Adjusting to new routines and schedules
- Meeting new people (adults and children)
- Participating in new activities
- Learning new rules
- Navigating norms, beliefs, or values that are different from those at home
- Trying new foods
- Riding the bus for the first time
- Being cared for by someone other than a family member for the first time
- Being introduced to a group setting in which individual time and attention from caregivers is given less frequently than they are accustomed to
- Adjusting to new naptime or rest-time routines

How children respond to each of these challenges depends on many different factors, including the child's age, personality, previous experiences with school or caregivers other than family members, relationship with their teacher and peers, their family's reactions to challenges and change, and many others. For example, some children might find meeting new people very interesting and exciting, whereas others might find it nerve-wracking or even terrifying. Some children might thrive in an environment in which they are being exposed to new activities throughout the day, whereas others might find it overwhelming. Some children might experience mixed emotions during any given activity. Others might experience emotions that change throughout the day—for instance, thriving in a new environment at the beginning of the day when well-rested but melting down by the middle of the day when exhausted.

Experiencing a major transition, such as transitioning to school, is taxing for children, no matter how they respond to each challenge that arises. Imagine now how the challenges that come with starting a new school year might be heightened for a child who is a DLL. Not speaking the dominant language may make it challenging for children to express their emotions and their needs, making every task that much more difficult. They may also be unfamiliar with the cultural norms or expectations in the classroom or school.

Along with being unfamiliar with the language, children who are dual language learners may also be unfamiliar with the cultural norms or expectations in the classroom or school.

Teacher characteristics, beliefs, and values can also affect a child's experience at school. One study found that teachers rate relationships with children as being more positive when they share the same ethnicity (Saft & Pianta, 2001). It's important for early childhood educators to be aware of this potential for bias and be mindful of how they create and maintain positive relationships with all children. Without meaning to, early childhood educators may also bring biases to the way they interpret interactions that may affect their relationships with children. Let's think about one scenario.

Damien loves his new teacher, Ms. Lindsey. She smiles and hugs him whenever he comes up to her. She uses gestures and pictures to help him communicate when he needs something and she even tries to use words in his home language. He wants her to like him and is excited to learn new things from her. During free-play time, Damien starts wrestling another boy in his class in the block area. The other boy seems to be enjoying it as much as Damien, so he feels surprised when Ms. Lindsey comes over to them scowling and pulls the two of them apart. Her face, tone of voice, and body language tells Damien that he has done something wrong. He feels confused and worries that Ms. Lindsey no longer likes him.

In this example, Damien feels confused because he was participating in an activity (wrestling) that was perfectly acceptable at home, but that did not seem to be acceptable at school. In Damien's home culture, adults actively encourage young boys to have fun in physical ways, noting that "boys will be boys" and encouraging them to build their strength. Damien and his brothers, male cousins, and uncles regularly engage in play wrestling matches as a way of bonding and spending time together. Over the next few weeks, Damien continues to wrestle other children in the classroom and on the playground. Each time he does, he sees the same negative reaction and, with time, he learns that wrestling is okay and even encouraged at home, but not at school.

Some rules, like "no wrestling," are easier to communicate than others. As children from diverse linguistic and cultural backgrounds navigate new situations, the spoken and unspoken rules take time to learn. When a language barrier is present, it can take even longer than expected for these rules to be learned, because communicating what a rule is and why it is important may be challenging. An important part of helping all children learn classroom expectations and norms is helping them learn what *to do* instead of just what *not to do,* and that takes many more skills than just saying "no" or "don't do that."

There are many ways early childhood educators can help children who are DLLs adjust to school, navigate the challenges that arise on a daily basis and throughout the school year, learn new routines and expectations, and form meaningful relationships with the adults and children in the classroom. In this chapter, we recommend four strategies for creating a classroom community supportive of diverse learners:

- Strategy 10: Set the Foundation for Warm and Trusting Relationships
- Strategy 11: Anticipate Children's Challenges and Needs
- Strategy 12: Create a Classroom Community
- Strategy 13: Frame Diversity as a Strength

STRATEGY 10: Set the Foundation for Warm and Trusting Relationships

At the heart of effective early learning environments are the relationships between teachers and young children. Having a warm and trusting relationship with one or more of the adults in their lives helps children feel safe and secure, enabling a child to be ready for learning.

In research, a child's relationship with his or her parent or caregiver is called an "attachment relationship" (Bowlby, 2008). **Attachment** relationships with parents and caregivers start from birth, and some would argue that these relationships begin even before birth. Most research on attachment focuses on the relationships between parents and their children, but research also shows that early childhood educators are an important part of children's early social experiences and can form a **secondary attachment** (sometimes called **earned attachment**) with young children (Bowlby, 2007). When young children have a secure relationship with a caregiver or educator, they are more likely to want to be like and emulate that individual, they are more likely to turn to that individual for comfort and help, and they are more likely to want to learn from that individual. Building positive and warm relationships is also foundational to developing culturally responsive practices (Han & Thomas, 2010). Getting to know children helps you learn what they need to feel supported.

Although 60%–65% of children are estimated to have a **secure attachment** with a parent or caregiver, 35%–40% of children have other types of attachment relationships, including insecure attachments (Berk, 2012). Having a secure attachment with a teacher at school can help protect children from the negative effects of having an insecure attachment at home (Mitchell-Copeland, Denham, & DeMulder, 1997). Creating and maintaining secure attachment relationships with young children who are DLLs may be especially challenging because of possible language barriers, but they are still very important. One study including 468 Hispanic American preschool children (ages 3–5) examined children's relationships with their parents and teachers and the association between those relationships and children's language abilities. Children who had higher-quality relationships with their teachers had higher English language abilities than children who had weaker relationships with teachers (Oades-Sese & Li, 2011). It is important to note that this study was correlational, which means that the direction of this relationship is unknown. It is possible that having a stronger relationship with teachers helped children benefit more from language instruction and learn language more quickly. It is also possible that having stronger English language skills made it easier for children to build relationships with teachers. Either way, there are many things early childhood educators can do to promote warm and trusting relationships with the children in their classrooms, verbally as well as nonverbally, to foster secure and trusting relationships and support children's language development.

> *At the heart of effective early learning environments are the relationships between teachers and young children.*

Apply Strategy 10

- Get to know each child in your classroom as an individual. This is a strategy that we mention at multiple points throughout the book because of the importance of building positive relationships with children and families. Although the focus of this book is on children who are DLLs, building a secure attachment is important for all children in your class. Take time to ask questions of children and families about their likes and dislikes and the things that are important to them. These conversations will facilitate deeper connections with children while also helping families feel involved and supported.

- Show interest in a child's home language and culture. As mentioned in Chapter 2, incorporating children's home languages is an important best practice for supporting DLLs. It is also a way to help facilitate a positive relationship with children as well as their families. When children who are DLLs arrive in a new environment, they may initially try to communicate in their home language. If these attempts fail (e.g., children are not able to communicate their needs effectively; children's attempts are ignored by peers or teachers), they may stop trying and instead enter a period of time during which they are nonverbal (Tabors, 2008). During this nonverbal period, you may observe children communicating primarily by gestures as they develop their receptive language skills. Incorporating children's home language when possible (e.g., during storybook reading, at circle time, by labeling classroom objects, etc.) sends the message to children that you value their language and models to them that you are trying to communicate in their home language just as they are also trying to learn English to communicate with you.

- Use **nonverbal cues,** including facial expressions, body language, and gestures, to build warm and supportive relationships with children. There are many ways that you can build relationships with children and adults through nonverbal methods. Getting down at a child's level, making eye contact, smiling, and using a kind and calm tone of voice can help children feel comfortable around you even if they are unable to understand the words you use. It is important to note, however, that nonverbal cues and gestures may have different meanings in different cultures. For example, in some cultures, children may be taught that making eye contact with an adult is disrespectful, whereas in others, children may be taught that it is respectful and required. Watch children and families for the nonverbal cues they are using and ask others if you are unsure if nonverbal cues you are using are appropriate.

- Get to know children's nonverbal cues. In her observations of children who were dual language learners, Tabors (2008) noted that children who are DLLs most often used nonverbal cues to ask for attention, make a request, protest or show they do not want or like something, and make jokes and show their sense of humor. Observing the nonverbal cues that children in your class use and taking note of those cues can help you get to know children and their needs. You can also use these opportunities to provide individualized attention and support to DLLs. For example, if you notice that a child pulls on your hand to ask for help, this may be an opportunity to teach and practice new phrases for asking for help in English and the child's home language.

- Help children get to know you as well. Share with children your own likes and dislikes. Use photographs and pictures as a way to bring your stories to life and to supplement auditory information for DLLs. For example, share pictures of your own family with the class on sharing days.

STRATEGY 11: Anticipate Children's Challenges and Needs

Early childhood educators play a critical role in helping children navigate the challenges related to adjusting to early childhood learning settings as well as the challenges that arise throughout the school year. Because young children—and especially children who are

Need	What It Might Look Like	How to Anticipate It	How to Manage It
Danny needs to go to the bathroom.	Crossing his legs, holding himself between his legs, trouble concentrating, crying	Give children a tour of the classroom at the beginning of the school day, and show children key areas, such as the bathroom, hand-washing sink, and cubbies.	Offer children regular opportunities to go to the bathroom throughout the day, using a picture of the bathroom and incorporating each child's home language to help communicate the message.

Figure 4.1. Identifying student needs: Danny.

DLLs—may not be able to express themselves effectively, early childhood educators might have to work harder to anticipate their emotions and recognize their needs throughout the day as they are adjusting to school.

Think about a child who is having difficulties expressing a need. Danny is 3 and a half years old. He was recently toilet-trained. His family just moved to the United States from France, and with such a big transition, he has started having regular accidents again. Danny speaks only French. How can his teacher identify Danny's need, anticipate this need, and manage the need in the moment?

Figure 4.1 provides four columns focused on identifying a need (Danny needs to use the bathroom), considering what the need might look like, anticipating this need, and managing the need in the moment. Thinking about the needs children might have difficulty communicating throughout the day is one way to anticipate these needs and consider ahead of time what you can do to help.

Here is another scenario. Ella is 4 years old and primarily speaks Spanish, although she knows a few English words. Right before naptime, another child takes her special stuffed bear. No one else notices what happened. Ella sits on her cot and starts to cry, sobbing and repeating the words "Mi oso. Mi oso." Figure 4.2 presents some strategies for supporting Ella's needs in this situation.

Think about other needs that might arise in your classroom. Figure 4.3 is a blank chart you can use to reflect on strategies for anticipating and supporting children as needs arise

Need	What It Might Look Like	How to Anticipate It	How to Manage It
Ella is feeling upset that her special toy was taken from her.	Crying, pointing at another child, acting out aggressively toward another child or even acting withdrawn	Teach and practice expected behavior in the classroom.	Help calm Ella by getting down at her level and speaking to her in a soothing voice. Attend to her hand gestures (e.g., look at who she is pointing to). Try to understand what she is communicating and ask questions, if appropriate.

Figure 4.2. Identifying student needs: Ella.

Need	What It Might Look Like	How to Anticipate It	How to Manage It
A child misses mother/father/family or is experiencing separation anxiety.			
A child is having trouble sitting still for an activity or at circle time.			
A child is trying to communicate something to you, but you are not able to understand what he or she is saying.			

Figure 4.3. Identifying student needs: You try it exercise.

throughout the day. For the first three rows, complete the boxes to the right of each need. Additional rows allow you to add your own list of needs that you expect might to arise.

Apply Strategy 11

- Begin getting to know children even before the school year begins. Use surveys from families collected at the beginning of the year to provide information that can help you to anticipate children's needs. Sample parent questionnaires in English and Spanish are provided in Chapter 3 appendices.

- Consider the emotions that underlie children's behaviors. According to emotional intelligence theory, emotions affect children in many ways, including their ability to pay attention and their behaviors (Salovey & Mayer, 1990). In fact, children's behaviors are often preceded by an emotion. For example, a child who hits another child may have done so because he felt *angry* when another child took his toy. A child who refuses to sit at the lunch table may be feeling *disappointed* that she cannot sit by her best friend. Consider learning words for basic emotions in the languages represented by families in your classroom (e.g., sad, happy, angry, calm, frustrated, disappointed). In addition, have pictures of faces showing different emotions available for children to use to share their feelings. Pinpointing a child's emotions can help you to figure out how to best manage their behavior in a situation. For example, if Carlos is having trouble sitting through circle time because he is bored and does not have the attention skills to focus for long periods of time, perhaps the lessons you are planning at the beginning of the year are too long. If Carlos is having trouble sitting through circle time because he is uncomfortable and needs to use the bathroom, a different strategy is needed, such as encouraging him to try using the bathroom each day before circle time begins.

- Recognize that children may show the same needs in different ways. For example, Amelia may get very quiet when she feels nervous or overwhelmed in the classroom and withdraw to the quiet corner. Kyle may become physically agitated when overwhelmed and run from place to place in the classroom. Getting to know each child's individual cues can help you identify his or her feelings.

- Recognize that children who are dual language learners may not have the words to express themselves at the beginning of the year, so you may play a larger role in helping to manage their emotions and meeting their needs. In addition, children may come from cultural backgrounds in which they are encouraged to express their needs to adults *or* from cultural backgrounds in which children are discouraged from expressing their needs to adults. Being aware of this fact can also help you consider questions you might ask families in order to learn more about their practices at home so that you can better understand and support children's behavior in the classroom.

> *Getting to know each child's individual cues can help you identify his or her feelings.*

- Show children how to use the quiet corner as a place to calm down or have quiet time, connect with an adult, or reflect. Avoid using the quiet corner as a punitive spot. Take children to the quiet corner when they experience intense emotions or if they are having trouble expressing themselves or getting along with others. Use images or books that depict various feelings to help children identify how they feel by pointing to pictures and using feeling words in English as well as a child's home language. The quiet corner should also be a place where children can use "transitional objects" from home (e.g., stuffed animals, blankets), which may ease their adjustment to school.

STRATEGY 12: Create a Classroom Community

Creating a **classroom community** involves putting in place supports for DLLs as well as for all children in the classroom. Involving all children in creating a supportive classroom community is essential to ensuring that all children have the feelings educators would like them to have—feelings that will help children be ready to learn, such as security, support, happiness, excitement, curiosity, and interest. Creating a classroom community goes beyond giving DLLs the support they need to feel like part of the classroom. It also involves helping children develop the skills they need to have access to the same social and educational experiences as other children. Finally, creating a classroom community includes ensuring that all children learn to value their own culture as well as the culture and values of peers from backgrounds that are similar and different, showing genuine curiosity and interest in one another and viewing other beliefs and values with interest and compassion.

Children have a natural curiosity about one another, and many children are eager to make friends and build relationships with other children. Although it may seem like friendships will occur naturally in a classroom (they will!), support from educators is needed to ensure that children have the skills they need to build and maintain relationships in a way that is inclusive of all children in a classroom. Fostering positive relationships across diverse groups of children takes skill development, practice, and encouragement from educators. There are many factors that affect a child's ability to make friends with others, including the social skills that they have as well as their personality traits. Language difference is another possible factor. Children make adjustments to how they play with others based on the other children's language abilities. For example, children who speak the dominant language in a preschool classrooms have been observed to treat children who are dual language learners like infants (Tabors, 2008). By being aware of this potential, early childhood educators can help children learn and practice skills to reach out to their classmates in an appropriate way.

Although it may seem like friendships will occur naturally in a classroom (they will!), support from educators is needed to ensure that children have the skills they need to build and maintain relationships in a way that is inclusive of all children in a classroom.

Apply Strategy 12

- Help children learn one another's names as well as the names of teachers in the classroom. Sing songs or play games that encourage children to practice saying each other's names. Some names may be more challenging for children to say than others, depending on their language abilities and familiarity with the sounds in a language. Practice pronouncing each child's name accurately and help children do the same.
- Talk openly with children about the different languages that are spoken in your classroom. Share with children that some children in our class are learning English and that they may need our help practicing new words. Remind children who speak English as a first language that, just as they can help their classmates practice English, their

classmates can help them learn words in their home language. Encourage language learning to be a reciprocal relationship between children rather than a one-way exchange that only values English learning.

> *Encourage language learning to be a reciprocal relationship between children rather than a one-way exchange in favor of English learning.*

- Provide children with varied opportunities to get to know one another. For example, use a **think-pair-share** or "turn and talk" approach during large or small group times. Ask children to turn to the person next to them and share an answer to a question that you ask. As children are developing their comfort in the group and learning new vocabulary, keep questions simple or ask questions that only require nonverbal responses. These types of activities can help children practice language and vocabulary skills with their peers in a way that is not as intimidating as speaking in front of the large group.

- During partner opportunities, alternate between pairing children who speak the same home language (if possible) who can serve as conversation partners to help promote one another's language development together with pairs who do not speak the same home language.

- Provide children with opportunities to teach one another in their native language. For example, if you count the days on the calendar together as a class every morning, alternate the language. Ask children in your class who speak Spanish or other languages to help the class count together in their home language. Providing leadership opportunities for all children (those who speak English as well as those who speak other languages) can help them develop pride in their own culture and language, convey competence to peers, build confidence in their ability to share their home language, and show that they are valued members of the learning community.

- Help children learn words in multiple languages that help them interact prosocially with one another. For example, at the beginning of the year, use books or role play to have children practice asking, "Want to play?" or "Can I play too?" in English, Spanish, or other languages spoken by children in the classroom. A list of vocabulary words in English and Spanish related to **prosocial behaviors** is included at the end of Chapter 3 (see Appendix 3.1).

STRATEGY 13: Frame Diversity as a Strength

It is natural for children to notice similarities and differences between themselves and their peers as they learn about the world. They may notice something about the way another child speaks, they may want to reach out and touch another's child's curly hair if they have straight hair, or they may stare at another child who wears different clothing from theirs or at another child whose skin color is different from their own, especially if they have never seen this difference before. Many studies have shown that young children look longer at people, items, or phenomena that are new or unexpected.

When adults see young children stare, it sometimes makes them feel uncomfortable. As a result, an adult may tell them that it is not polite to stare or shush them if they are making a comment about someone else ("Why is he wearing that?"). In doing this, however, we are sending children a message that talking about differences is not okay and is something that is frowned on or discouraged. To help children learn to appreciate both the similarities and differences between themselves and others (and use a strengths-based approach when considering the world), educators can help children learn appropriate ways to talk about differences and similarities. We can do this in a way that shows a genuine curiosity to learn about others as well as a desire to understand and appreciate other cultures, values, and beliefs.

Apply Strategy 13

- Choose classroom themes that celebrate the similarities and the differences within your class as strengths. Embedding multicultural messages as part of regular themes and classroom practices communicates the message to children that culture is all around them, not just a part of certain times of year (such as holidays) (Souto-Manning & Mitchell, 2010). For example, rather than inviting children's families to share their favorite traditions with the class once a year during the winter season, consider making this a regular occurrence throughout the school year. The conversations that accompany these experiences are critical to helping children view multicultural lessons with an open mindset (e.g., "This is a holiday that my family does not celebrate. I think it is really fun to learn about new holidays and traditions.").

- Talk about similarities and differences within your class. Chart eye color, hair color/length, favorite foods, likes/dislikes, favorite stories, or family traditions. Point out how wonderful it is to have so many children in the class with similarities as well as differences and that it is these differences that make each of us unique and special. Finding a way to creatively display artwork or classroom graphs and charts that highlight similarities and differences is one way to celebrate the message that "as a class, we value our similarities and differences."

- Help children identify and share things that make them special. Giving children an opportunity to share their strengths and to celebrate those strengths as a class can help build children's cultural and personal identity and boost self-esteem. Talk with the class about how important it is to help other people feel good about themselves. Share that it can be scary to feel like you are different from other people, so it's very brave to share things that are unique about yourself or your family. Teach children words they can say to support one another when they share (e.g., "Thank you for sharing." "That's cool! I never knew that before!" "I like the way you do that." "Can you tell me more about that?"). Communicate to children that by helping other people share and feel good about who they are, they can help one another feel proud, accepted, and valued.

- Teach children how to ask questions about differences and similarities they notice between themselves and their classmates and families. For example, if you overhear a child pointing out something he or she notices about another classmate (e.g., "Why does he wear glasses?), guide the two children in having a conversation about the difference ("Walter was wondering why you wear glasses. Can you tell us about your glasses?").

- Have open conversations with children about stereotypes and biases. For example, as you paint class portraits, talk about how great it is to see so many similarities and differences (e.g., "we all have two eyes, but our eyes come in many different colors"), but also share that sometimes people treat other people badly because of how they look, especially when they look differently or act differently from one another. Sometimes people treat one another differently because of the color of their skin or because they are a boy or a girl. Share with children that this is unfair and not how people should treat one another. Intentionally tackling stereotypes and biases during early childhood when children are developing their beliefs about the world will help them to be aware of and less likely to adopt biased viewpoints. This is critical to helping support the development of compassion and understanding in an increasingly diverse global society.

> *Intentionally tackling stereotypes and biases during early childhood when children are developing their beliefs about the world will help them to be aware of and less likely to adopt biased viewpoints.*

- Model a positive perspective toward diversity. When children share something about themselves, their home value, or culture, show and express genuine interest. You might say, "Wow. I never knew that before! That is so interesting." "I am really glad to learn about that." "I really like that tradition." "My family does things differently from yours, but isn't it great that there are so many different ways families can show each other they love each other?"

- Diversity exists within many forms in the classroom. It exists in terms of language, culture, abilities, socioeconomic status, age, and developmental levels as well as in other ways. Regardless of their background, treat all children in your classroom as competent, capable learners. When children experience challenges throughout the day (e.g., having difficulty communicating) or demonstrate difficult behaviors (e.g., having a temper tantrum), use empathy to frame the child's experience to the child and to other children. Use words that consider the child's perspective: "I know you wanted a turn. It's disappointing that we ran out of time."

- Other children look to you to set the example regarding how they should interpret their classmates' challenges. Children are often curious about the challenges that others are having. Watching others experience challenges, seeing how other children manage these challenges and how these challenges are supported (or not supported) by adults teaches children about effective and ineffective strategies, as well as who they can look to for support in the classroom. During and after experiencing a challenging situation with a child, it is important to realize that other children are likely to have taken away important messages from the interactions. Framing children to one another as learners helps children empathize with their classmates and see you as a source of support and understanding (e.g., "Sometimes Turner has tantrums. He's learning how to show us when he's angry. Maybe we can help him practice telling us with his words so that we can help him.").

CHAPTER CONCLUSIONS

There are many ways early childhood educators can help create a supportive classroom community for children from diverse backgrounds. Getting to know children as individuals, anticipating their needs as you get to know them, and helping children to build positive and supportive relationships with one another can create a classroom environment in which all children feel safe and supported. Framing diversity as a strength in your classroom can also help children to develop skills they need to effectively communicate with others from diverse linguistic and cultural backgrounds and ultimately lead to a more compassionate and understanding classroom community.

> *Framing diversity as a strength in your classroom can also help children to develop skills they need to effectively communicate with others from diverse linguistic and cultural backgrounds and ultimately lead to a more compassionate and understanding classroom community.*

Chapter 4: Check Your Learning

1. What percentage of children are estimated to have a secure attachment relationship with a parent or caregiver?
   a) 20%–25%
   b) 45%–50%
   c) 60%–65%
   d) 95%–100%

2. Who can children develop a secure attachment relationship with?
   a) A parent
   b) A teacher
   c) A grandparent
   d) All of the above

3. When introduced to a new environment, children who are dual language learners (DLLs) may first try to communicate in their home language and then _____.
   a) Give up and never speak their home language again
   b) Speak very loudly and slowly in their home language
   c) Enter a temporary nonverbal period
   d) None of the above

4. Studies have shown that for DLLs, high-quality relationships with teachers have a correlation with _____.
   a) Stronger relationships with peers
   b) Weaker English language abilities
   c) Stronger English language abilities
   d) Weaker abilities in the child's home language

5. Children who are DLLs most often use nonverbal cues to do which of the following? Select all that apply.
   a) Ask for attention
   b) Make a request
   c) Protest or refuse
   d) Make jokes

6. Children's _____ are often preceded by _____.
   a) Emotions . . . requests
   b) Behaviors . . . emotions
   c) Friendships . . . beliefs
   d) Needs . . . relationships

7. Creating a supportive classroom community means helping children find similarities between themselves and their classmates while ignoring the differences.
   a) True
   b) False

8. Which of the following statements made by teachers communicates diversity as a strength?
   a) "I saw you noticing his crutches. Would you like to ask him a question about them?"
   b) "I love learning about different ways that families do things. Does anyone else want to share what they are doing for the holidays?"
   c) "Look at all the different colors of hair we have in our classroom! Let's make another chart all together to see how we are the same and different."
   d) All of the above.

9. Talking with children about differences between classmates (even when handled in a supportive way) is harmful to children's self-esteem.
   a) True
   b) False

10. Incorporating children's home language into activities is considered to be a best practice for supporting DLLs.
    a) True
    b) False

For answers to this chapter quiz, please refer to the Answer Key on pages 182–183.

Chapter 4: Reflection Questions

1. What are your favorite nonverbal methods for building relationships with children and families?

   _____
   _____
   _____
   _____

2. How do you help children to get to know you? How can you share information about yourself in a way that is accessible to dual language learners?

   _____
   _____
   _____
   _____

3. What strategies do you use to help build an inclusive and supportive classroom community?

   _____
   _____
   _____
   _____

4. What new ideas are you excited to try in your own classroom after reading this chapter?

   _____
   _____
   _____
   _____

Chapter 4: Classroom Activities

ACTIVITY 1: Around the World With Our Classroom Community

MATERIALS: Map of the world

INSTRUCTIONS: Display a world map on the wall of your classroom. During group or circle time, talk about all the different places that the children in your classroom and their families come from. Place a mark on the map with a pen or small sticker for each child and his or her family. Consider letting each child make the mark that represents his or her family. When children travel to visit family or go on vacation, add additional marks to show the different places that your class has visited around the world. Ask children to repeat after you when you say the name of each new city, state, or country that you talk about. Talk with children about the fact that in our country, there are 50 different states, and each one has many different cities and towns inside of it. There are many other countries too! Talk about some of the similarities and differences across countries (e.g., "In some countries, people wear different types of clothing. Even in our own country, people wear different clothing. Let's look at pictures of different types of traditional clothing people wear around the world."). Model to children your own positive interest and curiosity about learning about each new place (e.g., "I wonder what children like to eat for lunch in school in this country? I love trying new foods!"). Add pictures or postcards to the side of the map to show images representing different cities, states, and countries.

SKILL DEVELOPMENT: Activities like this help children learn about the breadth of the world around them and develop a curiosity about the world. They begin to hear, learn, and recognize the names of different towns, states, and countries. They can also learn about geography and the location of various parts of the world, get a glimpse of culture, and learn about the relationship between cities or towns, states, countries, and continents.

APPLYING CULTURALLY RESPONSIVE PRACTICES TO THIS ACTIVITY: Carefully choose the words you use to talk with children about other cultures and countries. Avoid making statements that are definitive, such as "I hear all Mexicans like spicy food," or "Asians eat rice every day." Help children recognize the diversity that exists within and across cultures and countries. You might use statements like "Every time I try Mexican food, it is too spicy for me! I wonder if a lot of food in Mexico is spicy?" or "In my family, we eat potato pancakes called latkes when we celebrate a holiday called Hanukkah. What foods do you and your family eat when you celebrate holidays together?"

ACTIVITY 2: Celebrating Our Classroom Community Through Art: Self-Portraits

MATERIALS: Paper, drawing materials (markers, paints, or crayons), and mirrors

INSTRUCTIONS: Have children in your class create self-portraits using markers, crayons, or paints. Be sure to make crayons, markers, and paints available in a range of colors, including multicultural skin tones. Provide mirrors that children can use to see themselves or provide printed pictures of each child. Once the self-portraits are completed and dry, give children an opportunity to share their pictures in small groups or with the class during circle time. Ask each child to share one thing that is special about him- or herself. Find a place on the wall to display the pictures together. You may want to create a classroom community tree and hang the pictures on the branches. Together with the children in your class, talk about how wonderful it is to have so many different friends together in one class who all have their own special qualities.

SKILL DEVELOPMENT: Classroom themes like "I am special" are commonly used at the beginning of the school year as a way to help children to feel comfortable sharing about themselves and get to know one another. Building children's self-esteem and self-confidence related to their linguistic and cultural

(continued)

Chapter 4 Classroom Activities *(continued)*

background can help them to see the unique aspects of their family and culture as strengths. What is especially important when selecting these themes are the conversations that accompany each activity. While sitting around the snack or lunch table or in small groups, ask children to share about what makes their family special, what their family does to show they love one another, or what they do to celebrate birthdays or different holidays. Making these conversations a regular part of the classroom experience provides all children with the opportunity to share about themselves and their families and hear about their classmates. These conversations help normalize talking about what makes each of us unique as well as what helps connect us.

APPLYING CULTURALLY RESPONSIVE PRACTICES TO THIS ACTIVITY: As with each activity, take time to think about the different aspects of the activity that children might be especially excited about or that might make children uncomfortable based on individual or cultural differences. For example, in some cultures, it may not be appropriate or encouraged for young children to talk about themselves in front of others. Offering children the opportunity to say their name or share, but not forcing any child to share, can help avoid making children feel uncomfortable. Additionally, this may be an activity that works best in the middle or at the end of the year once children have had a chance to get to know one another, once you have gotten to know them, and once they have had other opportunities to share with the class.

ACTIVITY 3: Think-Pair-Share

MATERIALS: No materials required.

INSTRUCTIONS: During morning meeting or group or circle time, give children a chance to respond to questions that you ask by turning and talking with a partner. Ask children a question (e.g., "What happened that made Felicity feel sad in the story?") and give children time to think about their answers. Ask children to turn to the friend next to them and share their answer, helping them to pair off. Provide children with an opportunity to share if they would like to do so (e.g., "Who would like to share what they talked about with their partner?").

SKILL DEVELOPMENT: Turning and sharing with a classmate provides children with a "low stakes" opportunity to practice oral language skills. When you first try this activity, start with questions that require very simple answers or nonverbal answers. For example, you might ask "Can you make a happy face? How about a sad face? Let's turn and show our faces to our partner." With time, ask questions about stories or lessons that are increasingly complex but that require simple answers (e.g., "Would you like to ride in a hot air balloon or would you rather stay on the ground?") and build to the point where you are asking more complex open-ended questions.

APPLYING CULTURALLY RESPONSIVE PRACTICES TO THIS ACTIVITY: Support dual language learners (DLLs) by preteaching key vocabulary. For example, if you are planning to read a story to the class about two friends who go to the zoo, show children (individually or in small groups) pictures of a zoo and practice saying the word together. Before asking children to demonstrate an action or respond to a question, make sure that children have had many different exposures to key vocabulary words and concepts. You might even ask the same question of children individually the day before asking the question in a think-pair-share situation to make sure children understand what you are asking and to give them a chance to practice their responses. Consider arranging pair groupings based on children's language abilities; children with more advanced English language skills can serve as valuable models for children who are still developing their English language skills. Alternately, being paired with another child who speaks his or her home language can be a nice opportunity for DLLs to speak with one another in their home language or in English and support one another in both languages.

(continued)

Chapter 4 Classroom Activities (continued)

ACTIVITY 4: Rotating Sharing Day

MATERIALS: A handout with a calendar showing the date each child is scheduled to share each month along with instructions for the activity typed in English, Spanish, and other languages spoken by children in your class

INSTRUCTIONS: Set up a rotating sharing day in your classroom so that each child has an opportunity to share an item, picture, or book from home with the class. You might choose one day a week to serve as a sharing day or designate a short amount of time during each school day as sharing time. Choosing more frequent sharing days (daily rather than weekly) allows children the opportunity to practice sharing with the group multiple times over the year. Create a calendar and send copies home with families so that children and families know when their child's sharing day will be each month. Along with the calendar, send instructions asking families to help children to pick an item, picture, or book to bring to school to share. Encourage families to help children to think of one or two things they would like to tell the class about what they picked and practice at home before sharing day.

SKILL DEVELOPMENT: Setting up a sharing day gives children a chance to share something special to them with the class. Sharing can help children get to know each other better and help you get to know them better as well. Planning for sharing days also gives each child a chance to practice at home and become more comfortable showing something or saying something to the group.

APPLYING CULTURALLY RESPONSIVE PRACTICES TO THIS ACTIVITY: Recognize that children will have varying levels of comfort sharing with the class. Children's comfort might be affected by their age, language abilities, individual personalities, and other factors. In advance of a child's sharing day, send home questions that they can practice answering (e.g., What did you choose to share with us? What is something special about your item?). Let children have the opportunity to share, but do not force them to share if they are uncomfortable doing so (e.g., "Alex, would you like to share? Would you like me to help you share? Not today? Okay. Maybe next time."). As children share items that they brought to school, help support their use of English as well as of their home language. If a child struggles to find words to communicate, ask questions or offer suggestions (e.g., "Can you tell us about what you brought? It looks like an owl. Is it your owl?"). Give children opportunities to share more by asking questions like "Is there anything else you would like to tell us?" Encourage children to share in their home language as well as in English ("I see you brought a bear. How do you say *bear* in Spanish?"). Have a back-up plan for children who have forgotten to bring an item on their share day, such as allowing children to share the next day. To help avoid forgotten items, remind children (and their parents) the day before it is their turn to share. Post the share day calendar in a place where it is easy to see during pick-up and drop-off.

ACTIVITY 5: Staff Show and Tell

MATERIALS: No materials required.

INSTRUCTIONS: Invite staff members from your school or program to share lessons with your class about their home language or culture. Colleagues might read a favorite book or share a story or activity related to their own family traditions. Be sure to share stories or activities from your own culture with the class as well and invite members of your teaching team to do the same. Leveraging the expertise, experience, and backgrounds of staff members in this way helps to build a school or program community that values the individuals within the program. Sharing in this way helps children get to know the adults in their classroom as well as the larger program and gain an awareness of the prevalence of culture in our lives. Hearing

(continued)

Chapter 4 Classroom Activities (continued)

others speak openly about their own family lives and cultural experiences also communicates the message to children and families that your program values the many different cultural backgrounds represented by staff and families. Use these opportunities to help children practice asking questions of the person sharing in a safe setting. Before each guest comes, prepare children for the guest by letting them know who is coming and what he or she plans to do (e.g., read a book, share a story, sing a song). Encourage children to think of questions they could ask that person. After each guest shares, give children an opportunity to ask questions.

SKILL DEVELOPMENT: You can model to children and families that you value the cultural backgrounds of all individuals and that you believe in the importance of sharing cultural values and teaching children how to celebrate the diversity present in your community.

APPLYING CULTURALLY RESPONSIVE PRACTICES TO THIS ACTIVITY: Families may have varying levels of comfort or experience in sharing a range of cultural beliefs and traditions with their children. Some families may be very open to and excited about the idea of their children learning about other cultures. Other families may have little exposure to other cultures and thus feel more reserved or cautious about this type of sharing in the classroom. Before starting "Staff Show and Tell," share with families that this will be happening, invite them to attend, and let them know that over the course of the year, they are welcome to share stories or activities with the class as well. Communicate with families that part of your classroom and program philosophy includes helping children gain awareness of and appreciation for their own home values and culture as well as those of others.

ACTIVITY 6: What's Your Name?

MATERIALS: No materials required.

Tune: "London Bridge"	
English	**Spanish**
My name is _____. What's your name?	Mi nombre es _____. ¿Cómo te llamas?
What's your name? What's your name?	¿Cómo te llamas? ¿Cómo te llamas?
My name is _____. What's your name?	Mi nombre es _____. ¿Cómo te llamas?
Do you want to play?	¿Quieres jugar?

INSTRUCTIONS: Introduce this song to children at morning meeting, circle time, or group time. Help all children learn the words in English and Spanish. Sing it with children throughout the day during play and to support social interactions.

SKILL DEVELOPMENT: Pairing prosocial words and phrases with simple songs is one way to help children learn vocabulary words that can help them interact with others by introducing themselves, asking the other child his or her name, and asking to play.

APPLYING CULTURALLY RESPONSIVE PRACTICES TO THIS ACTIVITY: Translate the song (or keywords) into a number of different languages that are spoken in your class. Help DLLs practice key vocabulary in advance of using the activity in a large group.

Chapter 4: Additional Resources

BOOKS:

Anti-Bias Education for Young Children and Ourselves
Authors: Louise Derman-Sparks, Julie Olsen Edwards
Year: 2010
Publisher: National Association for the Education of Young Children

Leading Anti-Bias Early Childhood Programs
Authors: Louise Derman-Sparks, Debbie LeeKeenan, John Nimmo
Year: 2014
Publisher: Teachers College Press

WEB-BASED RESOURCES:

Helping Children Play and Learn Together
Authors: Michaelene M. Ostrosky, Hedda Meadan
Year: 2010
Web site: https://www.naeyc.org/files/yc/file/201001/OstroskyWeb0110.pdf

Resources on Embracing Diversity in Early Childhood Settings
National Association for the Education of Young Children
Young Children on the Web
Year: 2005
Web site: https://www.naeyc.org/files/yc/file/200511/DiversityResourcesBTJ1105.pdf

Strategies for Supporting All Dual Language Learners
Authors: National Center on Cultural and Linguistic Responsiveness
Web site: http://eclkc.ohs.acf.hhs.gov/hslc/tta-system/cultural-linguistic/fcp/docs/dll-strategies.pdf

Identifying Student Needs

Appendix 4.1

Need	What It Might Look Like	How to Anticipate It	How to Manage It

5. Using Classroom Management Practices That Support Diverse Learners

Ms. Kilinda knew that transitions would be challenging at the beginning of the school year. Years ago, her favorite mentor had pointed out that one of the reasons classrooms were so chaotic during transition times was that children often did not know what to do and did not have appropriate direction in these situations. Ms. Kilinda had never forgotten that lesson. From the first day of school, she taught children songs and fingerplays that they could sing together while waiting in line to wash their hands or use the bathroom. She modeled how to ask questions and have conversations with one another around the lunch table while waiting for food. She gave each child a job during clean-up time and she modeled completing the job she was assigned while the students sang a clean-up song together.

STRATEGIES

14. Narrate Children's Actions to Promote Self-Regulation and Language Development
15. Apply Best Practices to Classroom Management
16. Plan and Support Transitions
17. Be a Positive Role Model for Behavior Standards
18. Keep a Sense of Humor and Be Flexible

Ms. Kilinda observed that many of the classroom management strategies she used worked well for all of her students, regardless of what language they spoke. She also found that she had to adapt several of her strategies with best practices for supporting DLLs to keep the classroom running as smoothly as possible and to support all of the children in her class. For example, she found that her classroom clean-up song worked well as a cue to let all children know it was time to put their toys and activities away. Some of the children who were DLLs, however, did not understand all of the words in the song (e.g., "Time to put the blocks away"), so they needed extra support in the form of gestures, pointing, and words spoken in Spanish to let them know what to do next.

In this scenario, Ms. Kilinda is using a range of classroom management strategies to support children throughout the day. Having a wide range of classroom management strategies in your toolbox can help you to identify those that are most effective for the children in your class. You may not be able to predict the way that individual and cultural differences will affect how children respond to your classroom management practices, but watching how children respond to the strategies you use can help you determine which ones work best to support the children in your class.

Classroom management refers to the process and approaches educators and programs use to help children maintain appropriate behaviors (Kratochwill, DeRoos, & Blair, 2015). Part of classroom management includes helping children regulate their emotions and behaviors by noticing when an individual child is struggling and giving that child individual attention or by managing the energy level in the classroom as a whole. For example, Ms. Kilinda might notice that the children in her class have an especially high level of energy and decide to lead her class in an active music and movement activity before having them sit down for a quiet read-aloud.

Emotion regulation refers to the ability to manage emotions effectively, including being able to shift from one emotion to another or maintain an emotion. When someone takes action to help another person regulate his or her emotions and behaviors, this is a form of **external regulation** (McClelland, Ponitz, Messersmith, & Tominey, 2010; McClelland & Tominey, 2015). An example of external regulation might be engaging children in a story before rest time to help them relax or coaching a child to take deep breaths to calm down when upset. An important part of classroom management is for teachers to provide this external regulation for children to help them navigate the many transitions they experience throughout the day.

Teachers also help students develop **internal regulation** abilities, which involve a person's ability to manage his or her *own* emotions and behaviors (McClelland & Tominey). One aspect of internal regulation is called **self-regulation**. Self-regulation refers to a set of skills that include attention (the ability to pay attention to what is important, ignore distractions, and switch tasks), working memory (being able to keep information in mind long enough to follow through with instructions), and inhibitory control (controlling impulses and making positive choices about behavior). Simply put, self-regulation is the ability to stop and think before acting. Effective classroom management techniques help children develop self-regulation so that they can display positive behaviors out of a sense of personal responsibility rather than out of fear of punishment or in order to receive a reward (Weinstein et al., 2004).

> *Effective classroom management techniques help children develop self-regulation so that they can display positive behaviors out of a sense of personal responsibility rather than out of fear of punishment or in order to receive a reward.*

The early childhood years are an important time for the development of self-regulation (McClelland et al., 2010). Children who have strong self-regulation abilities have an easier time remembering rules, following directions, and getting along with their peers. These skills are also important for school readiness and the transition to kindergarten (McClelland et al.). Research shows that children who are bilingual score higher on self-regulation assessments than their monolingual peers (Bialystok & Martin, 2004; Chen, Zhou, Uchikoshi, & Bunge, 2014; Morales, Calvo, & Bialystok, 2013). Navigating two (or more) languages and cultures requires significant self-regulation abilities. Children need to pay attention to and remember the vocabulary and grammar associated with each language as well as the rules and norms associated with each. Across different settings, such as school and home, children may need to switch back and forth between languages and cultural expectations. For example, children may learn that at school they are allowed to start eating as soon as food is served, but at home it may be seen as rude to start eating before everyone is served. The mental effort required to switch back and forth in this way gives children many opportunities to practice self-regulation skills.

There are many ways in which early childhood educators can help children who are dual language learners (as well as all of the children in their class) develop self-regulation. The strategies in this chapter focus on classroom management through a combination of external regulation techniques and techniques to promote self-regulation. The strategies included in this chapter are as follows:

- Strategy 14: Narrate Children's Actions to Promote Self-Regulation and Language Development
- Strategy 15: Apply Best Practices to Classroom Management
- Strategy 16: Plan and Support Transitions
- Strategy 17: Be a Positive Role Model for Behavior Standards
- Strategy 18: Keep a Sense of Humor and Be Flexible

STRATEGY 14: Narrate Children's Actions to Promote Self-Regulation and Language Development

Early childhood educators can use many different classroom management practices to support smooth classroom functioning as well as to help all children practice and develop self-regulation. Using **narration** to describe what you see throughout the day is an important tool for helping children to learn new vocabulary words and lays the foundation for self-regulation (McClelland & Tominey, 2015). By narrating children's experiences, you can model how to talk about actions and feelings in a way that strengthens their development of self-regulation.

Apply Strategy 14

- Use narration to describe what happens in the classroom throughout the day. You can narrate your own actions and provide reasoning for the choices you make (e.g., "I am going to sit here on the side to make sure there is space for everyone else"). You can also narrate children's actions and guide their decisions (e.g., "I see you are walking toward the swings. Be sure to walk around this area so you do not get hurt"). Focus on offering positive feedback (e.g., "I see you are sharing that toy with your friend. I like the way you play so nicely together"). You can also narrate challenges that children are having, offering words to describe how they might be feeling as well as strategies (e.g., "It looks like you are having a hard time cutting with those scissors. That looks very frustrating. I wonder what would happen if we tried it this way instead?").

- As you narrate experiences in your classroom, try to provide children with language that describes what they should do rather than what they should not do. For example, you might say, "I see you want the same truck as Monika. Let's find another truck that you could use." Telling children what they should *not* do is often easier to express, especially when a language barrier is present. So it may seem easier to resort to saying "no" and showing disapproval in your face and tone of voice. There are many times when it may be helpful to use the word *no* to let children know they are in danger, about to hurt another child, or doing something inappropriate. Saying "no" without additional explanation, however, does not help children learn *what to do* and to learn the vocabulary that corresponds with those actions. Providing children with language and reasoning by describing why they might choose certain actions, even before they have the language skills to understand, will become a useful habit as children develop the necessary language and communication skills.

STRATEGY 15: Apply Best Practices to Classroom Management

There are many ways that educators can embed a range of teaching strategies to support DLLs, but no single technique will work in the same way for every child. Having a toolbox of strategies to draw from helps teachers to accommodate children's unique needs in different situations. Using visual aids, audio cues, tactile experiences, speech, and even sign language will help ensure that all children have the support they need to benefit from formal and informal learning opportunities throughout the day.

> *No single technique will work in the same way for every child.*

Apply Strategy 15

- Use visual aids and props whenever possible. If you have already labeled items and objects around the classroom in English and other languages, as we recommend in

Chapter 3, you can use these labels throughout the day to remind yourself of words in other languages as well as to show children the words and objects. For example, label the baskets for napkins and utensils in different languages and provide associated visuals. When children are helping to set up lunch or snack, have both DLLs and native English speakers practice the vocabulary words that they see on the labels. In addition to improving their English skills, DLLs can have the opportunity to teach you and other children new vocabulary in their home language during informal learning opportunities, including transitions.

- Use the picture labels that you have placed around the room showing the number of children allowed in each area of the classroom during independent play and small group times (see Chapter 3, Strategy 8). When a child is approaching a new area, point to the label and say, "Remember that only three children can be in the block area. Let's see if there are three people here already!" Together with the child, count "One, two, three," as you point to the images on the card. Repeat counting in the child's home language if you are able to (e.g., "Uno, dos, tres"). Then, count the number of children in the area together in English and the child's home language. If the number is fewer than three, let the child know that there is room for him or her to join in. If the number is three or more, let the child know that he or she will have to wait until another classmate leaves the area. A "Go" or "Stop" visual can also provide a valuable cue.

- Teach children basic sign language to communicate key words. For example, teach children the signs for words like *go* and *stop* or *bathroom*. Children's understanding of these signs can help you communicate to children across the classroom without raising your voice. Sign language is another way to help support children's language development as their vocabulary continues to grow in English and their home language.

- Realize that classroom management strategies you typically use may not always be culturally responsive. For example, praising some children out loud (e.g., "I like the way that Samantha is putting blocks away") may help them feel proud of their actions and continue to seek out ways to receive praise. For other children, however, receiving praise may not be something that is approved of in their home culture and may leave them feeling uncomfortable, embarrassed, or singled out. In this case, praising a child could actually result in a child trying to avoid situations in which they might be praised (Weinstein et al., 2004). You may not be able to predict the way that individual and cultural differences will affect how children respond to your classroom management practices, but by using a range of strategies (e.g., acknowledgement for hard work and persistence, saying what you see without judgment, sharing how something makes you feel) and watching how children respond to each strategy, you can determine which strategies work best to support each individual child in your class.

> *Adjusting to a new classroom and routine can take time, especially for children who are navigating a new language or a new culture.*

- It may be helpful to keep in mind that adjusting to a new classroom and routine can take time, especially for children who are younger or who are navigating a new language or a new culture. Remember that a certain amount of "controlled chaos" is expected in every early childhood classroom. As you problem-solve the strategies and techniques that do not seem to work well, take time to focus on those that do work well and celebrate the successes—big and small—that occur in your classroom each day.

STRATEGY 16: Plan and Support Transitions

Transitions make up a significant part of the preschool day and can be tricky, even chaotic. Nevertheless, just like any other time in the day, transitions can be planned to help ensure that they will go as smoothly as possible. Keep transitions consistent and provide children with tasks (e.g., specific jobs or activities) during transitions or while waiting. Let children know what is expected of them during transitions and model these behaviors. Doing so will help children learn to navigate transitions themselves. It may be more challenging to communicate information about each transition with children who are DLLs. Embedding a few phrases from the children's home languages as well as using visual aids and props are critical to helping children understand and participate throughout the day.

Apply Strategy 16

- Use your picture schedule to help children with transitions throughout the day. During your first group time (e.g., morning meeting or calendar), use your picture schedule to briefly talk children through the day. Point to the picture and words that correspond with each activity; use phrases from all the languages children in your classroom speak, if possible. Continue to refer to the calendar throughout the day. With time and practice, children can learn to use the visual schedule themselves to identify which activity they are participating in and what is coming next.

- Let children know that a transition is coming and give warnings in advance. For example, give children a 5-minute warning before independent play and exploration ends and clean-up time begins. Rather than flashing the lights or shouting to the entire room, walk around the classroom to let individual children and small groups of children know that they should wrap up their activity and get ready for the next. When engrossed in an activity, children may tune out to the sounds around them and not hear an announcement. This is doubly so for DLLs. In addition to visiting each child or group with the 5-minute warning, use visual aids like holding up five fingers or displaying a picture of a child putting toys away to help communicate the message.

- Create a feedback loop in which children can let you know that they have heard the warning about an upcoming transition. This could be as simple as a "thumbs up" or a brief oral response from children (e.g., "Can anyone tell me what is happening next?"). Practice these skills before transitions to ensure that all children, including DLLs, understand the directive and can participate meaningfully. When you choose a gesture to represent positive reinforcement, it is a good idea to check with the child or the child's family to make sure the gesture (e.g., thumbs up) is not considered to be an insult in their culture and is instead understood as positive affirmation.

- Provide clear instructions to support transitions by making sure children know what is expected of them at the beginning and end of each activity. For example, children who choose a new science center with magnifying glasses and autumn leaves, acorns, and pinecones may need guidance to understand how to appropriately use the magnifying glasses. Demonstrate how to use the materials in the center before excusing children from circle time. Model this new behavior for children and verbalize what you are seeing in the magnifying glass. Pair the verbalizations with gestures to communicate how the magnifying glass enlarges the items. In addition, when possible, include images of children engaging in the activity for children to look at. You can also model putting away the magnifying glasses carefully and gently storing the delicate leaves and pinecones. As always, ongoing feedback and support will help ensure that children are successful.

- Give children activities to participate in during a transition such as clean-up time, waiting in line, or moving from one task to another. This might be a song to sing, a fingerplay, or even a short game that helps them practice new words (e.g., days of the week). Teach songs and fingerplays in English as well as in other languages, if possible (parents may be a great resource for short songs or fingerplays in their home language).

STRATEGY 17: Be a Positive Role Model for Behavior Standards

One of the ways in which children learn is through imitating adults or peers who are more skilled than they are at a task (Bandura, 1999). As you strive to teach children how to regulate their behaviors and emotions throughout the day, **modeling** these skills yourself provides them with an example to imitate in their own daily experiences. Modeling is especially important for DLLs, as it provides visual cues that support the language children are absorbing (Howard, Lindholm-Leary, Sugarman, Christian, & Rogers, 2007).

Modeling is especially important for DLLs, as it provides visual cues that support the language children are absorbing (Howard, Lindholm-Leary, Sugarman, Christian, & Rogers, 2007).

Apply Strategy 17

- Be a role model by following classroom rules. Think about the rules that you would like children to follow (e.g., waiting in line to use the bathroom, using kind words to ask for a turn). Take time to model these behaviors throughout the day. Avoid cutting corners (e.g., stepping in front of a line of children to wash your own hands rather than joining the line along with them) unless it is absolutely necessary, such as for safety reasons.

- As you model these behaviors, narrate your actions and choices and explain why you are doing them. Modeling in this way can help provide all children, including DLLs, with vocabulary words that help them describe their own actions. For example, when walking to the sink to wash your hands, say out loud, "I need to wash my hands too so that they will be clean for snack. I am going to stand right here behind Alesha and wait for my turn just like you."

- Describe the behaviors you model so that children understand what you are doing and why (e.g., "I am going to push in these chairs so that no one will trip on them."). This can help children develop reasoning abilities as they build their own inner monologue—their inner thoughts. Narrating your behaviors throughout the day can lay a foundation for children's critical thinking abilities and their ability to make intentional choices. If children have heard you say multiple times throughout the week that you are pushing chairs in to prevent friends from tripping on them, they are more likely to remember why you ask them to push in their chairs after snack or lunch and to follow through. It is important to note that understanding the reason behind rules and positive behaviors lays the foundation for children's ability to self-regulate (McClelland & Tominey, 2015).

- Model strategies for effectively managing frustrations. Young children may experience a number of potential frustrations or challenging feelings throughout the day. Think about how you would like children to act when they feel angry, frustrated, or disappointed. Children express their feelings in many different ways, ranging from physical expressions of emotions (e.g., kicking, stomping, screaming) to verbal expressions of emotions (e.g., saying "I am mad!"). If a child does not have the words needed to express an emotion effectively, he or she may have to rely on using physical expressions to communicate that feeling (e.g., frowning, crossing arms, throwing a tantrum). Using words to verbalize how you handle your own emotions is an important way that you can help children to learn the vocabulary they need to express their emotions. For example, if it is raining and your classroom cannot go outside, you might say, "Wow, I am really disappointed about the weather. I was looking forward to going outside on the playground, but we will have to stay inside today. I think I'll check out the new water toys we have at the sensory table instead. Maybe I will feel better by trying out some of the new things we have inside our classroom!" When modeling how to talk about feelings with children, it is also important not only to share your feelings but also to talk about what you are doing to regulate those feelings, as we discuss in greater length in Chapter 6.

STRATEGY 18: Keep a Sense of Humor and Be Flexible

Working in the early childhood education field can be challenging! When working with young children, unexpected events can occur on any given day. With the wide range of languages and cultures that are represented in many early childhood classrooms, there may be miscommunications (e.g., a child thinking that a teacher asked him to hold the scissors when she was asking him to put them away), misunderstandings (e.g., a teacher thinking that a child is misbehaving when the child is trying to ask the teacher a question), or unexpected events (e.g., a child having an accident because he or she could not remember the English word for *bathroom*). When situations arise, be forgiving of yourself (and of children), keep a sense of humor, and be open to unexpected changes. Flexibility is key for the early childhood educator who is continuously faced with unexpected moods, challenges, and opportunities that go hand in hand with managing a classroom full of young children with diverse needs.

Apply Strategy 18

- Consider children's mood and energy level throughout the day. How can you adapt your plan to meet children where they are? There may be times when children's energy levels do not meet the demands of the task at hand—so having strategies to address these challenges is essential. For example, if children have a lot of energy before rest time, it may be helpful to do a quick activity to help them use some of their excess energy. This could be a music and movement activity, like freeze dancing, or another way for children to appropriately use their energy.

- Be willing to change the goal. If children are unexpectedly struggling with an activity, be flexible and modify the activity accordingly. You may have expected to read an entire book during circle time but found that halfway through, the children are having a hard time sitting still, especially if the book is being read in English and this is not the native language for all children. Consider ways that you can adjust your plans. Perhaps you could read the second half of the book later in the day. Or take this opportunity to teach the children about a bookmark and mark your place for another time or day. Follow up by making bookmarks with the group to use in their own books.

CHAPTER CONCLUSIONS

Early childhood educators play an important role in managing children's emotions and behaviors throughout the day. There are many ways that educators can embed best practices for supporting DLLs and culturally responsive practices into the classroom management strategies they use to help children navigate the day smoothly. Developing your own toolbox of classroom management strategies is an important way to help children feel supported throughout the day as well as to help them develop their own self-regulation abilities. We end the chapter with ideas for classroom activities as well as additional resources (books and web-based resources) where you can learn more.

Early childhood educators play an important role in managing children's emotions and behaviors throughout the day.

Chapter 5: Check Your Learning

1. Children who are bilingual score lower on self-regulation assessments than their monolingual peers.
   a) True
   b) False

2. Which of the following is an example of external regulation?
   a) A teacher leading children in stretching and deep breathing to help them calm before rest time
   b) A parent rocking and soothing a crying infant
   c) A teacher talking a child through a temper tantrum by encouraging him or her to use words to say "I'm angry!"
   d) All of the above

3. Which of the following is true about using the word *no* in early childhood classrooms?
   a) Saying "no" often and loudly is one of the best ways to improve behavior in the classroom.
   b) The word *no* should never be used with young children.
   c) Using the word *no* followed by additional behavioral support can help children learn what to do instead of the undesired behavior.
   d) If children do not respond when you say "no," you should repeat the word several times slowly.

4. Giving children a 5-minute warning to prepare for a transition can hurt their self-regulation development.
   a) True
   b) False

5. Educators may be able to ease transitions throughout the school day by doing which of the following? Select all that apply.
   a) Letting children know in advance that a transition is about to happen (e.g., 5-minute warning)
   b) Providing a cue to let children know when a transition is beginning (e.g., a clean-up song)
   c) Explaining to children what is expected of them during and after the transition
   d) Giving children something to do during the transition, especially if they are waiting or finish a task before their classmates (e.g., sing a song or fingerplay)

6. Which of the following are challenges educators might experience if using the same classroom management strategy for all children?
   a) Some classroom management strategies may not be culturally responsive and therefore may be ineffective for some children.
   b) Children respond differently to different strategies, so it is helpful to try a range of classroom management strategies.
   c) Nothing—what's good enough for one child is good enough for another. An educator only needs one good classroom management strategy to be effective.
   d) a and b only

7. Teachers should model positive behaviors that they want children to emulate throughout the day, but they should not model or discuss their own unpleasant feelings.
   a) True
   b) False

8. Teachers who use language to describe what they are doing throughout the day, and why, are supporting the development of which of the following skills?
   a) Vocabulary and language
   b) Self-regulation
   c) Critical thinking
   d) All of the above

9. It is a child's responsibility to be ready to learn. No matter what energy level a child has, when it is time to calm down, he or she should be able to calm down without support from a teacher.
   a) True
   b) False

10. Effective classroom management techniques help children develop self-regulation so that they can display positive behaviors _____ rather than _____.
    a) Out of fear of punishment or desire for a reward . . . out of a sense of personal responsibility
    b) Throughout the school day . . . under the supervision of parents
    c) When they are with friends . . . when they are alone
    d) Out of a sense of personal responsibility . . . out of fear of punishment or desire for a reward

For answers to this chapter quiz, please refer to the Answer Key on pages 183–184.

Chapter 5 — Reflection Questions

1. How can classroom management strategies support children's self-regulation development?

2. What are your favorite transition activities or songs that you use in your classroom?

3. In what ways are you incorporating languages other than English in your classroom management strategies?

4. What new ideas from this chapter do you plan to try in your own classroom?

Chapter 5: Classroom Activities

ACTIVITY 1: Build Vocabulary and Language During Transitions

MATERIALS: No materials required.

INSTRUCTIONS: During transitions throughout the day, play a game in which you ask children to do simple actions, such as "touch your head . . . hop on one foot . . . tap your shoulders," in English, Spanish, or other languages. You can model the different actions at first and then use only words.

Another activity that can help during transitions is to ask children to count off one by one when waiting in line. Children can practice counting in different languages and can take turns counting off.

SKILL DEVELOPMENT: Activities like these can help give children something to do while waiting in line or for the next activity and promote vocabulary and language development. The counting activity can also be used as a way for children to build social skills as they work together to identify whether anyone in the class is missing.

APPLYING CULTURALLY RESPONSIVE PRACTICES TO THIS ACTIVITY: Try using as many languages as possible when asking children to do simple actions or when counting. Let children from diverse language backgrounds lead the counting in their home languages and then teach their peers.

ACTIVITY 2: Playground Model/Map

MATERIALS: A picture or collage of the playground equipment (e.g., slide, swings) that you have on your playground, labeled with words in English and Spanish

INSTRUCTIONS: Label each picture with words in English and Spanish. Before outdoor time, use the map to ask children to identify one thing they plan to do during outdoor time. Alternately, after outdoor time, ask children to share one thing they did while they were outside, using the visual images from the map to point to playground equipment or activities that they do not know.

SKILL DEVELOPMENT: Asking children to make a plan for what they will do during outdoor time not only helps develop vocabulary, it also encourages children to think ahead and follow through with that plan, an important component of self-regulation. In addition, children can practice listening and turn-taking as they share their plans and listen to what the other children have chosen to do. As each child identifies what they want to do or what they did, practice saying key words together as a class in English, Spanish, or other languages spoken in the class. This mapping skill can also be done with the classroom, identifying major areas (e.g., art, water, blocks, library) or locations in the larger community (e.g., fire station, grocery, library, pet store, pizza parlor).

APPLYING CULTURALLY RESPONSIVE PRACTICES TO THIS ACTIVITY: Using visuals strategically can support dual language learners' vocabulary development, aid with comprehension, and empower children to actively participate and engage in classroom activities.

(continued)

Chapter 5 Classroom Activities (continued)

ACTIVITY 3: Roll the Dice

MATERIALS: Two small (6–8 inches per side) square boxes (*note:* square gift boxes work well for large "dice"); large dice created with pictures of different facial expressions, colors, or numbers (see instructions)

INSTRUCTIONS: Use the dice as a small-group activity or during transitions. Create dice with different images, colors, and numbers on each side. The dice can be used in many ways. For example, if you have colors on each side, you can roll the dice and ask all children who are wearing "blue" to go over to one of the centers. If you have feeling faces on the dice, you can roll the dice and ask all children to make a face that corresponds with the die and also to name a strategy associated with that feeling. For instance, if an angry face is rolled, ask children to make an angry face and share something that they do to calm down when they feel angry. One by one, children can respond to the prompt based on the roll of the dice and then make the transition to the next activity.

SKILL DEVELOPMENT: The colors and images on the dice can provide visual support, help children develop new vocabulary, and practice new skills (e.g., expressing emotions).

APPLYING CULTURALLY RESPONSIVE PRACTICES TO THIS ACTIVITY: Label the colors and numbers on the dice in different languages to represent the languages of children in your classroom and their families. When you roll the dice, practice saying the colors or numbers together in each of the different languages.

Chapter 5: Additional Resources

BOOKS:

Stop, Think, Act: Integrating Self-Regulation in the Early Childhood Classroom
Authors: Megan M. McClelland, Shauna L. Tominey
Year: 2015
Publisher: Routledge Eye on Education

WEB-BASED RESOURCES:

Developing Young Children's Self-Regulation Through Everyday Experiences
Author: Ida Rose Florez
Year: 2011
Web site: http://www.naeyc.org/files/yc/file/201107/Self-Regulation_Florez_OnlineJuly2011.pdf

Empathy and Cultural Competence: Reflections from Teachers of Culturally Diverse Children
Author: Michaela W. Colombo
Year: 2005
Web site: https://journal.naeyc.org/btj/200511/ColomboBTJ1105.pdf

Helping Children Make Transitions Between Activities
Authors: M. M. Ostrosky, E. Y. Yung, M. L. Hemmeter
Web site: http://csefel.vanderbilt.edu/resources/wwb/wwb4.html

Planning Transitions to Prevent Challenging Behavior
Author: Mary Louise Hemmeter, Michaelene M. Ostrosky, Kathleen M. Artman, Kiersten A. Kinder
Year: 2008
Web site: http://journal.naeyc.org/btj/200805/pdf/BTJ_Hemmeter_Transitions.pdf

Replacing Time-Out: Part One—Using Guidance to Build an Encouraging Classroom
Author: Daniel Gartrell
Year: 2001
Web site: http://www.naeyc.org/files/tyc/file/Gartrell%2001.pdf

6. Supporting Social and Emotional Learning for Dual Language Learners

Juan loved being around other children. He lit up every time he walked into the classroom and saw his classmates. His teacher, Ms. Elena, saw Juan's excitement and wanted to make sure he had the communication skills he needed to make friends with his peers and that they had the communication skills they needed to reciprocate. She had been using circle time to focus on helping children ask and invite one another to join in playing. During the first few weeks of school, she talked with her class about many different things that made each child and family unique as well as the things they had in common with one another. She had focused on helping children get to know one another's names and helping them to ask one another to join in playing in English, Spanish, and Creole—the three languages spoken by children in her classroom. Juan had quickly learned a few words in English and was able to ask, "Can I play, too?" His classmates had also learned how to ask him in Spanish if he wanted to play: "¿Quieres jugar?" Ms. Elena was glad to see the skills they were practicing during circle time transfer to children's behaviors throughout the day. She was excited to continue helping children practice and develop their social and emotional skills.

STRATEGIES

19. Create an Emotionally Supportive Classroom
20. Recognize and Scaffold Children's Social and Emotional Needs
21. Teach Social and Emotional Skills
22. Support Social and Emotional Development in English and in Each Child's Home Language
23. Involve Families in Children's Social and Emotional Learning
24. Use a Growth Mindset to Teach Social and Emotional Skills

APPENDIX

6.1 Vocabulary Word List

Social and emotional skills are the skills children and adults need to recognize and manage their emotions, think about the feelings of others, develop empathy, and build positive relationships with other children and adults (Fabes, Gaertner, & Popp, 2006). Self-regulation skills (see Chapter 5) such as paying attention, remembering and following through with instructions, and controlling impulses often are also included as part of the definition of social and emotional skills.

Social and emotional skills are important for many reasons. Research shows that children who have stronger social and emotional skills are more likely to get along with peers and teachers and are better able to benefit from learning opportunities (Arnold, Kupersmidt, Voegler-Lee, & Marshall, 2012; Brackett, Rivers, & Salovey, 2011; Zins, Bloodworth, Weissberg, & Walberg, 2004). A focus on children's social and emotional skills has been identified as a critical component of high-quality early childhood education. NAEYC, the National Head Start Association (NHSA), and the vast majority of states recommend early learning standards that include social and emotional skills along with early academic achievement standards (NAEYC, 2009a; U.S. Department of Health and Human Services, 2015).

> *A focus on children's social and emotional skills has been identified as a critical component of high-quality early childhood education.*

Research findings support positive connections between being a DLL or bilingual and having strong social and emotional skills. For example, some research has shown that children who are immigrants have greater social competence (e.g., higher levels of self-control, ability to organize play with other children) and fewer behavior problems (e.g., temper tantrums, fighting with other children) than nonimmigrants (De Feyter & Winsler, 2009). Other studies have shown that children who are bilingual have higher self-regulation than their monolingual English-speaking peers (Bialystok & Martin, 2004). Still other studies have found that children who are dual language learners show greater gains than their monolingual peers in social and behavioral outcomes from kindergarten through eighth grade (Halle et al., 2012). What is concerning is that some studies have shown that not all DLLs demonstrate positive social and emotional outcomes. Some studies have found that DLLs with the lowest levels of English proficiency have the worst social and emotional outcomes in the long term (Halle et al., 2014). Specifically, one study found that children who were DLLs in kindergarten who had not mastered English by the end of the kindergarten year had the poorest interpersonal skills and self-control in comparison to their classmates by fifth grade (Han, 2010). These mixed outcomes stress the need for more research to help clarify the unique social and emotional needs of DLLs. The studies clearly indicate that children who are dual language learners have the potential to thrive socially and emotionally when they have the support they need at school and at home to fluently learn their home language and English.

There are many things early childhood educators can do to help children learn, practice, and develop social and emotional skills. Foundational to the development of social and emotional skills are the relationships children have with parents and caregivers. When children have a warm, trusting, and secure relationship (i.e., a secure attachment, discussed in Chapter 4) with one or more of the key adults in their lives, they are more likely to turn to those individuals for help and support and to strive to be like and learn from those individuals. It is in these early relationships that children learn about social norms as well as cultural, individual, and family values. In addition, children often look to the adults in their lives as models. It is from observing and imitating models in their lives that children begin to develop and practice their own social and emotional skills and strategies. Children who have secure attachments with adults, including educators, also have more positive relationships with their peers (Howes, Matheson, & Hamilton, 1994).

In addition to building secure and trusting relationships with young children, adults can support social and emotional development through intentionally teaching social and emotional skills and giving children the opportunity to practice those skills across many different contexts (Bierman & Erath, 2006). Adults can also provide supportive feedback to help children view themselves as learners of social and emotional skills rather than as "bad" or "problem children" when they make a misstep or have a breakdown in social and emotional skills.

Foundational to the development of social and emotional skills are the relationships children have with parents and caregivers.

Teaching social and emotional skills to children who are DLLs may come with additional challenges, including the need for educators to foster the development of warm and trusting relationships in both verbal and nonverbal ways when a language barrier is present between themselves and a child or family, helping children practice and apply social and emotional skills in the classroom with peers who speak a range of languages and come from various cultural backgrounds, and supporting social and emotional skill development in English as well as in each child's home language. In addition, educators must use culturally responsive practices to support not only each child's home language but also their home culture, which may or may not align with the social and emotional teachings at school. For example, a teacher may actively encourage children to talk about many different feelings at school, including feeling happy, excited, frustrated, and sad. Some families might do the same at home, but other families might have cultural beliefs or values that emphasize the importance of only talking about positive emotions, only encouraging one gender (boys or girls) to talk about emotions, or not talking about emotions at all. Recognizing that families vary in their beliefs and values related to social and emotional development is an important part of building positive connections between school and home.

In this chapter, we provide six strategies for supporting the development of social and emotional skills for diverse groups of children and for engaging families in the process:

- Strategy 19: Create an Emotionally Supportive Classroom
- Strategy 20: Recognize and Scaffold Children's Social and Emotional Needs
- Strategy 21: Teach Social and Emotional Skills
- Strategy 22: Support Social and Emotional Development in English and in Each Child's Home Language
- Strategy 23: Involve Families in Children's Social and Emotional Learning
- Strategy 24: Use a Growth Mindset to Teach Social and Emotional Skills

STRATEGY 19: Create an Emotionally Supportive Classroom

There are many ways in which early childhood educators can create an **emotionally supportive classroom environment**. Many of these strategies may be helpful not only to educators but also to families (and are helpful to share during parent–teacher conferences or at family workshops).

One strategy is to model social and emotional skills throughout the school day. Early childhood educators are often told they should "fake it 'til you make it"—to put on a smile regardless of how they may be feeling. Although sharing a smile and expressing pleasant feelings and emotions with young children are important, taking this approach may neglect an important learning opportunity when you are not genuinely having these feelings.

First, sharing feelings with children, both pleasant and unpleasant, communicates the message that it is okay to talk about feelings and that everyone has a range of different feelings. Second, emotions can be very challenging to hide and may "leak" out in the way educators interact with or respond to children and families. Children may pick up on the fact that you are feeling stressed, frustrated, sad, or upset, even if you do not openly share these feelings, through the way you respond to situations that arise. For children who are DLLs, sharing your own feelings as well as the causes of those feelings may be especially important because children who are DLLs often rely on nonverbal cues to help them understand and interpret interactions. If children pick up on cues like facial expression, tone of voice, or body language that point to unpleasant feelings, they may worry that they are the cause of these feelings. There are many strategies educators can use to model their own social and emotional skills, including managing their emotions effectively and sharing their emotional experiences with children in their class in developmentally appropriate ways.

> *Sharing feelings with children, both pleasant and unpleasant, communicates the message that it is okay to talk about feelings and that everyone has a range of different feelings.*

Apply Strategy 19

- Share your feelings with children throughout the day, as well as the causes of those feelings, in developmentally appropriate ways (e.g., "I am feeling really excited today because we are having a special guest!" "I am feeling tired today because I did not sleep well last night. Sometimes I get frustrated easily when I feel that way."). If you have an unpleasant feeling, talk to children about why—and what you are doing to manage that feeling. For example, let children know what happened that led you to feel disappointed and talk to children about what you are planning to do about it (e.g., "I felt disappointed this morning when we did not get to have outdoor time because it was too cold. Going outdoors helps me use up my energy well!").

- Share your regulation strategies with your class and involve them in problem solving (e.g., "What do you think I could do to feel less disappointed? What helps you feel better when you are disappointed?"). Talking openly with children about your feelings and providing them with a chance to help you problem-solve can help children feel more comfortable talking about their own feelings and models language that they can use to express themselves. If possible, embed Spanish or other languages represented in your classroom in these conversations (e.g., "I feel ... excited, frustrated, disappointed" translates in Spanish to "Me siento ... emocionado/a, frustrado/a, decepcionado/a").

Ms. Elena loved being a teacher and felt energized and upbeat most days in her classroom. She was proud that she was known at her school as the teacher who was always smiling and always supporting others with positive words. She arrived at school one day feeling deeply saddened—a close family member had been diagnosed the night before with a very aggressive form of cancer. Ms. Elena's instinct was to try and put a smile on her face and fake her way through the day with her class, but she thought it would be impossible. She realized that doing so would lead to a missed opportunity to teach children how to manage their own sad feelings. Ms. Elena also realized that talking about her own sad feelings as well as strategies for managing those feelings could help children learn that all feelings are okay, that even their teacher feels sad, and that there are things you can do when you have feelings like this. During group time, Ms. Elena decided to tell the children about her feelings. She shared that she was feeling sad because one of her family members was sick. She asked children if they ever felt sad and if there were things that helped them feel better. She was surprised by the number of ideas children came up with, which included getting a hug, making a card for her family member, and talking to a friend.

The discussion turned into an activity starting with hugs for Ms. Elena and an art activity focused on making a card for someone special. Several children shared things that made them feel sad and others shared that there were people in their family who were sick, too. Not only did Ms. Elena feel closer to the children in her class, she felt better. She worried that the conversation may have been too complicated for some of the DLLs in her class to understand, but she did her best to incorporate words from other languages into her story (e.g., *triste,* which means *sad* in Spanish) and noticed that all of the children seemed to be very engaged.

- When you talk with children about your feelings, convey the emotion through your facial expressions, body language, and tone of voice to help children attach meaning to the feelings. You might even try this in front of a mirror so that you can practice communicating emotions nonverbally to children. Showing your emotions through nonverbal expression is important, not only for when you talk about your own feelings but also for when you read books and talk about the experience of the book's characters. Using nonverbal expressions of emotions can help bring your words and the books you read to life and help facilitate children's understanding.

- Develop your own toolbox of emotion regulation strategies, both those that support stress management long term (e.g., taking care of yourself, getting enough sleep, seeking social support) as well as those that support stress management in the moment (e.g., taking deep breaths, considering the other person's perspective in a conflict situation). Think about the strategies that work best for you. What helps you to calm down when you feel stressed in the middle of the school day, and what helps you to manage your stress when you are at home? Remind yourself of these strategies throughout the day and model these strategies for children.

- As you model your own social and emotional skills, explain to children what you are doing and why. If you model social and emotional skills without letting children know what you are doing, they may not be aware enough of the situation to learn from it. Narrating your emotional experience to children throughout the day gives them insight into your thinking process and ultimately can help them develop critical thinking skills and their own internal monologue. For example, try saying out loud, "I felt really frustrated when that happened. I'm going to count to five and take a deep breath to calm down." Talking about and modeling your strategies for managing emotions can help children build their own set of emotion regulation strategies. When possible, incorporate emotion words from the home languages of children in your classroom. A list of emotion words is included in Appendix 6.1.

- Give genuine apologies when you make a mistake. Find opportunities to model to children how to give an apology. Sometimes adults also struggle with managing their own emotions, especially in trigger situations (e.g., when doing something that makes them feel threatened or stressed). If you find yourself in a situation where you have responded sharply to a child, raised your voice inappropriately, or behaved in a way that you did not feel good about, point it out to the children in your classroom. For example, try saying, "Earlier today when the class was having trouble listening at group time, I felt very frustrated. When I was frustrated, I yelled for everyone to 'stop it right now!' and I should not have done that. I want to tell you I am sorry for doing that. Next time, I am going to take a deep breath and use a calm voice instead." It would be ideal for children to be able to develop this level of self-reflectiveness and to have the language and the social and emotional skills to do this themselves. Seeing models of adults doing this effectively is critical for that to happen.

STRATEGY 20: Recognize and Scaffold Children's Social and Emotional Needs

As children develop and practice social and emotional skills, early childhood educators play a critical role in recognizing children's social and emotional needs and scaffolding those needs throughout the day. When children are young, the adults in their lives (teachers and parents) help provide regulation for children, known as external regulation, as discussed in Chapter 5. Research highlights the importance of external regulation for children developing their own internal or self-regulation. The same is true for many other aspects of children's social and emotional skills.

Apply Strategy 20

- Learn to recognize each child's emotion cues. Emotion cues include facial expressions (e.g., smiling, frowning, eyebrows drawn in), vocal tones (e.g., soft and low voice, loud and high voice), and body language (e.g., clenched fists, drooping shoulders). Children express emotions in different ways. Some children cry when they are sad and others become withdrawn or show increased aggression. Recognizing the emotion behind a child's behavior is key to offering them the appropriate language to express themselves as well as strategies to help them manage their emotion. For example, when a child acts out by pulling another child's hair during outdoor time, a teacher should consider the emotion driving the behavior. Different emotions may require different responses or intervention techniques. First, most teachers in that situation would stop the child from pulling hair and likely draw the child's attention to the other child's feelings. Second, the teacher should also consider why the child was motivated to pull hair—how was he or she feeling that led to doing that? If a child was feeling lonely and pulled hair to engage the other child in play, the teacher might help the child practice strategies to join in playing ("Can I play too?"). If the child pulled hair in response to feeling angry from being pushed, the teacher might help the child practice strategies to express that anger, such as using words to say, "I don't like that. Please stop!"

- Consider how children are feeling throughout the day. Think about their energy level before each activity. Assess whether children are ready and at the appropriate energy level to participate in an activity. For example, will your class be able to productively engage and attend to a read-aloud if they have a lot of pent up energy? Use transition activities when needed to help children shift from one energy level to another. For example, if your students are feeling really energetic and you are hoping to engage them in a quiet reading activity, try using a physical activity followed by stretching and deep breathing to help children find a way to expend some energy so that they can be ready to focus.

- Spend alone time with children who are upset. Use books and images of children in your class or characters showing different feelings to help the children in your class identify how they are feeling. Even if children do not have the words to express their emotions using English or their home language, they may be able to point to a feeling face that matches their expression or demonstrate nonverbally how they are feeling.

- Support children before, during, and after emotionally charged situations (e.g., temper tantrums). When children experience intense emotions such as anger, rage, or frustration, stay calm and model the behavior you would like them to exhibit (e.g., using a calm voice, using words to describe what you see, taking deep breaths). Realize that when children are in those moments, their body's stress system has been activated. They may have difficulty hearing, focusing, and learning in those moments. After children have calmed down, revisit the issue and talk through what happened and what could be done differently next time. Help children learn to express their emotions in appropriate ways (e.g., verbalizing how they are feeling) and develop strategies for calming down (e.g., taking deep breaths, squeezing a pillow) outside of emotionally charged moments, such as while acting out a story following a read-aloud or during dramatic play time. If children have the opportunity to practice these skills outside of emotionally charged moments, they may be more likely to be able to use these skills during those challenging moments.

- Help children learn to make amends beyond saying, "I'm sorry." Guide children in asking others "Are you okay?" and "Can I help you feel better?" in English as well as in their home language. Use visual images of ways to help a classmate feel better. A picture mural can include images of items like a box of tissues, a cup of water, a stuffed animal, and one child hugging another to demonstrate ways children can help each other. Label the pictures in English, Spanish, and other languages represented in your classroom. Show children the pictures as you guide them through asking the other children if they would like a tissue or a hug.

STRATEGY 21: Teach Social and Emotional Skills

As mentioned at the beginning of the chapter, the phrase *social and emotional skills* covers a broad range of skills. Some especially helpful social and emotional skills to teach young children include helping children to develop a rich vocabulary of feeling words so that they can talk about their emotions, helping children to manage intense emotions, and helping children to learn about the emotions of others and develop empathy.

As children learn the words, phrases, and actions needed to interact prosocially and build relationships with their classmates, it's important for educators to provide children with opportunities to put these strategies into action.

Apply Strategy 21

- Help children to develop a vocabulary of feeling words. In many emotionally laden situations, a teacher's goal is to help children use words to tell us how they are feeling. This is an important task and one that may be challenging for all children—monolingual English speakers as well as DLLs. To support children's development of a sophisticated emotion vocabulary, try a combination of the following:

    - Modeling
    - Talking about emotions throughout the day
    - Sharing stories about experiencing different emotions
    - Pointing out the emotions of characters when reading books with children

- Have conversations about emotions during daily routines, such as during lunch. Ask children how they are feeling and what happened that led them to feel that way. Alternately, ask children what led to different feelings throughout the day (e.g., "What was the most exciting thing that happened today? What was the most disappointing?"). Children are often told "use your words" or "tell me how you feel." Having conversations with children is one way to help them practice using their words, develop their vocabulary, and learn to converse with others.

- Integrate social and emotional learning concepts into read-alouds and dramatic play. In Chapter 7, we provide recommended practices for supporting DLLs through read-alouds. In addition, read-alouds can be used to support social and emotional development through teaching children emotion-related vocabulary, encouraging children to think about the feelings of others, and talking about strategies that can be used in response to different emotions. When children are in the middle of emotionally charged moments, they may be too upset or stressed to hear new information, remember it, and learn from it. Helping children to practice social and emotional skills outside of those moments, such as through read-alouds and role-plays, can help them develop skills to manage their emotions in those trigger moments when they do arise.

- Choose books that show characters in social situations that are relevant to young children. For example, look for books that focus on social interactions, including making new friends, feeling left out, taking turns, or managing intense emotions. Point out to children the feelings that the characters in the book are having and discuss with children what happened that led to those feelings. Together, practice making faces that match the feelings of the characters or act out scenarios from books (e.g., "Can you make a sad face?").

- Give children opportunities to practice prosocial words in small- and large-group settings. For example, after reading a book focused on taking turns, talk about ways that students can take turns in the classroom. Try passing a ball or stuffed animal around the circle and giving each child the opportunity to say "Can I have a turn?" and "Thank you" as the ball is passed from one friend to the next. Teach children prosocial phrases in English, Spanish, and other languages represented in your classroom.

- Support children's social and emotional development as they interact with peers throughout the day. In the classroom, DLLs who are nonverbal or struggle with expressing themselves verbally may be misunderstood by their peers. For example, peers may think a child who does not have the words to ask if he or she can join in playing is not interested in playing with them. Helping children to learn and practice the words they need to engage in social interactions can improve their ability to build peer relationships.

> *DLLs who are nonverbal or struggle with expressing themselves verbally may be misunderstood by their peers.*

STRATEGY 22: Support Social and Emotional Development in English and in Each Child's Home Language

To scaffold the social and emotional development of DLLs, it's critical to incorporate the use of a child's home language. The use of children's home language is associated with higher levels of closeness between teachers and young children (Chang et al., 2007), and having a close relationship is a predictor of social and emotional development. In addition, a child's home language is the mechanism through which children learn about and have access to their family's cultural values, whether it is through their parents, grandparents, or other family members and friends.

> *A child's home language is the mechanism through which children learn about and have access to their family's cultural values.*

Apply Strategy 22

- Learn how to say basic feeling words in Spanish as well as other languages represented in your classroom. Staff members in your program or families may be a great resource to help you translate key words and work on your pronunciation. Incorporate these words into conversations with children and when reading stories depicting various feelings.

- Create a feelings board (see Classroom Activities section at the end of this chapter). Label the faces on the feelings board with words in English, Spanish, and other languages. Pictures of a range of feeling faces along with the corresponding labels can be used to help children identify their feelings and develop a vocabulary of feeling words.

- When possible, provide children with opportunities to practice social and emotional skills with different partners. Pairing children with peers who speak the same language can provide children with an opportunity to practice new words in their home language with one another. Relationships with peers who speak the same language can help children to practice new vocabulary in a safe space. In addition, interacting with

English-speaking peers may not only have a positive social impact but also help children to improve English skills (Chesterfield, Chesterfield, & Chavez, 1982) and help English-speaking children to learn words in other languages.

Strategy 23: Involve Families in Children's Social and Emotional Learning

As with any other learning area, finding ways to involve families in collaboratively supporting children's social and emotional development is an important part of building effective school–home partnerships. Share with families the ways in which you are helping children to expand their vocabulary to talk about emotions as well as ways that they can support children's ability to express their emotions at home.

Apply Strategy 23

- Share with families the social and emotional "rules" that are followed at school. Let families know that children are encouraged to express and share their emotions at school. Communicate with families that the social and emotional rules used at school help children get along with one another and help children have the skills they need to be ready to learn.

- Ask families to help translate a list of feeling words that you can use in the classroom. Choose words that are commonly used in your classroom that you would like to be able to teach children in their home language as well as in English. These feeling words might include words such as *happy, sad, angry, frustrated, disappointed, calm, excited, surprised, scared, lonely,* and *curious.*

- Encourage families to share what they do at home regarding their child's emotions. Recognize that if their "rules" do not align with the "rules" at school, they may not be comfortable sharing them and instead may opt to agree with your rules in the moment. For example, some families might encourage children to talk about their feelings and discuss emotions openly. Other families might believe it is inappropriate to have these kinds of conversations and might even discourage children from showing or expressing emotions. Find ways to help families to feel comfortable sharing their traditions and expectations with you—early relationship building with families will facilitate this process. Express that what they do at home is important and that learning more about what they do may help you to support their child at school. Let families know that you value and respect their home culture and family rules, even when those rules differ from the rules at school. Realize that even within a home, the emotion rules may differ across family members.

- Support each family's ability to be *intentional* in their approach to social and emotional learning at home by sharing developmentally appropriate expectations regarding self-regulation and understanding the perspective of others. Emphasize the fact that children need lots of practice and support to develop these skills. Share with families ways that they can support your school's emotion rules at home if they would like to, including sharing stories about their own feelings with children (if they feel comfortable doing so) and asking children how they are feeling. You can also offer to share your classroom steps for calming down and other regulation strategies that families may be interested in practicing and applying at home.

- As you share with families how you approach social and emotional learning at school, maintain respect and appreciation for each family's decision as to how it approaches these skills at home. It is important to realize that the rules that families use at home may be deeply grounded in culture and tradition or they may be a result of families doing what they know from their own experiences. Teaching families about research-based practices that work well at school can help families, in some cases, learn new strategies to use at home. For some families, the strategies you share may be similar to those that they are already using, but for other families they may not. Strategies you share may be welcomed and incorporated into what families are doing at home or they may be discarded. The ultimate goal should be to help families expand their knowledge and strategies, in a way that is respectful, and ultimately to support their child's social and emotional development.

STRATEGY 24: Use a Growth Mindset to Teach Social and Emotional Skills

Social and emotional skills are challenging to teach and challenging to learn. They are skills that need to be learned and practiced, just like any other. If a child is struggling with recognizing the letter A, for example, a teacher's response might be to incorporate the letter A into circle time, holding up a large letter A, talking about what the letter A sounds like, pointing out the letter A when it appears in the classroom and books, playing "I Spy" games to see if children can find the letter A around the classroom. The educator would provide children with lots of support, repetition, and examples to help them practice these skills.

One of the challenges of teaching social and emotional skills is that children struggling with these skills may be disruptive (e.g., have a temper tantrum) or do things that hurt other children physically or emotionally (e.g., hitting, calling someone a name). It can be harder for teachers to calmly respond to social and emotional struggles than to academic struggles. It's important to remember that children are learning social and emotional skills and to foster a **growth mindset**. A growth mindset is the belief that individuals can practice, learn, and grow their abilities. In contrast, a fixed mindset refers to the belief that one's abilities cannot be changed and are just part of who one is.

Apply Strategy 24

- Avoid getting discouraged if it takes time for children to develop key social and emotional skills. All children need repeated opportunities to practice and develop new skills, and early childhood is an especially important time to help children practice these skills. Consider Carol Dweck's recommendation to think about these skills as not "yet" developed and remember that children are on a learning curve (Dweck, 2006).

- Remind children who are struggling with social and emotional skills that they are practicing and learning these skills. Point out and celebrate their successes (e.g., "I noticed that even when you felt frustrated, you used your words to tell me you were upset instead of yelling. That's the first time you ever did that!") and help them to reflect on their challenges. For example, after an emotionally charged incident, ask a child, "What could we do differently next time? Let's make a plan."

- When you hear other children speaking negatively about a child who is struggling with social and emotional skills (e.g., "He always cries." "I don't want to play with her—she's mean! She always hits me."), let them know that the child they are talking about is still learning and that learning to be a good friend and to manage your emotions is really hard. Ask children to help one another practice and learn how to be a good friend at school (e.g., "She's learning how to stand in line without pushing. Maybe we could invite her to stand next to us and show her how! Let's practice together.").

CHAPTER CONCLUSIONS

Supporting children's social and emotional development is an important component of high-quality early childhood education settings. Early childhood educators can support children's social and emotional growth through modeling their own social and emotional skills as well as teaching these skills to children through a wide range of activities. Incorporating children's home language into social and emotional learning as well as other concrete supports (e.g., visual aids, storybooks, and props) can help ensure that all children have the opportunity to develop and practice these important skills.

Chapter 6: Check Your Learning

1. Which group of children tends to struggle the most in the United States socially and emotionally?
   a) Monolingual Spanish-speaking children
   b) Monolingual English-speaking children
   c) Children who are bilingual or dual language learners (DLLs)
   d) None of the above

2. "Secure attachment" is commonly used to describe _____.
   a) A warm and responsive relationship between a child and an adult
   b) The physical connection made when children stand together and hold hands in a circle
   c) The bond between two close friends at school
   d) All of the above

3. Best practices require teachers to "fake it 'til you make it" and smile regardless of how they are feeling.
   a) True
   b) False

4. Which of the following strategies are best practices that can be used to help support social and emotional development for children who are DLLs?
   a) Using books and visual images of characters experiencing different emotions
   b) Expressing emotions in your own facial expressions and vocal tones
   c) Incorporating emotion words from children's home languages
   d) All of the above

5. Which of the following is *not* an effective strategy for promoting social and emotional skills for young children?
   a) Building secure and trusting relationships with children
   b) Talking about emotions throughout the day—both children's as well as adults' emotions
   c) Encouraging children to make up their own rules
   d) Pointing out the emotions characters have during read-alouds

6. Which statement communicates to children that social and emotional skills need to be practiced and learned?
   a) "She is just being mean. I wouldn't want to stand next to her either."
   b) "That boy is a bully. Just stay away from him."
   c) "Lots of us seem to be yelling today when we get angry. Let's practice taking deep breaths together."
   d) "Quit crying. Everything's going to be fine."

7. Families who do not use the same approach as their child's school to promote their child's social and emotional learning are doing their child a disservice.
   a) True
   b) False

8. When a child is having a temper tantrum, it may not be a good time to try to teach him or her a new approach for calming down. Why is this?
   a) Children have trouble hearing, focusing, and learning when their stress system is activated.
   b) Children already know how to calm down without help from an adult.
   c) It is better to leave a child alone and walk away when he or she is upset.
   d) Other children might make fun of him or her.

9. Teachers who incorporate children's home languages into learning activities have closer relationships with children who are DLLs than teachers who do not.
   a) True
   b) False

10. A teacher should never apologize to a child.
    a) True
    b) False

For answers to this chapter quiz, please refer to the Answer Key on pages 184–185.

45 Strategies That Support Young Dual Language Learners by Shauna L. Tominey and Elisabeth C. O'Bryon.
Copyright © 2018 Paul H. Brookes Publishing Co., Inc. All rights reserved.

Chapter 6: Reflection Questions

1. What strategies help you regulate your emotions throughout the day?

   _____
   _____
   _____
   _____

2. What strategies do you use in your classroom for helping children manage intense emotions such as frustration or anger? What are your favorite activities for helping children calm down when they're upset?

   _____
   _____
   _____
   _____

3. Have you ever worked with families whose social and emotional rules at home differed from the rules at school? What strategies do you find most helpful for working together with families when home and school rules differ?

   _____
   _____
   _____
   _____

Chapter 6: Classroom Activities

ACTIVITY 1: Feelings Board

MATERIALS: Tag board or poster board; pictures of children or characters showing different feeling faces; labels of feeling words in English, Spanish, and other languages

INSTRUCTIONS: Create a feelings board showing children or characters making faces that depict many different feelings. Label each of the feeling faces with the feeling word (e.g., happy) in English, Spanish, and other languages represented in your classroom. Use the feelings board in the quiet corner to help children match their feeling to a visual image throughout the day, or use the feelings board to talk about the feelings of characters in books during read-alouds.

SKILL DEVELOPMENT: The feelings board can be used to help children match how they are feeling with an image. A book that depicts children having many different feelings could be used for the same purpose. Use the feelings board to scaffold children's abilities to talk about their own emotions by asking them to point to the picture that shows how they are feeling. Support children's ability to do so by describing what you see in their facial expression or body language that matches the expression they are making (e.g., smiling, frowning). Helping children to recognize how they are feeling and learn the vocabulary associated with their feelings can help them to better express themselves in English as well as in their home language.

APPLYING CULTURALLY RESPONSIVE PRACTICES TO THIS ACTIVITY: Children may have varying levels of comfort and skill with identifying and talking about their feelings. Following many of the tips presented in this chapter, including sharing and modeling your own emotions and talking with children about emotions through read-alouds and other activities, can help children become comfortable with talking about their own emotions. Incorporating children's home language whenever possible can help children learn to express themselves in English as well as in their home language.

ACTIVITY 2: Our Classroom Friend

MATERIALS: A stuffed animal or baby doll, soft music (optional)

INSTRUCTIONS: Let children know that you have a new (pretend) friend visiting in the classroom. Let them know that the new friend is a little afraid of meeting new people, so if they want to hold the new friend, they have to be very gentle and use a quiet voice. Play music that is soft and slow. Pass the new friend around the circle. Have each child ask, "May I have a turn?/¿Puedo hacerlo yo?" in English or Spanish when it is their turn and then say, "Thank you/Gracias."

KEY WORDS: "May I have a turn?/¿Puedo hacerlo yo?" and "Thank you/Gracias."

SKILL DEVELOPMENT: This activity offers children the opportunity to practice important social and emotional skills while also developing key language skills in English and other languages related to taking turns in a fun way.

APPLYING CULTURALLY RESPONSIVE PRACTICES TO THIS ACTIVITY: Try this activity using phrases in multiple languages to recognize the linguistic diversity in your classroom.

(continued)

Chapter 6 Classroom Activities *(continued)*

ACTIVITY 3: Paper Plate Feeling Faces

MATERIALS: Paper plates (not wax-coated), markers or crayons

INSTRUCTIONS: As a creative arts activity, have children draw faces showing different feelings and emotions. Children can either use crayons or markers to draw different expressions or you can place construction paper cut-outs of mouths, noses, eyes, and eyebrows for children to glue to their plates. Photos of people or book characters displaying different emotions can also be placed on the table as a model of different feeling faces. After the activity, children can share their feelings faces and the emotions that they chose to depict.

SKILL DEVELOPMENT: This activity gives children the opportunity to learn about the facial features and cues (e.g., smiles, frowns, eyebrows facing up, eyebrows facing down) that are associated with different emotions. Children can also practice learning new vocabulary associated with different emotions.

APPLYING CULTURALLY RESPONSIVE PRACTICES TO THIS ACTIVITY: As a circle time activity, have children share their feeling faces with one another. To accommodate children with varying levels of English language development, ask children different types of questions. For example, for children with less developed expressive language skills, ask, "Could all the children who drew sad faces please stand up?" You can also model a sad face to give visual cues to dual language learners. For children with more advanced skills, ask, "What makes you feel sad? What makes you feel happy?"

Chapter 6: Additional Resources

BOOKS:

Managing Emotional Mayhem
Author: Becky Bailey
Year: 2011
Publisher: Conscious Discipline

Me, You, Us: Social-Emotional Learning in Preschool
Author: Ann S. Epstein
Year: 2000
Publisher: National Association for the Education of Young Children

School Readiness and Social-Emotional Development: Perspectives on Cultural Diversity
Authors: Barbara Bowman, Evelyn K. Moore
Year: 2006
Publisher: National Association for the Education of Young Children

WEB-BASED RESOURCES:

Center on the Social and Emotional Foundations for Early Learning
Web site: http://csefel.vanderbilt.edu

Dual Language Learners and Social-Emotional Development: Understanding the Benefits for Young Children
Authors: Tamara Halle, Marlene Zepeda, Jessica Vick Whittaker
Year: 2014
Web site: http://www.childtrends.org/dual-language-learners-and-social-emotional-development-understanding-the-benefits-for-young-children

Teaching Emotional Intelligence in Early Childhood
Authors: Shauna Tominey, Elisabeth O'Bryon, Susan Rivers, and Sharon Shapses
Year: 2017
Web site: http://www.naeyc.org/yc/emotional-intelligence-early-childhood

Appendix 6.1: Vocabulary Word List

Feeling Words in English and Spanish		
English	Spanish	Other Language
happy	feliz/contento/a	
sad	triste	
angry	enojado/a	
scared	asustado/a	
surprised	sorprendido/a	
disappointed	decepcionado/a	
calm	tranquilo/a	
brave	valiente	
curious	curioso/a	
excited	emocionado/a	
frustrated	frustrado/a	

7 Enhancing Early Academic Skills for Dual Language Learners

Although Leila was often quiet at school, after only a few weeks, her family started noticing that she was engaging more in reading activities at home. She was excited to show her parents what she was learning about books, even with the Arabic books they read at home. Leila started surprising her parents with number knowledge at dinner by announcing (in Arabic) that if everyone took one falafel, there would only be two left, so there would not be enough for everyone to have two. Although she did not know the Arabic word for *octagon*, Leila taught her parents the English word and showed them that the stop signs they passed on the road had eight sides. Leila's parents knew her teacher did not speak Arabic, but they were impressed with her ability to share concepts with Leila in a way that transferred to their home language.

STRATEGIES

25. Make Learning Activities Accessible to Diverse Learners
26. Embed Best Practices into Read-Alouds
27. Embed Best Practices into Math and Science Activities
28. Draw Connections Between Activities and Children's Home Language and Culture
29. Engage Families in Children's Learning

APPENDICES

7.1 Vocabulary Word Lists

7.2 Books for the Dual Language Learner Classroom

With support from her teacher, Leila was experiencing a phenomenon called **cross-language transfer**, the ability to transfer skills developed in one language to another language. Cross-language transfer is a commonly observed process for DLLs and children who are bilingual when they are being effectively supported in both languages (Dickinson, McCabe, Clark-Chiarelli, & Wolf, 2004). In many classroom settings, a child's capacities to benefit from learning opportunities as well as interactions with teachers and peers largely depends on his or her language abilities (Ackerman & Tazi, 2015). Unfortunately, many children who are dual language learners may be at risk for not receiving adequate support in their home language or in English, which may put them at risk for falling behind their peers. When educators expose children to new concepts in the classroom and make concepts accessible through language, visual aids, and experiential learning, children are more likely to gain an understanding of the concept in a way that supports learning in both English and their home language. Cross-language transfer can apply to academic skills as well as to other learning areas that we have discussed throughout the book, such as social and emotional skills.

Although there is a need for more research on academic achievement and children who are dual language learners (Hammer, Jia, & Uchikoshi, 2011), some studies have found that early achievement gaps appear between children who are DLLs and their peers and that these achievement gaps can carry on into later schooling. For example, a longitudinal study examined a nationally representative sample of 4,690 children and compared early academic and social outcomes for children in white families and those in Latino families. Achievement gaps existed in preliteracy skills at 24 months and persisted through 48 months, with children from Latino families falling significantly below their white peers (Guerrero et al., 2013). These gaps are also evident on both state and national assessments. Students who are DLLs are less likely than their native English-speaking peers to score at or above a basic level in reading on fourth grade and eighth grade standardized tests (McBride, 2008)—and the differences are significant. One study found that (depending on the state) only 25%–52% of children who were DLLs scored at a basic reading level in fourth grade, in comparison with 66%–83% of their peers. In eighth grade, only 20%–41% of DLLs scored at a basic reading level, in comparison with 74%–84% of their peers (McBride, 2008).

Finding ways to meet the needs of diverse groups of students across all curriculum areas may help prevent or minimize early achievement gaps.

Given the diversity that exists within the population of students who are labeled as DLLs, more research is still needed. Many studies that examine outcomes for DLLs have small sample sizes and use loose and varied definitions of what it means to be a DLL (Hammer et al., 2014). Some studies measure children's language proficiency, whereas others do not. In addition, being a DLL is sometimes related to being from a low-income background, and the effects of being a DLL versus the effects of living in poverty may not be possible to untangle in the research (Wanless, McClelland, Tominey, & Acock, 2011). Regardless of the challenges associated with conducting research with DLLs, finding ways to meet the needs of diverse groups of students across all curriculum areas may help prevent or minimize early achievement gaps. Achievement gaps that emerge in preschool often persist and widen over time, so ensuring that students have the help they need in preschool is critical.

In this chapter, we provide recommendations for embedding best practices for engaging DLLs across the early childhood classroom curriculum, with examples of emergent literacy activities and read-alouds, early math activities, and others. This chapter's strategies are as follows:

- Strategy 25: Make Learning Activities Accessible to Diverse Learners
- Strategy 26: Embed Best Practices into Read-Alouds
- Strategy 27: Embed Best Practices into Math and Science Activities
- Strategy 28: Draw Connections Between Activities and Children's Home Language and Culture
- Strategy 29: Engage Families in Children's Learning

STRATEGY 25: Make Learning Activities Accessible to Diverse Learners

There are many ways that educators can embed best practices for supporting DLLs into learning activities to help make information accessible to diverse learners, but doing so takes intentional thought and planning.

> *There are many ways that educators can embed best practices for supporting DLLs into learning activities to help make information accessible to diverse learners, but doing so takes intentional thought and planning.*

Apply Strategy 25

- Think carefully about the language needs required by the themes and topics that you choose throughout the year. Complex topics that involve a large number of challenging vocabulary words (e.g., different species of bugs, undersea creatures) may be best saved for later in the year. At the beginning of the year, choose topics that have small vocabulary demands (e.g., weather, colors, seasons) or that include vocabulary critical to helping children navigate the classroom and peer relationships (asking to play, taking turns). In addition, pair new vocabulary words in English with the same word in each child's home language so that children are able to draw connections between these words. Pairing vocabulary can occur verbally and in writing (e.g., by labeling objects in the classroom).

- Embed learning activities into themes and topic areas that interest children. Choosing activities, games, and themes that help children get to know one another, learn about the classroom and school day, and develop vocabulary that helps them interact successfully at school is a great way to start. As you get to know the children in your class individually, look for ways to integrate their interests into classroom themes and learning activities. For example, if you are focusing on helping children to recognize letter sounds or learn the names of shapes, help children practice these skills in the contexts of what they are interested in throughout the day (e.g., robots, jungle animals) as well as across languages (e.g., "*Tiger* starts with a 't,' /t/. So does *tigre* in Spanish!").

- When introducing a new topic, concept, or idea, use pictures, visual aids, and props. This is important even if you speak the home language of children who are DLLs, as visual cues can make new concepts more accessible, help with recall, and reinforce new vocabulary. As we continue to emphasize, finding concrete ways to communicate the meaning of an activity is critical for all children but may be especially important for DLLs who are learning new content and new language at the same time. Speak slowly and clearly to give children an opportunity to practice their understanding of English and to learn new words in English. Repeat key words and incorporate children's home languages whenever possible so that children connect words across languages.

- Assess children's understanding of new vocabulary and concepts frequently. Ask children a range of different questions and have them demonstrate their learning in various ways. For example, after introducing a new vocabulary word to children (e.g., horse), show children a picture that includes the new word and ask them to point out the object or item (e.g., "Can you show me which one is a horse?"). To further assess children's learning, ask open-ended questions (e.g., "Does anyone know where a horse lives? How many legs does a horse have? What does a horse eat?"). Give children who are dual language learners a chance to connect the new word in English with their home language (e.g., "How do you say *horse* in Hebrew? Let's all try saying that together!").

STRATEGY 26: Embed Best Practices into Read-Alouds

Read-alouds and shared reading activities are one of the building blocks for early literacy development in early childhood classrooms (Cole, Dunston, & Butler, 2017). Read-alouds are also one of the ways that educators share information with children about many different concepts and topics, including social and emotional skills, early math skills, science and inquiry, social studies, and "the world around us" (i.e., community and culture). Before reading a book to your class, take time to consider how the best practices for supporting DLLs discussed in the following subsection can be embedded when you read with your class.

> *Read-alouds are one of the ways that educators share information with children about many different concepts and topics, including social and emotional skills, early math skills, science and inquiry, social studies, and "the world around us."*

Apply Strategy 26

- Choose storybooks carefully. When possible, find books that are available in more than one language (e.g., The Napping House/La casa adormecida; see Appendix 7.2 for a list of recommended books). Look for books that are short and repetitive or that have clear story lines that are easy to follow, along with descriptive pictures. In addition, choose books that represent people and characters from diverse and multicultural backgrounds. This does not mean that every book chosen must show a range of characters from multicultural backgrounds, but that the overall collection of books that you share should represent many different topics, peoples, ideas, and cultures.

- Read each book yourself before reading it out loud to your class. Not only does reading a book in advance give you the opportunity to identify key words and phrases to focus on and translate into other languages, prepare props and visual aids, and plan extension activities, it also gives you an opportunity to consider whether a book is appropriate for your class. You may find that some books written for young children are actually not appropriate for your class. Some books may teach messages that do not align with what you are teaching in your classroom. Others may be too long or have vocabulary that is too complex for your class at that time of year. Still others might present stereotypical viewpoints and characters.

- Don't choose a book solely because it's available in more than one language. Even books that have been translated in other languages may not necessarily be culturally relevant or interesting to children. Look for books that will be meaningful to children's lives (e.g., books about family, going to school, making friends) as well as books about topics that interest the children in your class. Avoid books or collections of books that perpetuate stereotypes. For example, if the children in your classroom are interested in learning about space, make sure that many different people (boys and girls, individuals from different racial and ethnic backgrounds) are represented as astronauts or characters in these books. If the only books children see about a topic include one gender or one race, they may think that the topic does not apply to them.

- Translate key words from the books you choose into Spanish and the other languages that children in your class speak before reading the book to students. Choose key words or a repetitive phrase as the focus of the book to practice with children repeatedly during and after reading. Books that have a rhyming scheme or phrases that repeat are often easy for children to learn. For example, try this with Eric Carle's *Brown Bear, Brown Bear, What Do You See?*, which repeats the phrases throughout the book. Writing key phrases on sentence strips so that children can see the words while saying them with you can help them practice the words as well as make the connection that letters can be put together to make words and words can be put together in a sentence.

- To support the ability of DLLs to understand books read in English during circle time, preread books with small groups of children in English and in their home language (if possible). You may be able to find audiobook versions of the books you are reading in Spanish or some of the other home languages. Many public libraries loan audiobooks just as they do hard-copy books. You may also find online videos of educators reading books in various languages.

- As you read to your class, use facial expressions, gestures, and a tone of voice that mirrors those of the characters in the book. For example, if a character is feeling happy or excited, smile and use an upbeat voice to communicate in your expression how the character is feeling. This provides an additional context cue that may help children pair the words you are saying with the meaning in the book.

- Add visual aids and props whenever possible to help bring the book to life for children (Castro et al., 2011; Magruder et al., 2013). For example, when reading *Caps for Sale,* use different colored hats or paper plates representing hats as props. In addition, let children hold the pictures or props as you practice new vocabulary words in English, Spanish, and other languages. If you do not know how to say a key word in one of the languages spoken by the children in your class, ask the children if anyone knows the word in a different language and have the child teach the new word to you and their peers.

- Read stories to your class multiple times so that books and new vocabulary become familiar to children. Talk about what happens in the story together, and extend the discussion beyond the storybook. When vocabulary words are discussed and reinforced throughout the day in many ways, children who are DLLs are more likely to understand the story and develop enhanced vocabulary from reading (Collins, 2005). For example, extend the story to role-play and dramatic play, encouraging children to act out the stories from books. Give children an opportunity to make puppets out of paper bags or paper plates as an extension activity following a story that they could use to enhance their role-plays.

- If additional copies of a book are available, send home copies of the book for parents of DLLs to read with the child in English or in their home language. One study found that pairing classroom storybook reading with at-home storybook reading in children's home languages actually enhanced children's English language vocabulary acquisition (Roberts, Jurgens, & Burchinal, 2005; Roberts, 2008). Parents may be able to help children understand key vocabulary words as well as the content of a story at home so that when the book is read at school, children are better able to connect the English words with their meaning. Sending books home could be a helpful way to encourage shared reading between all children in your class and their families, not just DLLs.

Ms. Delano speaks fluent Spanish, so Spanish-speaking children are often placed in her classroom. After reading books to her class in English, she would take the Spanish-speaking children aside and describe the story to them in Spanish, showing them the pictures in the book to help them connect the pictures with the story. However, after attending a professional development workshop on supporting DLLs, she realized that what she was doing might not be enough. Although Ms. Delano was reinforcing their Spanish language abilities and ensuring that the Spanish-speaking children were learning the content of each book, she was missing an opportunity to support their English language abilities. Following the workshop, she continued spending time explaining stories to children in Spanish, but she also incorporated words in Spanish into her read-alouds to help children connect English words with Spanish words to support vocabulary development in both languages. Ms. Delano was pleased to see that using this simple strategy started leading to improved English vocabulary for her Spanish-speaking children and an interest in learning Spanish vocabulary for her English-speaking children.

STRATEGY 27: Embed Best Practices into Math and Science Activities

The best practices discussed throughout this book can also be used to enhance children's learning related to any topic area or children's development of new concepts, including math and science and inquiry. Read-alouds are often the foundation for introducing new ideas in each of these topics, but there are many other ways to explore math and science and inquiry to enhance learning for DLLs.

Apply Strategy 27

- *Early Math:* In early childhood, the focus of math learning is often on numbers and counting, math language and vocabulary, comparisons (more/less), shapes, and basic addition and subtraction (De Feyter & Winsler, 2009). To support early math learning for DLLs, learn how to count from 1 to 10 or 1 to 20 in each of the languages represented in your classroom. Help children practice their counting throughout the day by counting together the number of children at school or the days on the calendar. Alternate counting in English with counting in other languages so that number knowledge of children who speak other languages is supported in their home languages. Children who are monolingual English speakers in your class can also develop counting skills in other languages.

- Play simple games or ask questions that encourage children to add or take away numbers (e.g., "We have four rolls. After I eat one, how many will be left?"). In addition, consider learning key words included in basic math language (e.g., more, less, longer, shorter, square, circle) in Spanish and other languages represented in your classroom. As you engage in different activities with children throughout the day, including play, use these words to talk about the activities (e.g., "Which one has more? Which is shorter?").

- *Science and Inquiry:* Helping children learn to think about the world around them is at the foundation of early science and inquiry development. When thinking about how to promote science and inquiry skills for children from diverse backgrounds, start with topics with which all children already have some familiarity. For example, most classroom teachers talk about the weather on a daily basis. Ask children questions about the weather (e.g., "What kind of clothes do you think we should wear outside today? Why do you think that? What do you think the weather will be like tomorrow?).

- Help children to practice asking and answering questions that encourage them to create hypotheses about the world around them. A hypothesis is an idea that can be tested through experimentation (e.g., "I think the snow will melt because the sun is shining and it is warm."). Help children test their hypotheses (e.g., "Let's check when we go outside for recess and see what is happening to the snow!").

- Provide hands-on opportunities to explore science and nature by bringing different items to the classroom (e.g., rocks and shells) or by making things like playdough or slime (e.g., "What do you think will happen when we mix these together? Let's see!"). In addition to offering tactile experiences, use visual images and props to help children understand different scientific phenomenon that you talk about in your class (e.g., the caterpillar–butterfly life cycle), especially when hands-on props are not available. As always, integrate children's home languages whenever possible (e.g., "Today we are going to talk about caterpillars and butterflies—*orugas y mariposas*.").

STRATEGY 28: Draw Connections Between Activities and Children's Home Language and Culture

Look for ways to embed items and artifacts that represent children's home languages and cultures into each aspect of your classroom, from dramatic play to the block area. Helping children to make cultural connections as they learn throughout the day as a regular part of your classroom routine helps to reinforce the message that culture is all around, increasing children's cultural awareness in experiential ways.

Apply Strategy 28

- *Dramatic Play:* Many early childhood classrooms have boxes or totes with items depicting various themes for use in the dramatic play area. Think about items that you might add to your existing dramatic play kits to make them culturally relevant to children from diverse backgrounds. Make sure that your collection of baby dolls and other play figures includes a range of races and ethnicities. Ask parents to bring in empty dry goods boxes that represent the foods they eat at home to add multicultural food items to your play kitchen. In addition, ask parents for donations of traditional fabrics or clothing that they no longer need to add to your collection of dress-up clothes.

> *Helping children to make cultural connections as they learn throughout the day helps to reinforce the message that culture is all around, increasing children's cultural awareness.*

- *Block Area:* Rotate the materials you use in the block or building area. Many classrooms have a standard set of wooden blocks. Try adding recycled materials (e.g., toilet paper tubes, empty boxes) to provide different shapes and materials for children to use. Display picture books in the block area that show different types of buildings from around the world, and encourage children to create different types of architecture.

- *Sensory Table:* Fill the sensory table with items that represent different cultures. Consider adding different types of rice, beans, or grains for children to touch and explore. Incorporating food items into play, however, may not be appropriate in under-resourced areas, especially if children in your class are at risk for experiencing food insecurity at home. Consider finding non-food items to include in your sensory table that represent a range of environments, including soil, dirt, sand, clay, twigs, and leaves. Through different combinations of natural materials and toys (e.g., plastic bugs, people, transportation toys), children can create and explore a range of creative environments and landscapes.

- *Creative Arts:* Provide children with a wide range of art materials to use in creative activities, including different types and textures of papers (e.g., origami paper) as well as recycled materials and items from nature. Make sure to have crayons and markers in multicultural skin tones available to children. When creating collages from magazines or newspapers, ask parents if they have these materials available in their home languages and include them in the materials available to children as well.

- *Listening Center:* Include books on tape in English, Spanish, and other languages so that children can hear stories in English as well as their home language. After reading a story in English to your class, play part of the story in another language so that all children can hear what the language sounds like, and let them know they can listen to the story in English or other languages at the listening center.

- *Music:* Include multicultural instruments in your collection of classroom instruments. Talk with children about where these instruments come from and what they are used for. Play instruments together while listening to a wide range of musical types and styles. (Chapter 8 focuses specifically on music and movement.)

- *Library:* Include books, newspapers, and magazines in a range of different languages as part of your classroom library. Even if you are unable to read the words in other languages, show children how the letters differ across languages. At your writing center, display the English alphabet as well as other alphabets and encourage children to try writing different types of letters.

- *Technology:* If you use technology-based activities in your classroom on a computer or electronic tablet, include games or apps that focus on vocabulary development in English as well as other languages. If your center uses technology such as computers or short videos in the classroom, consider using technology to help find photos or short videos to share with your class that reinforce learning concepts in class, including vocabulary, as well as images from different cultures and countries.

STRATEGY 29: Engage Families in Children's Learning

Families can be wonderful partners in helping to support children's learning across school and home. There are many ways that educators can engage families in the learning process. When you share with families new vocabulary words, classroom themes, and learning concepts, families will be better able to reinforce at home what children are learning at school. If families talk with children about what they are learning at school in their home language before, after, and during new learning experiences, children may be better prepared to benefit from learning experiences at school. They will have already had exposure to key vocabulary words and concepts in their home language. There are many things educators can do to help families have the information they need to be involved. We provide several additional strategies for engaging families in Chapter 9.

Apply Strategy 29

- Keep families informed of classroom themes or learning concepts. Send home a short weekly, biweekly, or monthly family newsletter that describes what skills and concepts the children are learning now and what they'll be working on in the coming weeks. Offer families specific tips or strategies for what they can do at home to enhance and extend their children's learning. For example, share a list of key vocabulary words in English and other languages associated with each new topic. If possible, have these words translated into Spanish and the home languages spoken by children in your classroom. Provide families with discussion questions that they can use at home as well as suggestions for children's books related to the topic that they could check out from your school or at the public library.

- Engage families in contributing to the learning process for all children in the classroom. Invite parents to send in books, magazines, or newspapers with child-friendly content to the classroom. Use these materials to talk with children about differences and similarities across languages. For example, you might show children that some languages (like English) are read from left to right. Other languages (like Arabic) are read from right to left and still other languages (like Chinese and Japanese) are read from right to left and top to bottom!

CHAPTER CONCLUSIONS

Meeting the needs of DLLs effectively involves making sure that all of the children in your classroom have access to the learning opportunities around them. In high-quality early learning settings, learning happens throughout the day during social interactions, small and large group activities, read-alouds, transitions, on the playground, and through play. Children who are DLLs need support throughout each of these activities to learn English vocabulary words as well as to ensure that they are learning new vocabulary in their home language.

Making sure content is interesting and relevant to children and that all children have access to new learning content is an important role of early childhood educators.

Chapter 7: Check Your Learning

1. What is cross-language transfer?
   a) The ability to learn words that sound similar in two different languages
   b) The ability to transfer skills learned in one language to another
   c) The ability to learn a third language quickly after learning a second language
   d) The ability to understand more words in a language than you can speak

2. In comparison to their English-speaking peers, children who are dual language learners (DLLs) are _____ to score at or above basic levels in reading on fourth and eighth grade standardized tests.
   a) More likely
   b) Less likely
   c) Equally likely

3. At-home storybook reading in children's home languages can enhance children's English vocabulary.
   a) True
   b) False

4. Which of the following is *not* one of the challenges associated with research that examines academic outcomes for DLLs?
   a) Studies may use different definitions of what it means to be a DLL.
   b) Many studies have small sample sizes, which makes it challenging to generalize findings.
   c) In some studies, it is difficult to untangle the effects of poverty versus the effect of language ability.
   d) The lack of research indicates that families of DLLs are not interested in being involved in research.

5. What are some of the reasons an educator should read a book first before reading it to his or her class? Select all that apply.
   a) Prereading allows a teacher to prepare props and extension activities to accompany the book.
   b) Prereading allows a teacher to determine whether the language demands of a book are appropriate for children in the class.
   c) Prereading allows a teacher to identify whether the book will be relevant and meaningful to the class.
   d) Prereading allows a teacher to translate key words into Spanish or other languages represented in the class.

6. Reading the same book to children more than once leads to poor attention and bored children.
   a) True
   b) False

7. Which of the following questions could a teacher use to support early math skill development? Select all that apply.
   a) Which one of these bananas is longer?
   b) Did you find any circles around our classroom?
   c) Who would like to count the number of days on the calendar?
   d) Can you jump up and down 12 times?

8. Learning more than one alphabet is too demanding for young children and thus children should be exposed to only one form of print language in early childhood (e.g., English or Arabic, but not both).
   a) True
   b) False

9. What is a hypothesis?
   a) An idea that can be tested
   b) A research question that cannot be tested and thus has no answer
   c) An established fact
   d) A research paper

10. Making sure children understand the content of a learning activity, such as by translating instructions into another language after you have explained the instructions in English, will sufficiently support all children's English vocabulary development.
    a) True
    b) False

For answers to this chapter quiz, please refer to the Answer Key on pages 185–186.

Chapter 7 — Reflection Questions

1. What strategies do you already use to support dual language learners (DLLs) during read-alouds and shared reading activities? How can you make these strategies and/or activities more engaging and effective?

   _____
   _____
   _____
   _____

2. What strategies do you already use to support DLLs during math and science and inquiry activities? How can you make these strategies and/or activities more engaging and effective?

   _____
   _____
   _____
   _____

3. In what ways do you incorporate multicultural artifacts and items into your classroom learning activities?

   _____
   _____
   _____
   _____

4. What is one new activity you would like to try in your classroom after reading this chapter?

   _____
   _____
   _____
   _____

Chapter 7: Classroom Activities

ACTIVITY 1: Charting and Graphing

MATERIALS: Large piece of chart pack paper or butcher paper, marker

INSTRUCTIONS: On the large piece of paper, visually depict the number of children in the class who prefer apples, bananas, and oranges (for example). On the x-axis (the horizontal axis from left to right), list the fruits using visuals and accompanying labels. Ask children which of the fruits they prefer and count the number of children in each fruit group. Write the number of children above each fruit (this can be done by writing, e.g., "6," by adding 6 apple icons, by coloring in 6 blocks, or a combination).

SKILL DEVELOPMENT: This activity can help with early math skills, including counting, sorting, and charting. This activity can also help children learn about similarities and differences between themselves and their classmates in a safe environment.

APPLYING CULTURALLY RESPONSIVE PRACTICES TO THIS ACTIVITY: Use visuals when possible to support new vocabulary. In this example, it would be helpful to bring in apples, bananas, and oranges as props or for tasting as part of the activity. In addition, use this activity to discuss with children the many things people have in common with one another as well as the differences. Acknowledge that having likes and dislikes is okay and part of what is special about each person.

ACTIVITY 2: Learning About Diversity Through Literacy

MATERIALS: Developmentally appropriate books that celebrate diversity

INSTRUCTIONS: Read books in your classroom that highlight diversity and culture as a strength throughout the school year. Integrating conversations about culture throughout the year (rather than limiting these conversations to the holiday season) sends the message to children and families that culture is found all around and is an important part of everyone's lives every day of the year (Souto-Manning & Mitchell, 2010).

SKILL DEVELOPMENT: Reading with children individually and in groups helps build emergent literacy skills and knowledge of print. Sharing books that highlight similarities and differences can help to show children that people can talk about these similarities and differences with genuine interest and curiosity, as similarities and differences are a normal and typical part of the world.

APPLYING CULTURALLY RESPONSIVE PRACTICES TO THIS ACTIVITY: Books that focus on the experiences of children and families from many different cultural backgrounds and that show many different family forms can spark conversations about the things that make people both all alike and different. When looking for books that highlight diversity, it is important to include books that depict cultural experiences related to the dominant culture as well as nondominant cultures. Sometimes it is easier to identify cultural diversity by looking specifically at nondominant cultures. This may leave children and adults who are part of the dominant culture with the impression that they do not have a culture, although this is not true. Help children from all cultures to identify what is special about their family traditions and values.

ACTIVITY 3: Learning Letter Sounds Simon Says

MATERIALS: No materials needed—just an open space where children can see and hear you and have space to move.

(continued)

Chapter 7 Classroom Activities (continued)

INSTRUCTIONS: Ask children to touch their heads if you say a word that starts with *H*, touch their toes if you say a word that starts with *T*, or put their hands up in the air if you say a word that starts with a different letter. Change the body parts that you choose, as well as starting letters, as children learn additional letter sounds (e.g., "Touch your nose if I say a word that starts with the *N* sound").

SKILL DEVELOPMENT: This game can be used to help children practice phonological awareness in English as well as other languages. In addition, this game can be used to help children learn vocabulary, including body parts.

APPLYING CULTURALLY RESPONSIVE PRACTICES TO THIS ACTIVITY: Say a combination of words in English, Spanish, or other languages. Let children lead the game by having them try to think of words that start with different sounds in English or their home language.

ACTIVITY 4: Nature Basket

MATERIALS: A basket, box, or bag; assorted items from nature (e.g., pinecones, rocks, shells, twigs, leaves)

INSTRUCTIONS: Share the basket of items with children during group time or at a learning center. You can use these items in many different ways. Teach children new vocabulary words in English as well as in their home language as they touch and hold different items. Help children practice vocabulary by playing guessing games with the items (e.g., "I am thinking of something in this basket that is green—verde. It is small and feels rough."). Let children choose items and describe them to their classmates, allowing others to guess.

SKILL DEVELOPMENT: Activities like this can help children learn about new objects in nature or from around the classroom as they develop their vocabulary. Having the items to hold and touch helps children to connect the vocabulary word with the item itself. In addition, guessing game activities like these help children to develop inquiry skills. Allowing children to take turns leading the activity provides them with additional opportunities to expand their vocabulary as well as to describe objects or ask questions of one another as they try to guess the object another classmate has chosen. Create other baskets with items from around the classroom to help children develop vocabulary related to classroom materials.

APPLYING CULTURALLY RESPONSIVE PRACTICES TO THIS ACTIVITY: Make multicultural baskets that include a range of items (or pictures of different items) that represent the cultures of children in the classroom. For example, ask children and families to send pictures to school of their favorite traditional foods. Look at the pictures together with the children in your classroom and use these pictures to take turns guessing each food. Make additional baskets with pictures of flags or traditional clothes from the different countries represented in your classroom.

ACTIVITY 5: Nature Walk Scavenger Hunt

MATERIALS: A picture list of objects labeled in English and Spanish (or other home languages) that can be found around the school (e.g., trees, grass, pinecones)

INSTRUCTIONS: Show children the list of objects and practice saying the name of each word in English, Spanish, or other languages represented in your classroom. Take the list outside and have children search for and collect the different items. Put items in a basket or bag to bring back in the classroom following outdoor time. Review the list again together and pass the items around the circle for children to touch and hold.

(continued)

Chapter 7 Classroom Activities (continued)

SKILL DEVELOPMENT: A scavenger hunt can be used to help children develop new vocabulary words in English as well as their home language. In addition, activities like these can expand children's knowledge of nature and increase awareness of the environment around them.

APPLYING CULTURALLY RESPONSIVE PRACTICES TO THIS ACTIVITY: Teach children the names of objects included in the scavenger hunt in English, Spanish, and other languages. Modify the objects on your list based on what is available around your school. If you are in an urban area, access to nature may not be possible. Instead, choose items that children are likely to see around them. The scavenger hunt can also be held inside the classroom or school.

ACTIVITY 6: Number Stomp

MATERIALS: A writing surface (chalkboard, dry erase board, or piece of paper); pen or marker

INSTRUCTIONS: During small or large group time, ask children to participate in an action (e.g., jumping) the number of times you indicate. Draw a number on the board and say the number together in English as well as in other languages spoken by children in the class. Count to that number together and jump that number of times. Write another number, count, and jump. Change actions (e.g., stomping, hopping on one foot).

SKILL DEVELOPMENT: Help children to practice counting and learn to recognize numbers. Allow children a chance to lead this by letting them choose an action or pick a number. Rather than writing a number, a child could hold up his or her fingers to show a number. Have all children hold up the same number of fingers before participating in the actions that number of times. This activity also helps children to practice self-regulation skills by having them jump only the number of times indicated.

APPLYING CULTURALLY RESPONSIVE PRACTICES TO THIS ACTIVITY: Practice counting in each of the languages represented in your classroom. Ask families to show you how the numbers 1 to 10 are written in their home languages, then practice counting in different languages with children and show them the different ways that numbers can be written.

ACTIVITY 7: Reading Books with Repetition and Incorporating Home Languages

MATERIALS: Developmentally appropriate books that include repetition

INSTRUCTIONS: Choose books that include lots of repetition of key words and phrases. As you read, incorporate key words in other languages as well as in English if you are able to do so. With books like *Brown Bear, Brown Bear,* incorporate the animal names and colors in English and Spanish as well as other languages represented in your class. Point out to children that in English, people say "red bird," with the color first and the animal second, but in Spanish, people say, "pájaro rojo," with the animal first and the color second. Create visual aids (e.g., sentence strips, flannel board characters, photocopies of images from the book) to accompany the book. Use the visual aids to enhance the story or to retell the story as a class or later as a small group activity.

SKILL DEVELOPMENT: Just like when singing songs, hearing phrases and words repeated and practicing saying these words can help children to develop phonological awareness of the sounds associated with a language as well as help them to learn and practice new vocabulary words.

(continued)

Chapter 7 Classroom Activities *(continued)*

APPLYING CULTURALLY RESPONSIVE PRACTICES TO THIS ACTIVITY: Whenever possible, find books that are available in multiple languages. If you or another staff member is able to do so, read the book in Spanish (or the child's native language) to a child who is a dual language learner before and after reading the book in a small- or large-group setting in the class. You might also consider sending the book home for families to read together with their children. You can also use reading opportunities to highlight similarities and differences between languages. For example, by learning that words are sometimes spoken in different orders or that some languages use different alphabets or are read in different directions (right to left or top to bottom versus left to right), children begin to gain an awareness of the similarities and differences that exist across languages and cultures.

ACTIVITY 8: Shape Hunt

MATERIALS: Classroom materials that are different shapes (could start with circular and square objects)

INSTRUCTIONS: After learning about circles and squares, ask children to go around the classroom and find objects that match those shapes. Provide a few examples first, such as a ball and a square block. Bring objects back to the circle and review why the objects fall in each category (e.g., "Let's count the sides on this square together! One, two, three, four. Now let's count them in Spanish. Uno, dos, tres, cuatro.").

SKILL DEVELOPMENT: Children can practice shape identification and develop social skills by working together to identify whether different objects are square or circular.

APPLYING CULTURALLY RESPONSIVE PRACTICES TO THIS ACTIVITY: Embed children's home languages into the shape hunt by teaching them the words for circle and square or other shapes in multiple languages. In addition, count the number of sides on each shape using multiple languages.

ACTIVITY 9: What's Missing?

MATERIALS: Four to eight items from around the classroom (items can correspond to a classroom theme); small blanket or piece of fabric to cover the items

INSTRUCTIONS: Lay the items out on the floor in front of the class. Practice saying the names of each item in English, Spanish, or other languages represented in the classroom. Use the blanket to cover the items and remove one of them without children seeing. Lift up the blanket and ask children to guess what is missing. This game can be played in small or large groups and with different types of items representing different classroom themes.

SKILL DEVELOPMENT: This game can be used to help children develop and practice vocabulary words. In addition, children are practicing self-regulation skills such as paying attention and taking turns as well as deductive reasoning skills to figure out what is missing.

APPLYING CULTURALLY RESPONSIVE PRACTICES TO THIS ACTIVITY: Play "What's Missing?" using a range of items that represent classroom themes or children's interests. In addition, you can use this game to increase children's multicultural awareness of foods, clothing, or other artifacts. Ask family members to bring in items that represent their home cultures that can be used when playing this game.

Chapter 7 Additional Resources

BOOKS:

Dual-Language Learners Birth to Grade 3: Strategies for Teaching English
Author: Angele Sancho Passe
Year: 2012
Publisher: Redleaf Press

Many Languages, One Classroom: Teaching Dual and English Language Learners
Author: Karen Nemeth
Year: 2009
Publisher: Gryphon House

WEB-BASED RESOURCES:

Early Childhood Mathematics: Promoting Good Beginnings
National Association for the Education of Young Children
Year: 2002
Web site: http://www.naeyc.org/files/naeyc/file/positions/psmath.pdf

The Essentials of Early Literacy Instruction
Authors: Kathleen A. Roskos, James F. Christie, Donald J. Richgels
Year: 2003
Web site: http://www.naeyc.org/files/tyc/file/Roskos.pdf

Many Languages, One Teacher: Supporting Language and Literacy Development for Preschool Dual Language Learners
Authors: Elizabeth S. Magruder, Whitcomb W. Hayslip, Linda M. Espinosa, Carola Matera
Year: 2013
Web site: http://www.naeyc.org/yc/files/yc/file/201303/Many_Languages_Margruder_0313_0.pdf

More, All Gone, Empty, and Full: Math Talk Every Day in Every Way
Author: Jan Greenberg
Year: 2012
Web site: http://www.naeyc.org/yc/files/yc/file/201205/RockingAndRolling_YC0512.pdf

Meeting the Home Language Mandate: Practical Strategies for All Classrooms
Author: Karen Nemeth
Year: 2009
Web site: http://eclkc.ohs.acf.hhs.gov/hslc/tta-system/teaching/eecd/domains%20of%20child%20development/language%20development%20and%20communication/meetingthehomelangage.pdf

Social Studies in Today's Early Childhood Curricula
Author: Gayle Mindes
Year: 2005
Web site: https://www.naeyc.org/files/yc/file/200509/MindesBTJ905.pdf

(continued)

Chapter 7 Additional Resources *(continued)*

Storybook Reading for Young Dual Language Learners
Authors: Cristina Gillanders, Dina C. Castro
Year: 2011
Web site: http://www.naeyc.org/files/yc/file/201101/GillandersOnline0111.pdf

Whatever Happened to Developmentally Appropriate Practice in Early Literacy?
Authors: Susan B. Neuman, Kathleen Roskos
Year: 2005
Web site: http://www.naeyc.org/files/yc/file/200507/02Neuman.pdf

Appendix 7.1: Vocabulary Word List

Numbers		
English	Spanish	Other Language
one	uno	
two	dos	
three	tres	
four	cuatro	
five	cinco	
six	seis	
seven	siete	
eight	ocho	
nine	nueve	
ten	diez	
eleven	once	
twelve	doce	
thirteen	trece	
fourteen	catorce	
fifteen	quince	
sixteen	dieciséis	
seventeen	diecisiete	
eighteen	dieciocho	
nineteen	diecinueve	
twenty	veinte	

Shapes		
English	Spanish	Other Language
circle	círculo	
triangle	triángulo	
square	cuadrado	
rectangle	rectángulo	
oval	óvalo	

(continued)

Appendix 7.1 Vocabulary Word List *(continued)*

English	Spanish	Other Language
pentagon	pentágono	
star	estrella	
heart	corazón	
diamond	diamante	

Math Language

English	Spanish	Other Language
How many are there?	¿Cuántos/Cuántas hay?	
Which ones has more?	¿Cuál tiene más?	
Which one has less?	¿Cuál tiene menos?	
more	más	
less	menos	
big/bigger	grande/más grande	
small/smaller	pequeño/más pequeño	
long/longer	largo/más largo	
tall/taller	alto/más alto	
wide/wider	ancho/más ancho	
short/shorter	corto/más corto	
what do you think will happen?	¿Qué crees que pasará?	

Spanish Alphabet

Letter	Spanish name
A, a	a
B, b	be
C, c	ce
D, d	de
E, e	e
F, f	efe
G, g	ge
H, h	hache

Appendix 7.1 Vocabulary Word List *(continued)*

Letter	Spanish name
I, i	i
J, j	jota
K, k	ka
L, l	ele
M, m	eme
N, n	ene
Ñ, ñ	eñe
O, o	o
P, p	pe
Q, q	cu
R, r	ere
S, s	ese
T, t	te
U, u	u
V, v	uve
W, w	doble uve
X, x	equis
Y, y	i griega
Z, z	zeta

Appendix 7.2: Books for the Dual Language Learner Classroom

I. Classroom Books That Celebrate Diversity

All Kinds of Families by Mary Ann Hoberman
Abuela by Arthur Dorros
Before You Were Here, Mi Amor by Samatha R. Vamos
Chrysanthemum by Keven Henkes
The Colors of Us by Karen Katz
Families by Shelley Rotner and Sheila M. Kelley
Felicity & Cordelia: A Tale of Two Bunnies by Lisa Jahn-Clough
Friends at School by Rochelle Bunnett
Global Babies/Bebés del mundo by Global Fund for Children
I Love My Hair by Natasha Anastasia Tarpley
I Love Saturdays y Domingos by Alma Flor Ada
Making Friends by Fred Rogers
Oscar's Half Birthday by Bob Graham
The Relatives Came by Cynthia Rylant and Stephen Gammel
Round Is a Mooncake: A Book of Shapes by Roseanne Thong
The Sandwich Swap by Queen Rania of Jordan of Al Abdullah
Same, Same, But Different by Jenny Sue Kostecki-Shaw
Shades of People by Shelley Rotner and Sheila M. Kelly
What Can You Do With a Paleta? by Carmen Tafolla
What I Like About Me by Allia Zobel Nolan
Whoever You Are by Mem Fox
Who's in My Family? All About Our Families by Robbie H. Harris
Wild Berries by Julie Flett
Yoko by Rosemary Wells

II. Classroom Books That Are Published in English and Spanish

Are You My Mother?/¿Eres mi mamá? by P. D. Eastman
Big Dog, Little Dog/Perro grande, perro pequeño by P. D. Eastman
Brown Bear, Brown Bear, What Do You See?/Oso pardo, Oso pardo, ¿Qué ves ahí? by Bill Martin Jr.
Caps for Sale/Se venden gorras by Esphyr Slobodkina
Don't Let the Pigeon Drive the Bus!/¡No dejes que la paloma conduzca el autobús! by Mo Willems
The Dot/El punto by Esther Rubio and Peter H. Reynolds
From Head to Toe/De la cabeza a los pies by Eric Carle
The Giving Tree/El árbol generoso by Shel Silverstein
Goodnight Moon/Buenas Noches Luna by Margaret Wise Brown

(continued)

Appendix 7.2 Books for the Dual Language Learner Classroom (continued)

Head, Shoulders, Knees, and Toes/Cabeza, hombros, piernas, pies by Annie Kubler
The Kissing Hand/Un beso en mi mano by Audrey Penn and Ruth E. Harpe
Love You Forever/Siempre te querré by Robert Munsch and Sheila McGraw
The Napping House/La casa adormecida by Audrey Wood
Opposites/Opuestos by Sandra Boynton
The Rainbow Fish/El pez arco iris by Marcus Pfister
The Snowy Day/Un día de nieve by Ezra Jack Keats
The Very Hungry Caterpillar/La oruga muy hambrienta by Eric Carle

III. Classroom Books That Include Spanish and English Text

Abuela by Arthur Dorros
All the Colors We Are/Todos los colores de nuestra piel by Katie Kissinger
Arroz con leche by Lulu Delacre
Gracias/Thanks by Pat Mora
Hello Ocean/Hola mar by Pam Muñoz Ryan
The Lost Ball/La pelota perdida by Lynn Reiser
Quinito's Neighborhood/El vecindario de Quinito by Ina Cumpiano
¡Yum! ¡Mmmm! ¡Qué rico! by Pat Mora

For additional book suggestions, see the Multicultural Library List on page 189.

8. Engaging Dual Language Learners Through Music and Movement

Mr. David played a recording of traditional children's songs in Spanish that Andrea's mother had brought to share with the class. As the music started to play, a smile spread across Andrea's face. Usually quiet, Andrea started to talk excitedly in Spanish and English, saying, "My music! ¡Mi música!" During morning meeting, Mr. David helped Andrea to tell the class about her favorite song ("Patito"), and together the class talked about what they liked about the song, how the song sounded, and what they knew about the language. They also listened for key words that they had practiced together in English and Spanish while looking at pictures of the words ("*Patito* means *little duck!*"). Mr. David extended the activity to a learning center at which children had the opportunity to draw their own ducks and create a collage of a pond while listening to the song and practicing key words in English and Spanish.

STRATEGIES

- 30 Learn About Culture Through Music and Movement
- 31 Invite Children and Families to Share Music with the Classroom
- 32 Share Classroom Music with Families
- 33 Build Children's Vocabulary and Early Literacy Skills Through Music

APPENDICES

- 8.1 Music Vocabulary
- 8.2 Children's Songs in English and Spanish

Even though Mr. David did not speak Spanish himself, he was able to use music in many ways to make language learning engaging and effective for DLLs and the other children in his class. A small but growing number of studies have found that music can be used in early childhood classrooms to foster engagement in classroom activities and learning (Paquette & Rieg, 2008).

Music is a powerful learning tool for people of all ages. Music can evoke different feelings and energy levels and can be a wonderful way to practice new words or concepts by learning through repetition. In addition, music is an important aspect of many cultures and can help children and adults connect with culture—their own and that of others. Sharing music from a wide range of cultures with children in your classroom exposes them to diversity in another form. In addition, when used with intention in the classroom, music and movement can be used to promote positive relationships, enhance learning opportunities, encourage physical exercise, and much more.

> *Music is an important aspect of many cultures and can help children and adults connect with culture—their own and that of others.*

There are many ways in which music can be used in early childhood classrooms to engage DLLs and all children in learning activities. Music can help create a positive learning environment and provide opportunities for experiential learning, regardless of a child's language abilities (Paquette & Rieg, 2008). Studies suggest that music and movement activities enhance children's interest and engagement in games and classroom learning activities (Paquette & Rieg; Tominey & McClelland, 2013). Using music and movement also provides children with additional cues they can use to make sense of the instructions of an activity. These cues may include melodies that remind children that it's time for a classroom transition (e.g., "clean-up song" or "rest time song") or lyrics that give instructions to help guide children's actions (e.g., "time to line up at the door!"). Music and songs can also be used to reinforce language and vocabulary development. For example, giving children an opportunity to practice singing new words repeatedly can help those words stick! In addition, teaching children songs in English as well as in other languages is another way to extend learning from the classroom to the home environment. Children are likely to sing songs at home that they learned at school. Through singing these lyrics, they continue to practice what they learned at school while at home and may even be sharing new vocabulary words in this way with their families.

> *Music and songs can be used to reinforce language and vocabulary development.*

A growing number of research studies link music and movement with a range of outcomes for children. For example, one study found that English- and Spanish-speaking children who were randomly assigned to a creative dance class were rated higher by parents and teachers in social competence than their peers who were in a control group (Lobo & Winsler, 2006). Another study found that children who participated in community music classes scored higher on self-regulation assessments than a matched sample of children (e.g., children from similar socioeconomic backgrounds) who had not taken community music classes (Winsler, Ducenne, & Koury, 2011). That study made an interesting observation: when asked to wait for a period of time, children who had taken music classes were able to wait longer than their peers who had not taken music classes. Participating in community music classes taught children a skill that was helpful to them while waiting—singing songs. The researchers noticed that children who had taken music classes often passed the time spent waiting by singing to themselves. Just as we discussed in Chapter 5 regarding classroom management, having something to do during a transition or waiting period can help children stay focused and on task.

A few studies have examined the effects of music specifically on outcomes for DLLs. For example, one study found significant gains in English language skills for 4-year-old children who spoke Chinese as a primary language, as a result of participating in an English-language music intervention (Lee & Lin, 2015). The intervention took place over an 18-week period, with children participating in 45-minute sessions twice each week. The sessions included a hello and good-bye song, musical storytelling, and musical movement activities. Both teachers and parents reported observing significant improvements in children's English language skills. The study's authors concluded that music served as a powerful tool to provide children with a nonthreatening way to help make language learning fun. They noted that even children who were normally introverted or slow to warm up participated in music activities. In addition, singing songs and playing musical instruments provided children with repetitive practice of vocabulary words. Through these activities, children also practiced other skills, such as paying attention, which may have also related to improved language abilities.

Studies like these provide ideas for creative ways that language learning can be practiced and reinforced. It's exciting that these techniques can be used not only to help children learn English but also to expose English-speaking children to other languages and cultures.

The strategies shared in this chapter are as follows:

- Strategy 30: Learn About Culture Through Music and Movement
- Strategy 31: Invite Children and Families to Share Music with the Classroom
- Strategy 32: Share Classroom Music with Families
- Strategy 33: Build Children's Vocabulary and Early Literacy Skills Through Music

STRATEGY 30: Learn About Culture Through Music and Movement

Music can be used to build cultural awareness and cultural competence in your classroom for both children and yourself (NAEYC, 1995). Playing a range of musical types and styles provides children with another lens through which to view different cultures. In this chapter, we provide strategies and suggestions for embedding multicultural music into the early childhood day as well as turning these listening experiences into activities that intentionally promote multicultural experiences.

> *Music can be used to build cultural awareness and cultural competence in your classroom for both children and yourself (NAEYC, 1995).*

Apply Strategy 30

- Play music from a broad range of styles and cultures. There are many opportunities throughout the school day to play and listen to music. Music may be appropriate during individual play and exploration, movement and dancing activities, at lunch or during snack, before rest or naptime, and during transitions. Incorporating different types of music and music from different styles (classical or modern) and from many cultures is another way that educators can teach children about one another and the world around them.

- In addition to playing a range of musical styles, be sure to talk with children about what makes each new piece of music interesting, unique, or special. Just like tasting different kinds of food can expand children's palates, giving children exposure to different styles of music will help them to broaden the range of music they enjoy listening to. Teach children vocabulary that allows them to talk about what they are hearing. At the end of this chapter, in Appendix 8.1, we provide a table of music-related vocabulary words in English and Spanish. Here are some possible discussion points you can use in your classroom:

  - Have you heard this song before, or is this a new song to you? Does it sound like other songs you have heard?
  - The speed of a song is called the *tempo*. Is the tempo of this music fast or slow?
  - Are people singing or do you only hear instruments? If you hear singing, what language do you recognize?
  - Do you know what the song is about? Let's talk about the story!
  - What instruments do you hear as you listen to the music? Do you hear a piano? Guitar? Violin? Flute? Trumpet?
  - What do you like best about this song?

- In addition to listening to music, give children opportunities to dance and move their bodies to a wide range of musical styles. Encourage children to freely explore their own movements to diverse music (e.g., moving quickly, slowly, jumping, moving their arms), or teach children about different types of dance (e.g., folk dancing, flamenco, tap dancing, traditional and native dances, salsa, African dance). You may not have knowledge of any or all of these dances, so using this strategy might require a community effort. Ask colleagues if they know one or more dances they could share with your class or invite families to share dances they know.

- Over time, build a collection of multicultural classroom musical instruments for children to play and explore. Different styles of music, cultural traditions, and countries use different instruments to make music. Introducing a new musical instrument to your class that children can play and explore gives them another lens through which to view culture. Buying musical instruments may not be feasible, as instruments can be costly, so you might also consider inviting families to share different musical instruments they have at home (e.g., tuba, djembe, gong) and look online for ideas for musical instruments that students could make out of recycled materials at classroom learning centers.

STRATEGY 31: Invite Children and Families to Share Music with the Classroom

Each family likely has its own musical tastes and preferences. These musical tastes may align with the dominant culture, their home culture, their personal preferences, or a combination. Invite each of the families of children in your classroom to share their favorite music or one of their favorite family songs with your class by sending in a recording or by visiting your class and singing a song with the class as a special activity. This can be a wonderful way to provide families with another opportunity for school engagement. It is also another way to communicate to *all* families that their home culture, heritage, and interests are valued in the classroom.

Apply Strategy 31

- Invite parents to teach the class a song from their childhood or a song in their own language. If the song is in a language other than English, ask parents to provide you with the words and translation ahead of time, if they are able to do so. To prepare for the visit, consider making visual aids that help support the words in the song. For example, if the song is about a train, draw or print a picture of a train labeled with the word in English as well as the language the song is in, if it is not in English.

- Invite parents to send in recordings of their child's or family's favorite song to share with the class. If a parent feels uncomfortable teaching the class a song him- or herself or if the parent's schedule does not allow for being present during the school day, sending music to school provides the parent with another option for sharing. Allow the child to share the song during group or circle time. Ask the child to talk about the song—what he or she likes about it and/or how it is a part of family time.

- Share music with your class that is special to you as well. Sharing music with your class that you like or that has been important in your own family models to children that everyone (including their teacher!) has music that is special to them and that taking pride and sharing that music is important and valued in your classroom.

STRATEGY 32: Share Classroom Music with Families

In addition to asking families to share music with your classroom, share with them the music that you play and sing in your classroom. Sending music home provides parents with another way to feel connected with what is happening in the classroom during the day. This also provides children with an opportunity to share with and teach their families and may help families expand their own linguistic and cultural knowledge.

Apply Strategy 32

- Print copies of the lyrics that you sing often in the classroom for children to take home and share with their families. Having the words available to see may help families to practice these songs with their children. Children can help teach parents the tunes and the words to the songs themselves. Be sure to share with children that you are sending the lyrics home to their families and ask them to identify someone they would like to teach a new song to so that they will be more likely to do so. Using a smartphone or digital recorder, you can also provide families with recordings of your class singing the song so that they can practice the songs together with their children.

- Ask for parent volunteers for help in translating words from songs that you sing in your classroom in English into their home language. Asking parents to translate the full set of lyrics from every single song you sing in your classroom may be overwhelming and too much to ask from a single family, but it may be worthwhile to hire a translator to do this one time or to find a staff member at your school or program who is able to do so for languages that are commonly spoken by families at your center. Once translations are available, send them home with families along with lyrics in English.

STRATEGY 33: Build Children's Vocabulary and Early Literacy Skills Through Music

Just as children like reading books again and again, children often enjoy singing the same song over and over and over again. This can be a wonderful and fun way to learn the sounds (phonology) of a language as well as to practice new vocabulary words and grammar with repetition.

Apply Strategy 33

- Choose songs to sing that are repetitive and lend themselves to using actions and making facial expressions. The repetition inherent in many songs will make them easier for children to learn, especially children who are DLLs. As you sing these songs, model the physical actions and facial expressions that correspond with the song. Encourage children to copy your expressions and movements as well. Not only does this help children to be engaged in the song, regardless of their language ability, it helps communicate the meaning of the song in nonverbal ways that will help reinforce the vocabulary in the song as children learn new words.

- When possible, sing songs in more than one language or incorporate words from children's home languages in songs. Songs that are available in more than one language (e.g., "Head, Shoulders, Knees, and Toes") provide an easy starting point. You can also choose select words from common English songs to translate into different languages. We provide translations in Spanish for several common children's songs in Appendix 8.2 at the end of this chapter.

- Help children practice phonemic awareness skills—the ability to hear, identify, and express the different sounds in a language—by identifying rhyming sounds that are the same or different in songs from various languages. For example, have children identify the rhyming sounds in "The Itsy Bitsy Spider" *(spout, out)* and "La araña pequeñita" *(subió, llevó)*.

- Create a picture songbook for your class. Add pages to a three-ring binder to make your songbook. On each page, include a picture or symbol that represents the song (e.g., a picture of a star for "Twinkle, Twinkle, Little Star"). Include the name of the song in English, Spanish ("Estrellita, ¿dónde estás?"), and other languages (when possible) and print the lyrics to the song on the back of the song page. Add a page for each song that you sing routinely in your classroom. The songbook can be used to support recognition of songs using visual images. It can also be used to give children an opportunity to choose a song by selecting a picture before they have the vocabulary to communicate which song they would like to sing. In many ways, using a classroom songbook also promotes emergent literacy skills. Children have an opportunity to practice turning pages and learn that the images in the book represent songs, just as letters on a page represent words and stories.

CHAPTER CONCLUSIONS

Music can be used in many different ways to help children learn about diverse languages and cultures and to support language learning and vocabulary development. Using music to foster intentional conversations about culture can help avoid using the **"tourist approach"**—sharing culture with children by providing them with limited exposure through celebrations and artifacts. For example, using a song like "The Mexican Hat Dance" to introduce Mexican culture to children with no other exposure to the culture could result in children seeing Mexican culture very narrowly.

> *Using music to foster intentional conversations about culture can help avoid using the "tourist approach."*

Sharing music and artifacts from other cultures expands children's knowledge of that culture and can help ensure that the knowledge children build about each culture is not limited to stereotypes. Children who are only exposed to one small aspect of another culture may believe that China is only about Chinese New Year or that Mexico is only about Cinco de Mayo. The tourist approach can be limiting and may actually contribute to perpetuating stereotypes, rather than fostering an appreciation of other cultures and values. Exposing children to a wide range of cultures in many different ways and through many lenses helps them to realize the depth that comes with various cultures.

Chapter 8: Check Your Learning

1. A study found that English- and Spanish-speaking children who were randomly assigned to a creative dance class were rated higher by parents and teachers in _____ than peers who were in a control group.
   a) Academic skills
   b) Social competence
   c) Self-help skills
   d) All of the above

2. Music can be used to build cultural awareness and cultural competence in early childhood classrooms for both children and teachers.
   a) True
   b) False

3. Research suggests that in the early childhood classroom, music and movement can enhance _____.
   a) Children's singing ability
   b) Children's ability to dance
   c) Children's engagement in learning activities
   d) Children's friendships

4. Having something to do during a transition time, such as singing a song, can be distracting to children and lead to more chaos in the classroom.
   a) True
   b) False

5. Results from a comparison study found that children who had taken music classes had _____ than children who had not taken music classes.
   a) Fewer behavior problems
   b) More behavior problems
   c) Lower self-regulation
   d) Higher self-regulation

6. What is the hypothesized reason why children who had taken community music classes were able to wait longer than children who had not taken community music classes?
   a) They were used to waiting because they spend a lot of time waiting in music class.
   b) They had strategies to keep themselves occupied, such as by singing songs.
   c) They were tired from being overscheduled in too many activities and often fell asleep.
   d) All of the above

7. What is the term for teaching children about a culture through limited exposure to celebrations or artifacts?
   a) Stereotyping
   b) Cultural awareness
   c) The tourist approach
   d) Sightseeing

8. You should only play songs for children in another language if you are able to speak that language.
   a) True
   b) False

9. What is phonemic awareness?
   a) The ability to make a rhyme
   b) The ability to understand a language without being able to speak the language
   c) The ability to sing different pitches
   d) The ability to hear and make the different sounds in a language

10. Introducing a wide range of musical styles, musical instruments, and dances to children is a way to expand their knowledge and appreciation for other cultures.
    a) True
    b) False

For answers to this chapter quiz, please refer to the Answer Key on page 186.

Chapter 8: Reflection Questions

1. What role did music play in your own family?

   _____
   _____
   _____
   _____

2. Do you remember specific songs or styles of music that were important in your family?

   _____
   _____
   _____
   _____

3. In what ways do you currently use music and movement to support dual language learners (DLLs) in your classroom? What would you like to do more often?

   _____
   _____
   _____
   _____

4. What are new ideas that you would like to apply to incorporate music more intentionally into your classroom as a way to engage DLLs?

   _____
   _____
   _____
   _____

Chapter 8: Classroom Activities

ACTIVITY 1: Freeze Dancing

MATERIALS: Music, a music player (e.g., CD player, smartphone)

INSTRUCTIONS: Play music with your class and ask them to dance when the music plays and to freeze when it stops.

SKILL DEVELOPMENT: Playing games like Freeze Dance gives children exposure to many different types of music and helps them develop other skills, including self-regulation. In this game, children are required to pay attention to and follow directions as well as start and stop to musical cues.

APPLYING CULTURALLY RESPONSIVE PRACTICES TO THIS ACTIVITY: Dancing to music from many different cultures over the school year can help expose children to culture through music and help children gain appreciation for different musical styles. In addition, playing songs in different languages can introduce children to the sounds and vocabulary of other languages as well as their own.

ACTIVITY 2: Sing Songs in English, Spanish, and Other Languages

MATERIALS: Simple songs in English and Spanish (or other languages)

INSTRUCTIONS: Use simple songs in English and Spanish (or other languages) in your classroom. You can teach your class an entire song in Spanish; if you do not speak Spanish, consider asking a colleague, friend, or a family from your program to help you practice your pronunciation of the Spanish words. If you are not comfortable singing entire songs in Spanish, try adding a few Spanish words into the songs. For example, you can include the names of animals in both English and Spanish when singing "Old MacDonald." When singing "If You're Happy and You Know It," use both English and Spanish for the feeling words: happy/feliz, sad/triste, and so on.

If You're Happy and You Know It/Si estás feliz y lo sabes

English:

If you're happy and you know it, show your face.

If you're happy and you know it, show your face.

If you're happy and you know it then your face will surely show it.

If you're happy and you know it, show your face.

If you're sad and you know it, show your face.

If you're angry . . .

If you're scared . . .

Spanish:

Si estás feliz y lo sabes, muestra tu cara.

Si estás feliz y lo sabes, muestra tu cara.

Si estás feliz y lo sabes, muestra ytu cara, pues tu cara claro la anseñará.

Si estás feliz y lo sabes, muestra tu cara.

Si estás enojada...

Si tienes miedo...

(continued)

Chapter 8 Classroom Activities (continued)

As you sing, model a tone of voice and facial expression that shows the feeling you are singing about. A list of feeling words in English and Spanish is included at the end of Chapter 6, in Appendix 6.1. Invite children to make faces that match the feeling word as well.

SKILL DEVELOPMENT: Singing songs, especially those with repetitive words, helps children to practice new vocabulary and develop key skills such as phonological awareness. Incorporating actions and facial expressions helps support children's understanding of the meaning of new vocabulary words. By alternating English and Spanish words (or words in other languages spoken by children in your classroom), you can provide opportunities for children to lead who typically take the role of follower. For example, you might sing one line, "If you're triste and you know it . . ." and then say, "Can anyone show me a face that is triste? Does anyone know what *triste* means?" The Spanish-speaking children in your classroom will have the opportunity to model the word for other children and be leaders in their own language.

APPLYING CULTURALLY RESPONSIVE PRACTICES TO THIS ACTIVITY: Embedding words from different languages into the songs you sing gives children exposure to the sounds and vocabulary words in other languages as well as their own. If you speak a language other than English, share traditional children's songs from the language or languages you speak with your class. When singing songs that emphasize emotion, recognize that children and adults express emotions in different ways and to varying degrees based on individual and cultural differences. Some cultures may encourage open expression of a wide range of emotions, whereas others may not. Asking children to show an angry face or a sad face may be uncomfortable for some children, so you might consider inviting children to do so, but not singling out individual children if they choose not to.

ACTIVITY 3: Music Maps

MATERIALS: Music, music player (e.g., CD player, smartphone), drawing paper, crayons or markers.

INSTRUCTIONS: This activity works well as a learning center station with individual or small groups of children. Provide children with individual pieces of paper or a large shared piece of paper to color or draw on while listening to music. Encourage children to draw along with the music, drawing quickly when the music is fast and drawing slowly when the music slows down.

SKILL DEVELOPMENT: Through this activity, children can work on developing fine and gross motor skills as well as attention skills and an appreciation for music. Asking children to draw along with the music can encourage them to attend to the music and pay attention to details they might otherwise ignore if music is playing in the background during play.

APPLYING CULTURALLY RESPONSIVE PRACTICES TO THIS ACTIVITY: Use activities like this to help children listen to a wide range of music and musical styles. Include songs in English, Spanish, and other languages so that children are receiving exposure to the sounds of different languages as well as the sound of different musical styles. In addition, use phrases in children's home languages to reinforce the activity. For example, you can employ Spanish words alongside English for words like go/*vete*, stop/*para*, fast/*rápido*, slow/*lento*.

Chapter 8: Additional Resources

BOOK:

The Bilingual Book of Rhymes, Songs, Stories, and Fingerplays
Authors: Beverly J. Irby, Rafael Lara-Alecio, Pam Schiller
Year: 2004
Publisher: Gryphon House

WEB-BASED RESOURCES:

Learning by Leaps and Bounds: Make a Little Music
Author: Rae Pica
National Association for the Education of Young Children
Young Children
Year: 2009
Web site: https://www.naeyc.org/files/yc/file/200911/LeapsandBoundsWeb1109.pdf

Music Play: Creating Centers for Music Play and Exploration
Authors: Kristen M. Kemple, Jacqueline J. Batey, Lynn C. Hartle
National Association for the Education of Young Children
Young Children
Year: 2004
Web site: https://www.naeyc.org/files/tyc/file/MusicPlay.pdf

Music Resources for Dual Language Learners
Author: Karen N. Nemeth
Web site: http://www.naeyc.org/content/music-resources-dual-language-learners

Appendix 8.1: Music Vocabulary

English	Spanish	Other Language
music	música	
song	canción	
sing	canta	
dance	baila	
listen	escucha	
fast	rápido	
slow	lento	
high	alto	
low	bajo	
piano	piano	
guitar	guitarra	
orchestra	orquesta	
band	banda	
violin	violín	
trumpet	trompeta	
drums	batería	
Go!	¡Vete!	
Stop!	¡Para!	

Appendix 8.2
Children's Songs in English and Spanish

"Head, Shoulders, Knees, and Toes"	"Cabeza y hombros rodillas y pies"
Head, shoulders, knees, and toes, knees and toes Head, shoulders, knees, and toes, knees and toes Eyes and ears and mouth and nose Head, shoulders, knees, and toes, knees and toes	Cabeza y hombros, rodillas y pies, rodillas y pies Cabeza y hombros, rodillas y pies, rodillas y pies Ojos y orejas y boca y nariz Cabeza y hombros, rodillas y pies, rodillas y pies

"The Itsy Bitsy Spider"	"La araña pequeñita"
The itsy bitsy spider went up the water spout. Down came the rain and washed the spider out. Out came the sun and dried up all the rain And the itsy bitsy spider went up the spout again.	La araña pequeñita subió, subió, subió. Cayó la lluvia y se la llevó. Salió el sol y todo lo secó Y la araña pequeñita subió, subió, subió.

"Old MacDonald Had a Farm"	"En la granja del Tió Juan"
Old MacDonald had a farm. E-I-E-I-O. And on that farm he had a cow. E-I-E-I-O. With a moo moo here and a moo moo there. Here a moo, there a moo, everywhere a moo moo. Old MacDonald had a farm. E-I-E-I-O. Old MacDonald had a farm. E-I-E-I-O. And on that farm he had a dog. E-I-E-I-O. With a woof woof here and a woof woof there. Here a woof, there a woof, everywhere a woof woof. Old MacDonald had a farm. E-I-E-I-O. Old MacDonald had a farm. E-I-E-I-O. And on that farm he had a cat. E-I-E-I-O. With a meow meow here and a meow meow there. Here a meow, there a meow, everywhere a meow meow. Old MacDonald had a farm. E-I-E-I-O.	En la granja del tió Juan, I-AI-I-AI-O. Muchas vacas tiene allí, I-AI-I-AI-O. Con un mu mu aquí, y un mu mu alla. Aquí un mu, allí un mu, en todas partes un mu mu. Tió Juan tenía una granja, I-AI-I-AI-O. En la granja del tió Juan, I-AI-I-AI-O. Un perrito tiene allí, I-AI-I-AI-O. Con un guau guau aquí, y un guau guau alla. Aquí una guau, allí una guau, en todas partes un guau guau. Tió Juan tenía una granja, I-AI-I-AI-O. En la granja del tió Juan, I-AI-I-AI-O. Cuatro gatos tiene allí, I-AI-I-AI-O. Con un miau miau aquí, y un miau miau alla. Aquí una miau, allí una miau, en todas partes un miau miau. Tió Juan tenía una granja, I-AI-I-AI-O.

(continued)

Appendix 8.2 Children's Songs in English and Spanish (continued)

"Twinkle, Twinkle, Little Star"	"Estrellita, ¿dónde estás?"
Twinkle, twinkle, little star. How I wonder what you are Up above the world so high, like a diamond in the sky. Twinkle, twinkle, little star. How I wonder what you are.	Estrellita, ¿dónde estás? Quiero verte titilar en el cielo, sobre el mar, Un diamante de verdad. Estrellita, ¿dónde estás? Quiero verte titilar.

"The Wheels on the Bus"	"Las ruedas del autobús"
The wheels on the bus go round and round, round and round, round and round. The wheels on the bus go round and round, all through the town!	Las ruedas del autobús giran y giran, giran y giran, giran y giran. Las ruedas del autobús giran y giran, ¡por toda la ciudad!
The wipers on the bus go swish, swish, swish, swish, swish, swish, swish, swish, swish. The wipers on the bus go swish, swish, swish, all through the town!	Los limpiaparabrisas del autobús hacen swish swish swish, swish swish swish, swish swish swish. Los limpiaparabrisas del autobús hacen swish swish swish, ¡por toda la ciudad!
The people on the bus go up and down, up and down, up and down. The people on the bus go up and down, all through the town!	La gente del autobús salta y baja, salta y baja, salta y baja. La gente del autobús salta y baja, ¡por toda la ciudad!
The doors on the bus go open and shut, open and shut, open and shut. The doors on the bus go open and shut, all through the town!	Las puertas del autobús se abren y se cierran, se abren y se cierran, se abren y se cierran. Las puertas del autobús se abren y se cierran, ¡por toda la ciudad!

45 Strategies That Support Young Dual Language Learners by Shauna L. Tominey and Elisabeth C. O'Bryon.
Copyright © 2018 Paul H. Brookes Publishing Co., Inc. All rights reserved.

9 Engaging Families from Diverse Backgrounds

Gabriel's mother, Paulina, dropped him off and picked him up from school every day. Although Gabriel's English- and Spanish-speaking skills were developing rapidly, Paulina felt very self-conscious about her own ability to communicate in English. She wanted to be involved in Gabriel's schooling but was not sure how to be involved. In fact, she did not even feel comfortable asking Gabriel's teacher questions because of her limited English abilities. She was also not sure whether asking the teacher questions was respectful, as it was not respectful to question teachers in her home culture. Fortunately, Gabriel's teacher, Ms. Svea, recognized that families might be feeling this way and approached each family individually to talk about their expectations, ways they could be involved in the classroom, and the families' thoughts on what engagement meant to them.

STRATEGIES

- **34** Help Children Prepare for the Transition to School
- **35** Promote Regular Communication with Families
- **36** Provide Families with Ways to Be Engaged in School
- **37** Approach Challenging Conversations with Empathy and Understanding
- **38** Ask Families for Feedback

Providing opportunities for families from diverse backgrounds to be involved in their child's education is an important task for early childhood educators. Because early childhood learning settings are often a family's first opportunity for school involvement, early childhood educators and leaders have an important job to help promote a collaborative, welcoming environment. Nurturing families' early engagement in their child's education can pave the way for ongoing positive experiences with school involvement. Early interactions and experiences are especially important, given that families that engage early in their children's academic career are more likely to stay involved as their children continue their schooling (Weiss, Caspe, & Lopez, 2008).

> *Nurturing families' early engagement in their child's education can pave the way for ongoing positive experiences with school involvement.*

Helping families to feel welcome has the potential to affect not only the relationships between a family and school but also the way a child feels about coming to school. Studies have found that when families are involved in their children's school, children are more likely to have positive feelings about their teachers and more positive feelings about school (Dearing, Kreider, & Weiss, 2008). This is important because the relationships children have with their teachers lay a foundation for learning. The teacher–child relationship predicts positive relationships with peers, engagement in learning, and future academic achievement (Bowlby, 2008; Commodari, 2013; Drake, Belsky, & Fearon, 2014; Howes, 2000; Mashburn et al., 2008).

Before jumping in to talk about promoting family engagement, it is important to define what is meant by **family engagement.** According to the National Association for the Education of Young Children, "Family engagement occurs when there is an on-going, reciprocal, strengths-based partnership between families and their children's early childhood education programs" (Halgunseth, Peterson, Stark, & Moodie, 2009, p. 3). The words we want to highlight in this definition are *ongoing* (i.e., helping families feel a continual connection with their child's school), *reciprocal* (i.e., ensuring that engagement is a two-way relationship), and *strengths-based* (i.e., recognizing the many strengths families bring to a relationship between school and home).

> *When families are involved in their children's school, children are more likely to have positive feelings about their teachers and more positive feelings about school.*

Family engagement in school has consistently been associated with positive short-term and long-term outcomes for children. Short-term outcomes span many different domains and include improvements in academic achievement (Henderson & Mapp, 2002; Jeynes, 2005), positive effects on social and behavioral skills (McWayne, Hampton, Fantuzzo, Cohen, & Sekino, 2004), and more positive attitudes about school for children (Christenson & Havsy, 2004; Patrikakou, Weissberg, Redding, & Walberg, 2005). Some of the long-term effects of parent engagement include lower rates of high school dropout, increased on-time school completion, and higher grade levels completed by students—even after controlling for child and family background characteristics and risk factors (Barnard, 2004). It is important to note that family engagement that begins early in a child's education has also been identified as a potential pathway through which to narrow income-based achievement gaps (Wong & Hughes, 2006).

ENGAGING FAMILIES FROM DIVERSE BACKGROUNDS

To effectively engage families from diverse backgrounds, it is important to recognize that across racial, ethnic, and socioeconomic backgrounds, parents want their children to succeed in school and want to engage in behaviors that support their child's academic success (Mapp, 2002). Schools and families may think about family engagement in different ways, however. The ways in which families approach and interact with their child's school can differ based on their cultural backgrounds, beliefs, and personal experiences with the educational system. For example, parents who have had negative personal experiences with schools (e.g., their own experience; experiences with an older sibling) may approach relationship building with their child's teachers with anxiety or reluctance. Some parents may be ready to jump in to any engagement opportunity that arises, whereas others may worry that they do not have the skills they need to support their children's education, which may hinder their involvement. Some parents may try to "stay out of the way" so that they do not interfere with the education children are receiving from their teachers. Keeping in mind that the vast majority of parents have positive intentions and *want* to support their child's education can be helpful as you try to find ways for all parents to be involved in the way they can and would like to be involved.

Across racial, ethnic, and socioeconomic backgrounds, parents want their children to succeed in school and want to engage in behaviors that support their child's academic success.

Research with families of children who are dual language learners has shown that parents are involved in their child's education in many different ways, including nontraditional forms of family involvement or engagement that they believe supports their child's learning (Halgunseth, Jia, & Barbarin, 2013). For some families, supporting their child's education might include making sure children get enough sleep at night, are on time for school, treat their teachers with respect, or interact well with their classmates (Halgunseth et al., 2013). What do you think of when you hear the terms *family engagement* or *family involvement*? Take a look at the following list and note which items you typically consider when you think of the things families do to support their child's education.

- ❏ Volunteer in the classroom
- ❏ Check in with the teacher at drop-off or pick-up to ask about their child's day
- ❏ Attend parent–teacher conferences
- ❏ Share family values or strategies from home with teachers at school
- ❏ Read school newsletters, handouts, or updates that are sent home
- ❏ Ensure children get enough sleep and are well fed for school
- ❏ Budget for child care tuition
- ❏ Transport children to school on time
- ❏ Buy school supplies and clothes
- ❏ Ask children about their day at school
- ❏ Emphasize to children the importance of listening to their teacher at school

- ❏ Read books to children at home
- ❏ Make donations (materials or money) to school
- ❏ Serve on school committees or boards

Take time to recognize the many different types of family involvement that exist—those on this list as well as others. Technically, not all of these examples of family involvement meet the definition of family engagement, as they are not all ongoing and reciprocal, but they are still important to recognize. A mismatch between the expectations held by parents and teachers around family involvement can create a tension that hurts the formation of positive relationships between teachers and family members. As an educator, communicating your expectations and the expectations of your program for family engagement as well as taking the time to hear from families about their perspectives can help build relationships that are collaborative and supportive of children's growth and learning.

A primary goal of the strategies provided in this chapter is to foster positive relationships between educators and families to ensure effective communication between home and classroom. Another goal is to help all families have the same access to information about their child's education and have a wide range of opportunities to engage in their child's school in a way that best recognizes their family values, culture, strengths, and needs.

In this chapter, we provide five specific strategies for engaging families from diverse backgrounds using a culturally responsive lens:

- Strategy 34: Help Children Prepare for the Transition to School
- Strategy 35: Promote Regular Communication with Families
- Strategy 36: Provide Families with Ways to Be Engaged in School
- Strategy 37: Approach Challenging Conversations with Empathy and Understanding
- Strategy 38: Ask Families for Feedback

STRATEGY 34: Help Children Prepare for the Transition to School

Just as it is important for you to learn about the children and families who will be coming to your classroom, it is important for them to get to know you. As you prepare for a new school year or for a new family to arrive in the middle of the school year, think about how the family will be feeling as they bring their child to school for the first time. For families who do not feel confident in their ability to communicate in English or for those who are unfamiliar with the school system in the United States, unpleasant feelings such as nervousness, anxiety, worry, or fear may be heightened.

There are many things educators can do to learn how families may be feeling about their children's transition to school and strategies educators can use to foster a positive experience for all involved. Simply being available is a good first step. Offering families an opportunity to meet with you and visit the classroom as well as providing them with information about what to expect during the first few days and weeks of school may help ease the transition to school for families and children.

Apply Strategy 34

- Making personal contact with children and families can be a valuable way to help children and families feel more comfortable in a new school. If possible, offer an opportunity for family members and children to meet with you before the child's first day of school. Invite children and families to visit the classroom or consider making a home visit. Use this time to begin building a relationship, answer questions for families, and share information about what to expect. Connecting with parents early and in person is essential to laying the foundation for working together to promote children's success (Magruder et al., 2013). It can also help parents to feel more comfortable and can facilitate the formation of collaborative relationships between families and teachers.

- In addition to a visit with families, send an e-mail to families or give families hard copies of pictures of the classroom and teachers so they have images to prompt talking with their children about school before starting school or even throughout the school year.

- If an in-person visit is not possible, or in addition to an in-person visit, send a short letter home to families in English and their home language to introduce yourself and express your excitement for welcoming them to your classroom. Include information about what they can expect on the first day of school, what to bring, and who to ask if they have questions, and encourage families to talk about what to expect with their child.

STRATEGY 35 — Promote Regular Communication with Families

Communicating regularly and often with families is one way to promote positive relationships across school and home (Baker & Manfredi-Petitt, 2004; Minke, Sheridan, Kim, Ryoo, & Koziol, 2014). Share regular updates with families on what is happening in the classroom, including classroom themes, activities, and special events. In addition, let families know about upcoming classroom or school events as well as opportunities for involvement in the classroom.

It may be helpful to include prompts for families with questions that they can ask their child (e.g., "Ask your child what his or her favorite snack is at school" or "We had a special guest in class yesterday. Ask your child who came to read a book in our class."). Giving families prompts that encourage open-ended responses, rather than a yes or no response, can help support conversations with their child about school. Use multiple methods of communication (e.g., paper handouts, phone calls, e-mails, text messages) to share the information you send home to ensure that all families have equal access to being involved in and supporting their child's educational experiences. Maintaining regular communication between a program and families can take a significant amount of time. To limit the burden on any one person, consider how this responsibility could be divided among teachers in a classroom (e.g., each teacher is responsible for communicating with a small number of families) as well as shared with school leaders.

Apply Strategy 35

- Ask families verbally as well as through written communication how they would like to receive information from the school and how they would prefer to communicate with the school. If possible, use family recommendations to help guide the way you share ongoing information with families.

- When possible, provide families with information in English as well as in their home language. Identify bilingual staff who can assist with translations for families when needed, in-person or in written materials. Alternately, ask families who are fluent in English as well as other languages to help translate for other families who are not.

- If families have limited proficiency in English, ask them if they are able to identify someone in their lives who speaks their language and English who would be willing to help them to interpret and understand written material that is sent home when translations are not available.

- Consider alternative means of communication. Families may prefer text messages, short phone calls, bulletin board postings, e-mails, or touching base in person when time allows. Communicating with families using multiple means increases the likelihood that all families will be reached.

> *Communicating with families using multiple means increases the likelihood that all families will be reached.*

- Include pictures and images in your communication to families over e-mail, in newsletters, or on a bulletin board. Seeing images of their child engaged during the school day is something most families will appreciate. Images can help families to feel connected with activities that are happening at school and can be used by families to prompt conversations about school with their children.

- Let families know when the best times are to connect with you in person during or after the school day (if those times exist). For example, if drop-off time before 9 a.m. is fairly quiet and an easy time to discuss issues because children are occupied with getting settled and the number of staff members is high, then let the families know you are available to communicate then.

STRATEGY 36: Provide Families with Ways to be Engaged in School

Offer a number of ways for families to be involved at school. Ask families about how they would like to be involved, and use this information to provide opportunities that meet each family's needs when possible. By providing families with different options and opportunities for engagement, educators are more likely to reach and connect with a larger number of families from diverse backgrounds. Communicating these options to families is essential to encourage participation and strong home–school connections.

Apply Strategy 36

- Encourage parents to spend time in the classroom. Let parents know your classroom and program policies for classroom visits. Are parents welcome to visit and spend time in the classroom at any time or only on particular days or during particular activities? Invite parents to visit school to read a story with the class, share a talent (e.g., play a musical instrument), teach the class a song, or share a family tradition.

- Use interactive bulletin boards to encourage ongoing, two-way communication with families. These boards provide key information about what is happening in the classroom and program so that parents have this information easily accessible at pick-up and drop-off time. Your interactive bulletin board can also include prompts to encourage parents to share with other families and the program. For example, you may encourage parents to identify and share community-based resources—such as free child-focused events or English language classes—that they have found helpful. This information can be valuable for other families as well as for your school.

- Schedule regular parent–teacher conferences. In-person opportunities to connect can facilitate relationship building as well as information sharing between teachers and family members. If necessary, seek out an interpreter to help facilitate communication at these conferences.

- Send home ideas for quick and easy activities that parents can do at home with their children to help build social and emotional skills as well as early academic skills. For example, ask families to write down the names of books they read together at home or stories they shared over the past week. You can also prompt parents to ask children questions about book characters when reading together, such as "How do you think he/she was feeling? How can you tell? Can you think of a time when you felt sad/mad/happy?" Then ask for parents' feedback: What did they try? What did their children enjoy most? What did they like best? Was there anything that worked well that you could try at school? This process can help promote at-home learning *and* two-way communication with your families.

- Hold family workshops or in-person group meetings. Workshops can cover a range of topics and can provide a forum for families to ask questions and learn more about what is going on in their child's classroom. Workshops can also help families to connect with other families in the school community. This has been found to be especially important for Latino families for promoting involvement (Durand, 2011). Here are some tips and considerations for holding family workshops with diverse families:

  - Survey parents to identify appropriate days and times to hold workshops—before or after school, on weekends, or at a time that overlaps the school day. Consider the schedules, responsibilities, and any constraints that may make it difficult for parents to attend in-person events at the school.

  - Provide child care if possible or consider hosting workshops that are child-friendly (e.g., a workshop on strategies for reading together with your child). If workshops are advertised as child-friendly, be sure to include activities appropriate for older or younger siblings, if possible.

- Consider the feelings that you would like families to have during and following a workshop. Families may be feeling stressed, overwhelmed, intimidated, or nervous to attend a workshop for the first time at their child's school. They may also be feeling excited and curious. Think about the feelings you would like them to have during a workshop (e.g., interested, supported) and the feelings you would like them to have when they leave the workshop (e.g., inspired, valued). Choose activities that you believe will help promote these feelings and those that will help calm their unpleasant feelings and promote those that are pleasant.

- Involve interpreters when necessary.

- Include "make and take" or "learn with me" activities that families can create as part of a workshop with their children. Ideas for "make and take" activities might include an art project that parents and children create together (e.g., a painting of their home, a sculpture of a favorite family food) or musical instruments created out of recycled objects that families can play together at home.

- Help families to connect with one another during workshops. Allow time for parents to introduce themselves and have time to visit with the families of their child's classmates. Encourage parents to share with one another through icebreaker questions such as "How would you like your child to feel at school?" or "What is your favorite activity to do together with your family?"

- Choose workshop topics that are relevant and meaningful to families from diverse backgrounds. Workshop topics might include English skills, supporting children's social and emotional development (e.g., managing challenging emotions), school readiness, or how to find community resources. Ask families for their input as to what they would like to learn more about.

- Even if families do not respond to your invitations for engagement, avoid assuming that families do not care or are not willing to be engaged in their child's school. Continue to seek out ways to share information with families and support their engagement in the way they would like to be involved. In addition, communicate with families that their engagement helps you to learn about their child and their family so that you can best support them.

> *Communicate with families that their engagement helps you to learn about their child and their family so that you can best support them.*

Family conferences can be tricky. Let's take a look at Mr. Alex, a first-year teacher who was eager to support the DLLs in his class, all of whom spoke Spanish at home.

Mr. Alex was excited to host his very first round of family conferences. The children in his class had learned so much, even during the first few months of school, and he could not wait to share this with their families. He prepared typed reports for each family detailing their child's social and emotional and academic milestones in English and Spanish (for Spanish-speaking families) and asked a Spanish-speaking interpreter to attend conferences for families who did not speak English.

During the first family's conference, Mr. Alex spent the entire time talking. Having an interpreter took more time than he expected, so he ran out of time before the parent was able to ask any questions. During the second family's conference, he spent less time talking and made time for the parent to ask a few questions. During the third family's conference, he decided to take a different approach. He asked the parents what they thought was going well and if they had noticed growth in their child. He was amazed to hear the family share many of the same milestones he was planning to share with them. In addition, the family shared with him some challenges they were experiencing at home (e.g., a recent move, the death of an extended family member) that they thought might be affecting their child's behavior. Mr. Alex told them how much he appreciated that they shared this information with him and that it would help him to better support their son. He then shared some additional milestones and growth he had noticed.

Mr. Alex left the conference with an impression that he knew the family and the child much better than he had before the conference. The family left feeling excited to hear how well their son was doing at school and also feeling confident that Mr. Alex cared for their son and was doing his best to meet his needs. This conference also served as an important reminder to Mr. Alex that conferences are not just a time to share with families but a time to learn from them as well.

STRATEGY 37: Approach Challenging Conversations with Empathy and Understanding

There are many different reasons why you might need to have a challenging conversation with a family. Some of these reasons might include having conversations about children's challenging behaviors in the classroom, concerns about a child's growth or development, the need to have a child evaluated for special services or potential delays, suspected abuse, school policies that are not being followed by the family (e.g., cell phone use, late pick-up), or other reasons. Although these conversations may be difficult, approaching them with empathy and a culturally responsive lens will help them be productive.

Apply Strategy 37

- Consider the family's cultural background and prior experiences as you consider the most appropriate way to deliver a difficult message. Be especially mindful of how hearing your message might affect a parent's feelings. If you are sharing with a family that they are breaking one of the school policies by picking their child up late every day, they may feel embarrassed for not understanding that time is not as fluid in the United States as it is in their home country.

- If you have been struggling with a child's challenging behaviors and have just come to the realization that the child likely needs special education services, this realization may be a relief to you, but it may have another effect on the family. It is important to realize that different cultures view special needs in drastically different ways. To some families, learning that their child may have delays or need special education services may be a shock or surprise or even a disgrace to their family. The path that parents commonly take to accepting that their child has special needs often includes anger and denial followed by grief and eventual acceptance (Heath, 2009). Knowing that families may follow this pathway to acceptance can help you to support them through those steps. For example, you may be able to connect families with support networks that can assist parents through grief that they may experience when learning about a child requiring special education services.

- Make sure that families understand the information you share. If families are not able to understand what you communicate, they may feel too embarrassed to ask for clarification and may instead show signs that they *do* understand so that they do not appear disrespectful to you. Consider involving an interpreter, if needed—either a member of your center's or school's staff, a family advocate, or a friend of the family who speaks English as well as the family's home language. Make sure family members are comfortable with that person hearing the message you have to share. In addition, make sure that families receive the message in multiple ways (e.g., send a note or e-mail after an in-person call summarizing what you shared).

- Encourage families to ask questions, and answer their questions honestly and to the best of your ability. Follow up with families at a later time to ensure that they understood what was discussed and to answer questions that have come up since the initial conversation. In the moment, the family member or members might feel overwhelmed or respond defensively. Providing time and space for them to consider the news you have shared and following up to have a conversation at a later time might help.

STRATEGY 38: Ask Families for Feedback

To encourage a reciprocal relationship, it is important to ask families for feedback. Ask what is working well for them. Do they feel connected to their child's school and engaged in their child's early learning? If this is not their first school, you may consider asking how they were involved in their child's last school and what worked well for them there. Not everything families recommend may be feasible. For example, you cannot have a 30-minute conversation with each family in your class each night or even each week, but perhaps an occasional phone conversation for special circumstances might be feasible, depending on your program's policies.

Apply Strategy 38

- Consider sending brief surveys home to families at multiple points during the school year. Be sure to have translations available in their home language or offer opportunities for families to complete the surveys with support from a translator, if needed. Use surveys to learn what is working well for families, whether they have questions, or whether they have recommendations of ways to improve the home–school partnership. For example, you may ask parents to respond to the following prompts: "I would feel more connected to what is going on in my child's classroom if _____." or "I wish

I received more information about _____." Consider giving families an opportunity to complete and return some surveys anonymously to ensure honest responses. Informal conversations can also serve this purpose, but some families may not feel comfortable sharing their honest opinions in person, particularly if something is not going well.

- One important note related to this strategy is that families may feel overburdened by too much paperwork (e.g., enrollment surveys, beginning of the year surveys, feedback surveys). For families who are not native English speakers, sending home many different surveys may feel taxing, especially if they are spending significant time looking up English words or if they are hiring a translator or depending on others to translate for them. Pick and choose the surveys you send home with care so that you are gathering information that will help you best support children without overtaxing families. Consider your classroom's specific needs when determining which surveys to send to families. You may have to create your own survey to gather feedback you need or there may be existing surveys available online that you can customize and send.

- Use in-person opportunities to check in with families or ask for feedback. This could take place one-on-one at drop-off or pick-up, during parent–teacher conferences, or at family workshops.

- Show families that you value their input by thanking them for providing feedback and by sharing how that feedback has been incorporated into your lesson plans and has shaped program decisions and adaptations.

CHAPTER CONCLUSIONS

Early childhood educators can promote family engagement in ways that recognize the strengths and meet the needs of diverse families. Remember to treat families as learners, just as both teachers and students are treated as learners. Parents are learning about how they can support their child's healthy growth and be engaged in their child's education as their child reaches each new developmental level. Share expectations clearly and help families to learn about the many different ways they can be involved in your school or program in a way that best fits their family.

> *Remember to treat families as learners just as both teachers and students are treated as learners.*

Approach interactions with families with empathy and understanding and maintain the belief that families want what is best for their children. Keep in mind that the vast majority of families are doing the best they can with the knowledge and resources that they have available to them. Families are doing this within the greater context of their lives, and it is important that educators acknowledge both the strengths and the challenges of their realities. Educators can help increase families' engagement through targeted efforts to promote ongoing, reciprocal, and strength-based partnerships.

Chapter 9: Check Your Learning

1. Families that are engaged in their child's education early on are more likely to remain engaged in their child's schooling.
   a) True
   b) False

2. When families are involved in school, children are more likely to have _____ and _____.
   a) A greater rate of illness . . . a higher number of school absences
   b) Positive feelings about their teachers . . . positive feelings about school
   c) Friends who speak their home language . . . fewer fights at school
   d) Higher-level English language abilities . . . difficulties in their home language

3. Which of the following statements about family engagement is true?
   a) Family engagement has been identified as a potential pathway to narrowing achievement gaps.
   b) Family engagement in early childhood lays the foundation for family engagement throughout a child's schooling.
   c) Family engagement relates to more positive attitudes about school for children.
   d) All of the above

4. Lower rates of high school dropout have been identified as a long-term effect of parent engagement.
   a) True
   b) False

5. Family engagement occurs when there is an _____ between families and their children's early childhood program.
   a) Open stream of communication
   b) Appreciation of language and cultural differences
   c) Ongoing, reciprocal, strengths-based partnership
   d) E-mail, phone, or in-person exchange

6. Which of the following examples would be considered family involvement but does *not* meet the definition of family engagement?
   a) A teacher regularly asking families about what is working well for their child at home during nap-time and then using this information to help support children at school
   b) A parent taking on an extra job to pay for a child's school supplies
   c) A monthly family newsletter sharing classroom information as well as columns written by families on topics related to parenting
   d) A classroom hosting "family traditions" sharing days at which families can share traditions with the class and other families

7. The teacher–child relationship has been found to predict what?
   a) Positive relationships with peers
   b) Engagement in learning
   c) Future academic achievement
   d) All of the above

8. Families who do not attend parent–teacher conferences are less interested in their child's well-being than families who do attend parent–teacher conferences.
   a) True
   b) False

9. In order to effectively promote family engagement for diverse families, it is helpful to do which of the following?
   a) Share your own and your program's expectations for family engagement.
   b) Ask parents how they would like to be engaged.
   c) Offer many different types of engagement opportunities throughout the year.
   d) All of the above

10. If a family does not speak English, it is their responsibility to hire a translator when needed.
    a) True
    b) False

For answers to this chapter quiz, please refer to the Answer Key on pages 186–187.

Chapter 9 Reflection Questions

1. How was your family engaged in your schooling when you were growing up?

   _____
   _____
   _____

2. What do you believe are the most important ways in which families can show involvement in their children's education?

   _____
   _____
   _____

3. What do you think are some of the barriers to family engagement in school?

   _____
   _____
   _____

4. What is one new thing you plan to do to support family engagement in your classroom?

   _____
   _____
   _____

5. What is one new thing you plan to do to support family engagement in your classroom?

   _____
   _____
   _____

Chapter 9: Additional Resources

BOOKS:

50 Strategies for Communicating and Working with Diverse Families (3rd edition)
Author: Janet Gonzalez-Mena
Year: 2013
Publisher: Pearson

Engaging the Families of ELLs: Ideas, Resources, and Activities
Authors: Renee Rubin, Michelle Abrego, John Sutterby
Year: 2012
Publisher: Routledge

Reaching Out to Latino Families of English Language Learners
Authors: David Campos, Rocio Delgado, Mary Esther Soto Huerta
Year: 2011
Publisher: ASCD

WEB-BASED RESOURCES:

The Importance of Home Language Series
Head Start: Early Childhood Learning & Knowledge Center (ECLKC)
Year: 2015
Web site: http://eclkc.ohs.acf.hhs.gov/hslc/tta-system/cultural-linguistic/home-language.html

Family Engagement, Diverse Families, and Early Childhood Education Programs: An Integrated Review of the Literature
Authors: Linda C. Halgunseth, Amy Peterson, Deborah R. Stark, Shannon Moodie
Year: 2009
Web site: https://www.naeyc.org/files/naeyc/file/research/FamEngage.pdf

Immigrant Parents and Early Childhood Programs: Addressing Barriers of Literacy, Culture, and Systems Knowledge
Authors: Maki Park, Margie McHugh
Year: 2014
Web site: http://www.migrationpolicy.org/research/immigrant-parents-early-childhood-programs-barriers

Reciprocal Relationships
National Association for the Education of Young Children
Web site: http://www.naeyc.org/familyengagement/principles/3

10 Continuing to Grow Through Professional Development

Ms. Miller loved learning about the culture and traditions of the families of children in her classroom. Coming from a predominantly white European American ancestry, she often told people that she did not grow up with a culture. What she did and believed seemed to be just like what everyone else around her did and believed, so she had never considered what her own culture and her family's culture might be.

STRATEGIES

- **39** Develop Cultural Awareness and Adopt Self-Reflective Practices
- **40** Expand Your Multicultural Knowledge
- **41** Participate in Professional Development Activities
- **42** Learn How to Effectively Conduct Assessments
- **43** Involve Families in Decisions Related to Assessments
- **44** Understand Mandated Reporting Laws and Regulations
- **45** Think of Yourself as a Lifelong Learner

Ms. Miller's parents had taught her to appreciate and value the culture and ideas of others. They had many friends from diverse backgrounds and celebrated traditional holidays along with them. Ms. Miller's parents had stressed the importance of education in her life and worked hard to ensure that she had the opportunity to go to college when she decided that she wanted to become a teacher. What Ms. Miller did not realize is that each of these family values is part of what makes up her own culture. Her family's acceptance and openness to welcoming other cultural beliefs into their household was a part of their home culture. Their belief in the value of education and the responsibility of parents to provide educational opportunities for their children was another part of their home culture. Each of these values and beliefs has the potential to affect the perspective Ms. Miller brings to working with children and families.

Just like Ms. Miller, every early childhood educator has beliefs and values shaped by their own culture and personal or family experiences that may affect their teaching. In this chapter, we present strategies focused on building your own professional development practices around cultural awareness to support your ability to use culturally responsive practices in the classroom. We include six strategies focused on professional development as well as considerations that may arise as part of your professional responsibilities, including considerations when using assessments with children from culturally and linguistically diverse backgrounds and the need to understand mandated reporting laws. At the end of the chapter, we include a list of resources to further enhance your professional development on these and other topics.

The strategies included in this chapter are as follows:

- Strategy 39: Develop Cultural Awareness and Adopt Self-Reflective Practices
- Strategy 40: Expand Your Multicultural Knowledge
- Strategy 41: Participate in Professional Development Activities
- Strategy 42: Learn How to Effectively Conduct Assessments
- Strategy 43: Involve Families in Decisions Related to Assessments
- Strategy 44: Understand Mandated Reporting Laws and Regulations
- Strategy 45: Think of Yourself as a Lifelong Learner

STRATEGY 39: Develop Cultural Awareness and Adopt Self-Reflective Practices

One of the steps important to developing cultural responsiveness is practicing cultural awareness—awareness of the impact one's own culture can have on interactions with others and one's teaching practices, as well as an awareness of culture in general (Han & Thomas, 2010). Your own culture tends to be easier to identify if you are a member of the nondominant

> *One of the steps important to developing cultural responsiveness is practicing cultural awareness.*

cultural group, because many of these cultural aspects stand out from the people and society around you. If you are a member of the dominant cultural group, however, sometimes it can be more challenging to determine what makes up your culture and your cultural beliefs.

Apply Strategy 39

- Take time to reflect on the values that are important in your culture. There are many different aspects of culture that you could consider. Try thinking about the holidays you celebrate (or choose not to celebrate); the values that are important in your family; the language or languages your family speaks; and the music, art, and food that are special or meaningful to your family.

- Next, consider some of the values that are most important to you and your family. How did your family view education and how do you view education? What skills do you value most in young children? What role do you believe parents and teachers each play in the lives of a child? Your answer to each of these questions is a reflection of your personal and cultural beliefs and values. These beliefs and values may also affect your approach to teaching. If you came from a cultural background in which girls were encouraged to participate in quiet activities (e.g., arts and crafts, playing dolls and house) and boys were encouraged to participate in more physically active games (e.g., building with blocks, playing with cars and trucks), without realizing it you may not be encouraging each gender equally to participate in and try all of the activities that are available to them in the classroom. On the flip side, if you feel strongly that all children should be encouraged to participate in all aspects of the classroom, this may clash with the values of certain families that focus on more traditional gender roles. Being aware of how your beliefs affect the choices you make when teaching and how your beliefs align or do not align with the beliefs of the families of children in your class can help you to be more intentional about the choices you make throughout the day.

- Make sure that the teaching choices you make are made with intention. Reflecting on why you are choosing each activity and why you respond to each child in the way you do can help you to consider how culture might influence your teaching choices. For example, as Ms. Miller spent more time thinking about her home culture, she realized that one of the values that was instilled in her from a young age was the idea that children could succeed academically in any topic regardless of their gender. Her parents encouraged her and her brother equally in math and sciences. She excelled in her math classes and did not realize until she was an adult that the field had traditionally been male-dominated.

  She also came to realize that her parents did not apply this same equitable lens to social and emotional development. She was allowed and encouraged to express her feelings at home, but her brother was not. Once she identified that this belief was part of her family culture, she realized that she was carrying it forward in her own classroom. She often spent time talking about feelings with the girls in her class, but made comments to boys like "Big boys don't cry! Don't you want to be a big boy?" She did not think there was anything wrong with this (after all, it was part of her family culture and her brother had turned out just fine), but her supervisor, Ms. Ginise, disagreed. Ms. Ginise shared that their curriculum and accreditation requirements shaped their school culture, which encouraged teachers to support social and emotional expression for all children. Ms. Ginise coached Ms. Miller on language she could use to support social and emotional language for children of all genders, but also shared with her that she valued her home culture. She even suggested that Ms. Miller tell the children in her class about her cultural beliefs about emotions ("In my culture, girls are allowed to talk about their feelings, but boys are not supposed to. The rule at our school is that this is a place where both girls and boys can talk about feelings.").

STRATEGY 40: Expand Your Multicultural Knowledge

The greater awareness that educators have about different cultural values and beliefs, the better able they are to support children and families based on those cultural backgrounds. One way to expand your multicultural knowledge is to start within your program. Use the expertise of program staff to share your own cultures with one another and expand your multicultural knowledge.

> *The greater awareness educators have about different cultural values and beliefs, the better able they are to support children and families based on those cultural backgrounds.*

Apply Strategy 40

- Take time to learn about and celebrate one another's home cultures and traditions during formal or informal staff meetings and gatherings. Hold staff potlucks or sharing days at which colleagues can share traditional foods or stories if they choose. This is often done during holidays (e.g., Thanksgiving, Christmas, Hanukkah), but these types of activities should be extended throughout the year. Take the opportunity to ask questions of your colleagues that help you learn about new and different personal and cultural beliefs and values. Practicing these skills in your own life can help you to better model and teach these same skills to the children in your classroom.

- Get to know one another to foster an emotionally supportive work environment. Creating a caring and supportive community among staff is just as important as creating a caring community in your classroom. Together with your classroom team or fellow staff members, have discussions about how you would like to feel at work. You may (or may not) be surprised to find out that you likely all want to have similar feelings. Most adults want to feel happy, safe, valued, respected, and other pleasant feelings during the day. What helps each individual have these feelings, however, may be very different based on individual and cultural values.

- For example, you and your colleague may both identify feeling respected as an important value; however, to one of you, feeling respected might mean having others make eye contact with you and offer compliments and praise to let you know when you have done well. To the other, feeling respected may mean *not* making eye contact (eye contact may be a sign of dominance or threat in some cultures) and being given the space to make decisions without criticism. Having these types of conversations with colleagues can help staff learn about one another's cultural values as well as what they can do to better support one another throughout the school day.

- Take time on your own to expand your knowledge about other cultures. There are many different ways in which you could go about doing this, including asking a friend from another background to lunch and sharing stories, reading books about the experiences of others, watching movies and documentaries, or exploring online resources and community-based supports. It is important to remember that even people who come from the same cultural background may not share the same personal beliefs and values, so getting to know every individual and family remains important. Taking time to expand cultural knowledge can help educators to learn more about the children and families they support and to better understand the role culture plays in their lives—as well as in the educators' own lives.

STRATEGY 41: Participate in Professional Development Activities

In addition to sharing your own cultural values and learning more about the cultural values of your colleagues, you might consider embedding intentional learning activities focused on cultural awareness into staff meetings and gatherings in order to institutionalize culturally responsive practices and make them an explicit part of your program's practices (Han & Thomas, 2010). If you do not feel comfortable leading these types of discussions with your colleagues, you can reflect on these types of questions individually.

Apply Strategy 41

- Consider having brainstorms or group discussions on the following questions with your colleagues and fellow staff members:
    - What are all the ways you think families can engage in their child's early education at school and at home? What are ways that families might be involved that educators may not be able to easily recognize?
    - What are all the barriers that you think might affect a family's involvement in their child's school?
    - What challenges typically arise during the school year that make it hard to connect with families?
    - What can educators do to help support families in the ways they want and need to be supported?
    - What are your favorite ways to connect with children and families?
    - What are your favorite multicultural books for use in the classroom?
    - What are your favorite "get to know you" activities to help children learn more about each other in the classroom?
- Whether or not you feel comfortable recommending activities to your colleagues focused on cultural responsiveness, you can serve as a model of these skills on a daily

basis. One of the ways that you can do this is by pointing out the impact of culture during conversations. For example, if a colleague shares that he or she is having difficulties with a certain family, you can help her or him consider how the family might be feeling in the situation or brainstorm ways that their cultural values or beliefs might be different from those at school. Avoid using language that perpetuates stereotypes and help colleagues do the same. If you hear a colleague making comments such as "I've worked with families from that group before—they never come to any of our family events," you might reply with a comment that helps your colleague acknowledge individual differences across families: "After we get to know them a bit better, maybe we can ask what would help them be more involved or how they would like to be involved. They might be experiencing some challenges that we don't know about."

- As a program, seek out organizations that provide professional development for early childhood educators and look for opportunities that specifically focus on supporting DLLs, culturally responsive teaching practices, and engaging families from diverse backgrounds. NAEYC, as well as state and local branches of the organization, often provides conferences and professional development opportunities on a wide range of early childhood topics. Get in touch with your local chapter and learn about other resources for early childhood educators in your area. At the end of this chapter, we provide a list of additional professional organizations along with their web sites, where you can learn more.

STRATEGY 42: Learn How to Effectively Conduct Assessments

Ms. Vaughn has two children in her class who are DLLs. Deepa and Mani were both about the same age when they started preschool for the first time this fall. Neither spoke a word of English. As the year continues, Ms. Vaughn is noticing significant differences between the two of them in terms of developing language and other skills, which has made her worry. Several months into the school year, Mani has a significant English vocabulary, but Deepa is only using about a dozen words in English. Mani has made several friends in the class, whereas Deepa seems content playing by herself. Deepa also appears to struggle with other activities, including basic sorting activities at center time. She has trouble following along with her classmates during large-group activities and does not always follow the other children when Ms. Vaughn is leading a transition, such as preparing the class to go outside.

Ms. Vaughn has tried providing more individualized support to Deepa, but she is surprised that the strategies she typically uses with success do not appear to be helping much. Ms. Vaughn is unsure if the differences she is seeing are due to normal variations between the two children or if she should be concerned that Deepa may have developmental delays or need special services.

Identifying when children need additional support and what type of support can be a challenging task. This can be especially difficult when working with children from diverse linguistic and cultural backgrounds. There are many factors that affect a child's ability to learn language and to learn more than one language, including a child's age, aptitude, personality, and more (Tabors, 2008). These same factors can affect children's growth in other areas of development as well. It is important to realize that children grow and develop at different rates and that children who appear to be at very different developmental stages may still fall within the typical range of development. It is also important to recognize that when delays are accurately identified and supported in early childhood, there can be tremendous benefit for children and their families.

Failing to appropriately identify the cause of a young child's challenges, however, can have serious implications. Because their ability to communicate in English can be behind that of their peers, it is not uncommon for DLLs to be referred for special education services. Providing a child who is a DLL with inappropriate special education services could be a disservice in many ways: the child would be receiving the wrong services and supports, his or her language needs would not be addressed, and the school's resources would not be appropriately utilized—potentially meaning that a child who needs those services would be denied access. Given the complicated and complex relationship between language and learning, the assessment process with DLLs can be a challenge (Wagner, Francis, & Morris, 2005).

There are many reasons educators might use assessments in early childhood, including to 1) promote learning and development for individual children, 2) identify children with special needs or health conditions for the purpose of intervention, 3) monitor trends in programs and evaluate effectiveness, and 4) obtain data from individual children, classrooms, or programs for accountability purposes (Espinosa & López, 2007). Many programs ask or require educators to assess children's abilities in the fall so that they can track children's progress over the year. One challenge with this is that educators may not know children well enough at the beginning of the year to determine what language should be used to assess a child. Another challenge is that the assessments developed for one group of children (such as children in the dominant cultural group) may not be appropriate or relevant for children from other groups. For example, an assessment measuring children's vocabulary that includes specific cultural references may not adequately assess the vocabulary of a child unfamiliar with that culture. In the next subsection, we recommend several approaches for educators who are considering using assessments with children who are DLLs.

Apply Strategy 42

- Before assessing a child, choose assessments carefully. Consider what your goals are and what the assessment is intended to measure, as well as whether it was developed for use with DLLs (Peña & Halle, 2011). If you have serious concerns, create an assessment team, including the child's family and at least one early childhood professional who understands the child's home language and home culture—specifically, someone who has experience and expertise in conducting nondiscriminatory bilingual assessments (Espinosa & López, 2007). Together, the assessment team can identify measures that will be most appropriate for individual children and work together to identify approaches to assessment that will give children the best possible chance to demonstrate their knowledge and abilities.

- Assess children in English as well as their home language whenever possible (Peña & Halle, 2011). Even if children seem equally comfortable in both languages or if they seem to have a preferred language, children often have access to different vocabulary words across languages. For example, a child may have received most of their knowledge about feelings at home with their family in their native language, but most of their knowledge about letters at school in English. Assessing a child in only one language may not show the range of abilities and knowledge that the child holds across both languages.

- Use multiple methods to gather information about children. There are many different types of assessments, including reports from parents or families and teachers, observational measures, and direct assessments in which children are asked to demonstrate a skill. Assessments can be formal and informal. Using only one assessment to gather information about a child may not accurately reflect the child's abilities (Ackerman & Tazi, 2015). When possible, gather information from assessments in combination with information from family observations at home as well as teacher observations in the classroom.

- Pair your assessment information with your own notes from observations and interactions with children in the classroom. Although many assessments have been developed to assess specific skills, the information gained from assessments is not always the same as practical information gained from observation of a child in the classroom and during interactions with peers. Teacher notes can be a very effective way to learn about the needs that individual children have in order to support them in the classroom and improve classroom planning (Espinosa & López, 2007).

- Leverage the knowledge and expertise of your colleagues and fellow staff members. Ask them about what assessments they typically use and find helpful. What advice do they have that might help address your concerns? Learn about your school or center's processes for assessment as well as support available to conduct assessments and follow-up.

- Use the resources of mental health professionals at your school, in the early childhood program, or in the school district. School psychologists and social workers can provide valuable information about different assessment options and what may be most appropriate given the presenting concerns. Seek out time for a consultation and bring specific questions to explore with mental health professionals.

- Have a plan for how you will use information gained from assessments to help support children. Early childhood educators have a responsibility to effectively and appropriately use the insights gleaned from the assessment process. This may involve classroom accommodations, implementing specific recommendations, or applying educational interventions. It is important that throughout the process, family members are informed and involved in key decision making.

STRATEGY 43: Involve Families in Decisions Related to Assessments

As we have emphasized throughout this book, building positive relationships with families and working together to support their child is an essential part of providing children with support. Promoting family engagement early on can help you to establish a relationship with families and a process for communication that can play an important role throughout the year when both successes and challenges arise with children in the classroom. Involving families in the assessment process helps ensure that you maintain open communication about a potentially challenging area where sharing information across the school and home contexts may be especially critical for children.

> *Building positive relationships with families and working together to support their child is an essential part of providing children with support.*

Apply Strategy 43

- When you suspect a child might be experiencing a delay or have concerns about a child's behavior, set up a time to talk with the family about the issue. You may want to set up a time to meet before, after, or during the school day at a time that is convenient for everyone. Whether a delay is present or not, it is better to discuss potential issues earlier rather than later. Conversations with parents may shed light on circumstances or background information that families have insight into that may provide context for your concerns. Family members may also suggest successful strategies employed at home that could be tried and applied in the classroom.

- Make sure the family has the supports in place that they need to understand the information you are sharing with them. The feelings that come along with discussing possible delays or difficulties that children might be experiencing at school can be heightened if parents are struggling to understand the information you are sharing and the implications. This might mean involving an interpreter or providing written information in their home language. Identify whether in-person meetings, phone calls, or written communication is most helpful when communicating with a family and ensure that parents have the opportunity to ask questions and speak with specialists, when appropriate.

- Apply a culturally responsive lens as you consider how families might feel discussing concerns you have about their child. Different cultures view emotional and behavioral challenges as well as special needs in very different ways. Families may feel relieved and thankful to receive additional support for challenges they are also observing at home—or ashamed and embarrassed about potential issues that could be considered shameful. Communicate honestly with families, keeping their feelings and perspective in mind, and provide them with opportunities to ask questions.

- Give families time and space during and after a challenging conversation. Realize that news about a child's delay might be a trigger for a family member and lead to angry words or outbursts. Stay calm during the conversation and be forgiving of immediate responses if they seem strong or uncalled for. After providing some time, ask families if they would like to talk again.

- Make a plan with families to have regular communication before, during, and after the assessment process, whether a delay has been identified or not. Even if a child is not deemed as needing additional services, there was likely a reason for conducting an assessment and a child may still need additional support across school and home, which can be best facilitated when educators and parents work together.

STRATEGY 44: Understand Mandated Reporting Laws and Regulations

Teachers are part of a special group of professionals known as mandated reporters. Being a mandated reporter means that you are legally required to make a report to the proper authorities (e.g., Child Protective Services, Department of Human Services) if you suspect child abuse or neglect. Knowing the federal and state regulations dealing with being a mandated reporter is critical for early childhood educators, regardless of their role in the classroom (e.g., lead teacher, assistant teacher, paraprofessional), and most early childhood centers provide training on this information in addition to having their own protocols.

Apply Strategy 44

- Communicate openly with families about what it means to be a mandated reporter and the types of behaviors that lead to a report of abuse or neglect. Families may not understand what it means to be a mandated reporter or have misconceptions about the role. Make sure to share this information in a way that is sensitive and supportive to families, rather than threatening or intimidating. Some families may come from countries or cultures where certain disciplinary actions or punishments that are considered illegal in the United States are not only legal but a respected form of discipline. Share information with families about what is allowed in the United States and what is not, as well as what is recommended by research (e.g., spanking children may be legal, but it is not done at school because there is no research supporting its effectiveness). Sharing a handout at the beginning of the school year may be helpful for some families; however, doing so may raise alarm for other families, leading them to think that teachers and staff are scrutinizing the way they discipline their children. A handout may also be hard to understand for families with low literacy levels or developing English skills. Consider instead sharing this information with families in in-person settings, such as during orientation meetings. Be sure to include an opportunity for families to ask question confidentially with a staff member they know and trust.

- Talk with your colleagues and supervisors about the policy at your center for making a report of abuse or neglect. Be sure to know when you should make a call and who you should speak with at your center for support before and after that call, or if you are not sure, whether or not you should make a call.

- If you suspect child abuse or neglect but are not sure whether what you have observed is something you should report, ask someone you trust at your center or school for support. If you do share your concerns with a colleague or supervisor, realize that your role in the process is not over. It is important to follow up to find out if he or she made a call or what was determined and why. You can also call Child Protective Services or the Department of Human Services, explain what you observed, and ask for information.

- When you notice something of concern (e.g., unusual bruising) or hear children talk about something that is concerning to you, share this information with families. Families may have information that helps clarify a situation that is legally acceptable (e.g., when a child says that she gets frustrated when she gets hit over and over, she may be in an abusive situation or she may be receiving regular spankings in a way that is legally acceptable; a child may have a physical condition that leads to easy bruising or birthmarks that appear bruise-like).

- If you do have to make a call to report a concern, consider letting the family know and asking if they would like to be involved in the phone call. Although it may seem easier and safer to make a call anonymously, the intention of Child Protective Services is to maintain the well-being of children and families. Families can call themselves to receive support and advice, and, if they are comfortable doing so, calling with you may provide them with additional support and information that helps them to better support their child's growth and development.

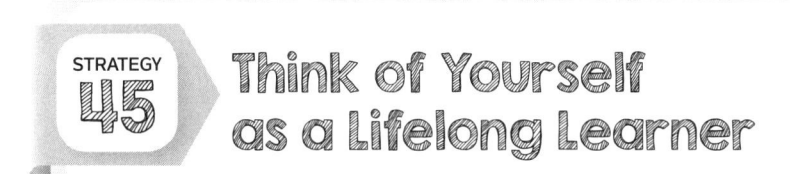

STRATEGY 45: Think of Yourself as a Lifelong Learner

In the way that you consider children to be learners of language, social and emotional skills, and academic skills, recognize and embrace yourself as a lifelong learner. The strategies and activities presented in this book are meant to expand your toolbox of best practices for supporting DLLs and their families. We hope that this book is one of many resources that you will use to expand your knowledge of culturally responsive practices and best practices for supporting DLLs as you continually grow and develop as an educator.

> *In the way that you consider children to be learners of language, social and emotional skills, and academic skills, recognize and embrace yourself as a lifelong learner.*

Apply Strategy 45

- Take time each day to reflect on your teaching practices related to supporting DLLs and families from diverse backgrounds. Ask yourself what is going well, and celebrate the successes you are having. In addition, ask yourself about what challenges you are having and what you would like to improve or learn more about.

- Seek out feedback from others. Share ideas with your colleagues for effectively supporting diverse learners and their families and ask them to share their ideas and strategies with you. When your colleagues share feedback, take time to reflect on it. Positive feedback often leaves people feeling proud and supported. Feedback that is negative may leave people feeling deflated and defensive. Reflect on all feedback that you receive and consider how you can use that feedback to improve your teaching practices by doing the things you do well more often, as well as by modifying approaches that are not effective.

- Seek out new information and additional resources to continue growing your professional knowledge and development. Each chapter in this book includes a list of additional resources, including books and web-based articles through which you can continue to expand your professional knowledge. Take time to read through these resources and identify those that can help you to expand your knowledge related to supporting DLLs and their families.

CHAPTER CONCLUSIONS

In this chapter, we highlight only a few of the professional considerations that might be helpful to you as you learn more about working with children and families from culturally and linguistically diverse backgrounds. Expanding your own multicultural knowledge as an individual and a staff member is an important part of professional growth. There are likely many resources at hand within your own classroom, program, or center, and using those resources as well as those that are available to you through professional development opportunities is another way to expand your toolbox. In addition, we encourage you to look for ways to bring a culturally responsive viewpoint to each of the different responsibilities that educators have when working with children and families throughout the day, including conducting assessments, complying with mandated reporting, and having challenging conversations.

Chapter 10: Check Your Learning

1. What is the definition of cultural awareness?
   a) The ability to determine when a child is from the nondominant or dominant cultural group
   b) Having awareness of the impact of your own culture and other cultures on your interactions and teaching practices
   c) Having knowledge associated with multicultural holidays
   d) All of the above

2. All members of the same cultural group share identical cultural values.
   a) True
   b) False

3. Which of the following is *not* a reason why an early childhood educator might use assessments?
   a) To promote learning and development for individual children
   b) To identify children with special needs
   c) To monitor trends in program effectiveness
   d) To gather evidence that could be used to kick a child out of a preschool program

4. Translating an assessment into another language ensures that the assessment is culturally responsive for that population.
   a) True
   b) False

5. Which of the following is *not* a best practice for using assessments with dual language learners (DLLs)?
   a) Assessing children in English as well as their home language
   b) Involving families in the assessment process
   c) Sharing only positive findings from assessments with families
   d) Using multiple methods of assessment to gather information (e.g., observations and direct assessments)

6. Only members of ethnic minority groups grow up having a culture.
   a) True
   b) False

7. In early childhood settings, which staff members are mandated reporters?
   a) Lead teacher
   b) Assistant teacher
   c) Paraprofessional
   d) All of the above

8. Which of the following is a risk associated with incorrectly providing a child who is a DLL with special education services?
   a) The child may be receiving the wrong services or support.
   b) The child's language needs would not be addressed.
   c) The school's resources would be misallocated.
   d) All of the above

9. Mandated reporters are required to make reports to Child Protective Services or the Department of Human Services anonymously without involving families in the decision to report or in the actual call itself.
   a) True
   b) False

10. Which of the following are methods used for assessing young children's abilities or needs?
    a) Reports from parents and teachers
    b) Direct assessments of children's abilities
    c) Classroom observations
    d) All of the above

For answers to this chapter quiz, please refer to the Answer Key on pages 187–188.

Chapter 10: Reflection Questions

1. What are some of the traditions and values that are important to you or your family?

    _____
    _____
    _____
    _____

2. What traditions from your family of origin do you still uphold as an adult or with your own family?

    _____
    _____
    _____
    _____

3. What new traditions do you uphold?

    _____
    _____
    _____
    _____

4. Which of your family's values were aligned with the dominant culture? Which were not?

    _____
    _____
    _____
    _____

(continued)

Chapter 10 Reflection Questions (continued)

5. Reflect on your own professional development. What courses or workshops have you participated in that specifically focused on supporting dual language learners (DLLs) and children from diverse families? What were the key messages you remember from these experiences?

   _____
   _____
   _____
   _____

6. After reading this book, what topics related to supporting DLLs and families from diverse backgrounds are you interested in learning more about? What is one thing you can do to learn more?

   _____
   _____
   _____
   _____

Chapter 10: Additional Resources

BOOKS:

Dual Language Development and Disorders: A Handbook on Bilingualism & Second Language Learning (2nd Edition)
Authors: Johanne Paradis, Fred Genesee, Martha B. Crago
Year: 2011
Publisher: Paul H. Brookes Publishing Co.

Young Dual Language Learners: A Guide for PreK-3 Leaders
Author: Karen N. Nemeth
Year: 2014
Publisher: Caslon Publishing

WEB-BASED RESOURCES:

¡Colorín Colorado! A bilingual site for educators and families of English language learners
WETA Public Broadcasting
Year: 2017
Web site: http://www.colorincolorado.org

Dual Language Learner Teacher Competencies (DLLTC) Report
Alliance for a Better Community
Authors: Antonia Lopez and Marlene Zepeda
Year: 2012
Web site: http://www.buildinitiative.org/Portals/0/Uploads/Documents/DualLanguageLearnerTeacherCompetenciesReport.pdf

Dual Language Learning: What Does It Take?
Head Start Dual Language Report
Authors: National Head Start Training and Technical Assistance Resource Center
Year: 2008
Web site: http://eclkc.ohs.acf.hhs.gov/hslc/tta-system/ehsnrc/docs/DLANA_final_2009%5B1%5D.pdf

Mandatory Reporters of Child Abuse and Neglect
U.S. Department of Health and Human Services Children's Bureau
Web site: https://www.childwelfare.gov/topics/systemwide/laws-policies/statutes/manda/

Preparing Teachers to Work With Culturally and Linguistically Diverse Children
Authors: Jerlean Daniels, Susan Friedman
Year: 2005
Web site: https://www.naeyc.org/files/yc/file/200511/DanielFriedmanBTJ1105.pdf

Program Preparedness Checklist Version 5: A Tool to Assist Head Start and Early Head Start Programs to Assess Their Systems and Services for Dual Language Learners and Their Families
The National Center on Cultural and Linguistic Responsiveness
Web site: http://eclkc.ohs.acf.hhs.gov/hslc/tta-system/cultural-linguistic/ProgramPreparedn.htm

(continued)

Chapter 10 Additional Resources *(continued)*

Responsiveness to ALL Children, Families, and Professionals: Integrating Cultural and Linguistic Diversity into Policy and Practice (Position Statement)
Author: Division for Early Childhood
Year: 2010
Web site: http://eclkc.ohs.acf.hhs.gov/hslc/tta-system/cultural-linguistic/Dual%20Language%20Learners/disabilities/inclusion/position-statement.pdf

PROFESSIONAL ORGANIZATIONS:

National Association for Bilingual Education
Web site: www.nabe.org

National Association for Multicultural Education
Web site: http://www.nameorg.org

National Association for School Psychologists
Web site: http://www.nasponline.org

National Association for the Education of Young Children (NAEYC)
Web site: www.naeyc.org

National Center for Cultural Competence
Web site: http://nccc.georgetown.edu

The National Clearinghouse for English Language Acquisition
Web site: http://www.ncela.us

National Head Start Association
Web site: https://www.nhsa.org

Glossary

attachment a child's relationship with his or her parent or caregiver

best practices for supporting dual language learners evidence-based techniques or methodologies used to promote the social and academic success of children who are dual language learners

bilingual learner an individual who speaks two languages equally well and fluently

classroom community a classroom environment in which all children feel supported in their learning, have equal access to social and academic opportunities, and feel appreciated for the individual and unique strengths as well as valued for their differences; see also *emotionally supportive classroom environment*

classroom management the strategies employed by educators to manage children's emotions and behaviors in the classroom as well as to help children develop skills to manage their own emotions and behaviors

cognates words that sound similar across different languages

cross-language transfer the process of transferring knowledge and skills learned in one language to another language

cultural awareness awareness of the impact one's own culture can have on interactions with others and with teaching practices, as well as an awareness of culture in general

cultural broker an individual who is able to help serve as a bridge between individuals or groups from different cultures

cultural responsiveness skills associated with supporting children and families from diverse linguistic and cultural backgrounds

developmentally appropriate strategies educational techniques that reflect knowledge and understanding of child development as well as the needs and abilities of individual children

discourse how sentences are put together in a language to create stories and dialogues

dual language learner (DLL) an individual who is learning more than one language at the same time

earned attachment the attachment relationship that children form with others outside of their immediate family; see also *secondary attachment*

emotionally supportive classroom environment a classroom environment in which all children feel supported in their learning, have equal access to social and academic opportunities, and feel appreciated for their individual and unique strengths as well as valued for their differences; see also *classroom community*

emotion regulation the ability to manage emotions effectively, including being able to shift from one emotion to another or to maintain an emotion

English language learner an individual who is learning English for the purpose of his or her education—most often an individual who speaks another language at home

external regulation the process through which adults regulate children's emotions and behaviors

family engagement an ongoing, reciprocal, strengths-based partnership between families and their children's early childhood education programs

family surveys questionnaires that are administered to parents and other caregivers for various purposes (e.g., to learn more about the home environment, the child's background, parents' needs)

grammar how words are put together to make sentences in a language

growth mindset the belief that abilities can be fostered and developed, as opposed to the belief that certain qualities are "fixed" and cannot be changed

internal regulation the ability to manage ones own emotions and behaviors

mandated reporters the group of professionals, including educators, who are legally obligated to report suspected or observed abuse or neglect of children

modeling a form of teaching that involves intentionally demonstrating specific actions, words, or behaviors the teacher would like to encourage others to emulate

monolingual a child who speaks one language or is learning to speak only one language

mutual accommodation a process through which educators determine when to accommodate a child or family versus when the child or family is expected to accommodate the needs of a classroom or school

narration an educational technique that involves the teacher describing aloud what he or she sees or what is happening

nonverbal cues communication that does not involve spoken words (e.g., gestures, facial expressions, body language)

phonology the sounds of a language

pragmatics the rules related to how people use language and have conversations

prosocial behaviors actions and behaviors that are intended to benefit others (e.g., helping, cooperating, taking turns)

quiet corner also called a "calm corner," a designated area in the classroom where children can seek out quieter activities, calm down, and gather their thoughts when they experience intense emotions, or seek one-on-one time with another child or teacher

secondary attachment the attachment relationship that children form with others outside of their immediate family; see also *earned attachment*

secure attachment   a relationship between a child and a parent or caregiver that is characterized by warmth, sensitivity, and responsiveness as well as clear guidance and boundaries

self-regulation   skills needed to regulate one's own thoughts, behaviors, and emotions, including the ability to pay attention, ignore distractions, remember and follow through with instructions, and control impulses

sequential language development   the process by which a child learns a second language after having learned a first language

simultaneous language development   the process by which a child learns two (or more) languages at the same time

social and emotional skills   the skills children and adults need to recognize and manage their emotions, think about the feelings of others and develop empathy, get along with other children and adults, and make prosocial decisions

strengths-based approach   an approach that focuses on abilities and capabilities and tapping into an individual or group's competencies, rather than focusing on deficits

think-pair-share   a learning strategy that involves having children turn to a partner and share the answer to a question or work with another child to discuss a topic or solve a problem

tourist approach   teaching children about a culture through limited exposure to celebrations or artifacts

vocabulary   the words included in a language

Quiz Answer Key

CHAPTER 2

1. b) False. Although "good teaching" and the use of developmentally appropriate practices in the classroom help support children who are DLLs, there are many different strategies and skills that educators need to support children from diverse backgrounds. These skills include strategies to support children's language development in English and their home language as well as cultural responsiveness.

2. Both a) and b) are true. In early childhood, children who are dual language learners tend to have a smaller vocabulary than their peers in each language that they speak, but a larger combined vocabulary across languages.

3. d) All of the above. Cultural responsiveness includes a) reflecting on your own personal beliefs and values and on how your home culture affects your teaching, b) expanding your knowledge of other cultures and the way culture may affect children's development and their family engagement in school, and c) developing multicultural skills that help you consider your own biases and support children and families in the way they want and need to be supported.

4. a) and b) only. The terms *dual language learner* and *English language learner* both use a strengths-based approach to acknowledge that children are learning more than one language.

5. b) False. Although some dual language learners in the United States are born in other countries, many DLLs are born in the United States.

6. c) Spanish is the next most common primary home language (following English) in the United States.

7. d) A child who has difficulty putting words together in the correct order is still learning grammar—how words are put together in sentences.

8. a) The percentage of children in Hispanic families living in poverty (32.3%) is higher than the national average of children living in poverty (21.6%).

9. d) All of the above. Research shows that children who are bilingual are likely to have increased self-regulation, greater empathy toward others, increased openness to other cultures, and high levels of social competence.

10. b) False. Best practices for supporting dual language learners include supporting children's language development in English as well as their home language and incorporating their home language whenever possible at school.

CHAPTER 3

1. c) An appreciation for diversity.

2. a), b), c), and d). There are many different ways that educators can get to know children and families before the school year begins, including conducting a home visit, sending family surveys home, engaging community organizations or cultural brokers, and offering opportunities to visit the classroom.

3. b) False. The Curricular Subscales Extension to the Early Childhood Environment Rating Scale (ECERS-E) includes a set of diversity-related questions that emphasize awareness related to gender and race in the classroom.

4. c) Labeling objects in the classroom with home languages of children in your class not only encourages literacy, it also communicates to children and families that their home language is valued. Supporting children's home language is a best practice for supporting DLLs.

5. d): a) and c) only. The quiet or calm corner can be used to benefit dual language learners by providing children with a space to calm down and gather their thoughts when they experience intense emotions; it can also serve as a place where children can seek one-on-one time with a teacher.

6. Considering children's energy level and access to materials when creating a classroom schedule and routine helps ensure smooth classroom functioning. Choosing activities that meet children's energy level throughout the day can support their ability to engage in each activity. Making sure children have access to materials when and where they need them allows children to develop self-help skills and may be especially important for DLLs who do not have the vocabulary to ask for what they need early in the school year.

7. a) True. At the beginning of the school year, children may not have developed the ability and attention span to focus on group activities for long periods of time. Keeping group lessons short and gradually increasing their duration each week helps children to practice these important skills.

8. b) Building relationships with families and getting to know children individually is foundational to creating an effective learning environment for all children, including DLLs.

9. b) False. At the beginning of the year, it is better to make sure materials that children need are easily accessible to them so that they can find the materials themselves or easily indicate to a teacher what they need as they develop their classroom vocabulary. In addition, teachers may need to give many children extra support at the beginning of the school year, so finding ways for children to be self-sufficient makes it easier for a teacher to provide support to children who need it most.

10. d) At the beginning of the year, planning more small-group activities rather than large-group activities may help teachers get to know children better and allow opportunities to provide individualized support.

CHAPTER 4

1. c) An estimated 60%–65% of children have a secure attachment relationship with a parent/caregiver.

2. d) All of the above. There are many different adults with whom children can develop a secure attachment relationship, including parents, teachers, and grandparents. These secondary attachments or earned attachments with caregivers and teachers can protect children from the negative effects of having an insecure attachment relationship at home.

3. c) Enter a temporary nonverbal period. It is not uncommon for children who are dual language learners to spend time listening and observing when introduced to a new environment.

4. c) Studies have shown that for dual language learners, high-quality relationships with teachers also relate to stronger English language abilities.

5. a), b), c), and d). Children who are dual language learners most often use nonverbal cues to ask for attention, make a request, protest or show they do not want something, or make jokes.

6. b) Children's behaviors are often preceded by emotions. Identifying the emotion that is motivating a behavior and helping a child to manage that emotion is important to modifying children's behavioral responses.

7. b) False. Creating a supportive classroom community involves helping children to appreciate similarities as well as differences between themselves and their classmates.

8. d) All of the above. Each of these statements models language that communicates to children that diversity within their classroom is a strength.

9. b) False. Talking with children about differences between classmates in a supportive way can help a child learn to view differences between others and differences between themselves and classmates as normal. With support, children can learn to talk about differences as well as similarities and view both their differences and similarities as part of what makes them special.

10. a) True. Incorporating children's home language into activities is considered to be a best practice for supporting DLLs.

CHAPTER 5

1. b) False. Children who are bilingual tend to score higher than their monolingual peers on self-regulation assessments.

2. d) All of the above. Each of these scenarios is an example of external regulation, the process by which adults help regulate children's emotions and behaviors.

3. c) Using the word *no* might be an effective way to stop children from engaging in a behavior; but if it is not followed by additional support, saying *no* does not help children learn what to do instead.

4. b) False. Giving children a 5-minute warning can actually support the development of self-regulation by giving them time to prepare for the transition.

5. a), b), c), and d). There are many ways educators can help children to prepare for transitions before they happen as well as guide children through transitions.

6. d): a) and b) only. If educators use only one classroom management strategy to support all children in their classroom, they may find that some classroom management strategies may not be culturally responsive and thus may have the opposite effect on some children. In addition, children respond differently to different strategies, so it is helpful to try a range of classroom management strategies (instead of using just one) to find those that work best for the children in your class.

7. b) False. Teachers should model positive behaviors that they want children to emulate throughout the day and also model and discuss their own unpleasant feelings. Sharing pleasant and unpleasant feelings with children and discussing how they are managing their feelings helps support children's social and emotional learning.

8. d) All of the above. Using language to describe what you are doing throughout the day, and why, supports development of vocabulary and language, self-regulation, and critical thinking.

9. b) False. The adults in a child's life are responsible for helping young children to be ready to learn. Teachers can provide external regulation to help regulate children's emotions and energy levels throughout the day to engage children and help prepare them for what is coming next. Supporting children in this way lays a foundation for them to be able to self-regulate.

10. d) Effective classroom management techniques help children to develop self-regulation so that they can display positive behaviors out of a sense of personal responsibility rather than out of fear of punishment or in order to receive a reward.

CHAPTER 6

1. a) In the United States, monolingual Spanish-speaking children tend to have greater social and emotional struggles than their peers who are monolingual English speakers, DLLs, or bilingual.

2. a) A secure attachment relationship refers to a warm and responsive relationship between a child and an adult.

3. b) False. Although smiling and expressing a pleasant mood is an important way to express warmth to young children, forcing this expression when not genuinely having these feelings may not be as effective as you think. When teachers have unpleasant feelings, they can use this as a learning opportunity to talk with children about these feelings as well as what they are doing to regulate these feelings.

4. d) All of the above. Using books and visual images of characters feeling different emotions, expressing emotions in your own facial expressions and vocal tones, and incorporating emotion words from children's home languages are best practices that can support social and emotional development for children who are DLLs.

5. c) Encouraging children to make up their own rules is not an effective strategy for promoting social and emotional skills in young children.

6. c) The following statement communicates to children that social and emotional skills need to be practiced and learned: "Lots of us seem to be yelling today when we get angry. Let's practice taking deep breaths together."

7. b) False. There are many ways to support children's social and emotional development. Some are more effective than others, and this may be dependent on the time, place, and cultural context. Many early childhood education programs use a social and emotional curriculum or shared approach to support children's social and emotional development. It is important to share this approach with families to help expand their personal strategies for supporting children's social and emotional development. It is also important to value a family's choice to use or not use these strategies based on their own family's values and beliefs.

8. a) When a child is having a temper tantrum, it may not be a good time to try and teach him or her a new approach for calming down, because children have trouble hearing, focusing, and learning when their stress system is activated.

9. a) True. Teachers who incorporate children's home languages into learning activities have closer relationships with children who are DLLs than teachers who do not.

10. b) False. Everyone makes mistakes, and apologizing to a child is one way to communicate that message. Showing children how to make a genuine apology when you make a mistake can help them learn to do so during interactions with their peers and with other adults.

CHAPTER 7

1. b) Cross-language transfer is the ability to transfer skills learned in one language to another.

2. b) Compared with their English-speaking peers, children who are dual language learners are less likely to score at or above basic levels in reading on fourth and eighth grade standardized tests.

3. b) True. Sending books home for parents to read in their child's home language that were read at school in English can enhance children's English vocabulary.

4. d) Families of dual language learners not being interested in research is *not* one of the challenges associated with research that examines academic outcomes for DLLs.

5. a), b), c), and d). Prereading a book allows an educator to prepare props and extension activities to accompany the book, determine whether the language demands of a book are appropriate for children in the class, identify whether the book will be relevant and meaningful to the class, and translate key words into Spanish or other languages represented in the class.

6. b) False. Children can benefit from multiple readings of the same book. Most children love repetition and enjoy reading books more than once. Each reading of a book can help children to learn and solidify new vocabulary as well as their understanding of the story and content. Teachers can use each reading to ask different types of questions and introduce extension activities.

7. a), b), c), and d). Each of the questions encourages children to think about math concepts, including measurement, counting, and math vocabulary.

8. b) False. Young children are capable of learning more than one language in oral and print form.

9. a) A hypothesis is an idea that can be tested.

10. b) False. Translating instructions for an activity into another language after providing an explanation in English is important to help ensure that children who are dual language learners understand the content of the activity and that they can benefit from the activity along with their peers. Providing a translation is not enough, however. Incorporating words from a child's home language and pairing individual words and phrases with English can help a child to connect the two languages and support the home language vocabulary development as well as English development.

CHAPTER 8

1. b) Social competence. A study found that English-speaking and Spanish-speaking children who were randomly assigned to a creative dance class were rated higher by parents and teachers in social competence than their peers who were in a control group.

2. a) True. Music can be used to build cultural awareness and cultural competence in your classroom for both children and yourself. Playing a range of musical types and styles provides children with another lens through which to view different cultures.

3. c) Research suggests that in the early childhood classroom, music and movement can enhance children's engagement in learning activities.

4. b) False. Having something to do during a transition time, such as singing a song, can help children to regulate their behaviors during a challenging time in the classroom.

5. d) Results from a comparison study found that children who had taken community music classes had higher self-regulation than children who had not taken music classes.

6. b) Children who had taken community music classes were able to wait longer than children who had not taken community music classes, likely because they had strategies to keep themselves occupied, such as singing songs.

7. c) Teaching children about a culture through limited exposure to celebrations or artifacts is commonly referred to as the tourist approach.

8. b) False. Whether or not you speak a language, playing songs that include different languages for the children in your class can help them to develop an appreciation for different musical styles as well as phonemic awareness of the sounds associated with other languages.

9. d) Phonemic awareness is the ability to hear and make the different sounds in a language.

10. a) True. Introducing a wide range of musical styles, musical instruments, and dances to children is a way to expand their knowledge and appreciation for other cultures.

CHAPTER 9

1. a) True. Families that are engaged in their child's education early on are more likely than those that are not engaged to remain engaged in their child's schooling.

2. b) When families are involved in school, children are more likely to have positive feelings about their teacher and about school.

3. d) All of the above. Family engagement has been identified as a potential pathway to narrowing achievement gaps. In early childhood, it lays the foundation for family engagement throughout a child's schooling and it relates to more positive attitudes about school for children.

4. a) True. Lower rates of high school dropout have been identified as a long-term effect of parent engagement.

5. c) Family engagement occurs when there is an ongoing, reciprocal, strengths-based partnership between families and their children's early childhood program.

6. b) A parent taking on an extra job to pay for a child's school supplies is considered to be family involvement, but it does not meet the definition of engagement. Family engagement requires involvement to be ongoing, reciprocal, and strengths-based.

7. d) All of the above. The teacher–child relationship has been found to predict positive relationships with peers, engagement in learning, and future academic achievement.

8. b) False. Families who do not attend parent–teacher conferences may be just as interested in their child's well-being as families who do attend parent–teacher conferences. There are many barriers that might affect a family's ability to participate in engagement opportunities such as parent–teacher conferences, including work schedule, transportation, child care issues, and others.

9. d) All of the above. In order to effectively promote family engagement for diverse families, it is helpful to share your own and your program's expectations, ask parents how they would like to be engaged, and offer many different types of engagement opportunities throughout the year.

10. b) False. Although it may be helpful to families to have a translator, it should not be their sole responsibility to hire a translator when needed. When possible, schools should help provide translation for families to help reduce the barriers families experience in securing education for their child and participating in engagement opportunities.

CHAPTER 10

1. b) Cultural awareness is defined as having awareness of the impact of your own culture and other cultures on your interactions and teaching practices.

2. b) False. All members of the same cultural group are likely to share many of the same cultural values, but even within the same cultural group, there can be diversity in values.

3. d) There are many reasons early childhood educators might use assessments. Gathering evidence that could be used to kick a child out of a preschool program should not be one of them.

4. b) False. Translating an assessment into another language does not ensure that the assessment is culturally responsive for that population. There are many considerations in addition to language that might affect whether an assessment is culturally responsive.

5. c) Only sharing positive findings from assessments with families is not one of the best practices for using assessments with dual language learners. When assessments are conducted, families should be involved in the decision to conduct an assessment and informed of the results, especially those that may affect decisions made about their child in relation to support services needed, whether the findings are considered to be positive or negative.

6. b) False. Everyone has a home culture, whether they come from a nondominant or dominant group.

7. d) All of the above. Lead teachers, assistant teachers, and paraprofessionals are all mandated reporters (as are administrators and any other staff working in early learning settings).

8. d) All of the above. Inappropriately providing a child who is a dual language learner with special education services may lead to the child receiving the wrong services or support, the child's language needs not being addressed, and the school's resources being misallocated, giving one child special services who does not need them and possibly denying services to a child who does.

9. b) False. Mandated reporters often choose to make reports anonymously because it can feel uncomfortable to share with a family that a report is being made. Mandated reporters can also consider discussing their concerns with families and encouraging families to make a call to Child Protective Services/Department of Human Services themselves or to be involved in the mandated reporter's call.

10. d) All of the above. Reports from parents and teachers, direct assessments of children's abilities, and classroom observations are all methods that can be used to assess young children's abilities or needs.

Multicultural Library List

Anansi the Spider: A Tale from the Ashanti by Gerald McDermott

Bee-Bim Bop! by Linda Sue Park, illustrated by Ho Baek Lee

Bringing the Rain to Kapiti Plain by Verma Aardema

The Desert Is My Mother/El desierto es mi madre by Pat Mora, illustrated by Daniel Lechon

Dumpling Soup by Jama Kim Rattigan, illustrated by Lillian Hsu

Golden Domes and Silver Lanterns by Hena Khan, illustrated by Mehrdokht Amini

Grandmother's Nursery Rhymes/Las Nanas de Abuelita by Nelly Palacio Jaramillo, illustrated by Elivia

Hairs/Pelitos by Sandra Cisneros, illustrated by Terry Ybáñez

How My Parents Learned to Eat by Ina R. Friedman, illustrated by Allen Say

Margaret and Margarita/Margarita y Margaret by Lynn Reiser

One Afternoon by Yumi Heo

Red Is a Dragon by Roseanne Thong

Somewhere in the World Right Now by Stacey Schuett

Thanking the Moon: Celebrating the Mid-Autumn Moon Festival by Grace Lin

The Tortilla Factory by Gary Paulsen, illustrated by Ruth Wright Paulsen

Two of Everything by Lily Toy Hong

We All Sing with the Same Voice by J. Philip Miller

What a Wonderful World by George David Weiss and Bob Thiele, illustrated by Ashley Bryan

What We Wear: Dressing Up Around the World by Maya Ajmera, Elise Hofer Derstine, and Cynthia Pon

Whoever You Are by Mem Fox, illustrated by Leslie Staub

Whose Toes are Those? by Jabari Asim, illustrated by LeUyen Pham

Yoko Writes Her Name by Rosemary Wells

References

Ackerman, D.J., & Tazi, Z. (2015). *Enhancing young Hispanic dual language learners' achievement: Exploring strategies and addressing challenges.* (Policy Information Report, ETS Research Report No. RR-15–01). Princeton, NJ: Educational Testing Service.

Arnold, D.H., Kupersmidt, J.B., Voegler-Lee, M.E., & Marshall, N.A. (2012). The association between preschool children's social functioning and their emergent academic skills. *Early Childhood Research Quarterly, 27*(3), 376–386.

August, D., Carlo, M., Dressler, C., & Snow, C. (2005). The critical role of vocabulary development for English language learners. *Learning Disabilities Research and Practice, 20*(1), 50–57.

Baker, A.C., & Manfredi-Petitt, L.A. (2004). *Relationships, the heart of quality care: Creating community among adults in early care settings.* Washington, DC: The National Association for the Education of Young Children.

Bandura, A. (1995). Social learning. In A. S. R. Manstead & M. Hewstone (Eds.), *Blackwell encyclopedia of social psychology* (pp. 600–606). Oxford: Blackwell.

Barnard, W.M. (2004). Parent involvement in elementary school and educational attainment. *Children and Youth Services Review, 26*, 39–62.

Berk, L.E. (2012). *Infants and children: Prenatal through middle childhood—Explorations in child development.* London, UK: Pearson.

Bialystok, E. (2001). *Bilingualism in development: Language, literacy, and cognition.* Cambridge, UK: Cambridge University Press.

Bialystok, E., & Martin, M.M. (2004). Attention and inhibition in bilingual children: Evidence from the dimensional change card sort task. *Developmental Science, 7*(3), 325–339.

Bierman, K.L., & Erath, S.A. (2006). Promoting social competence in early childhood: Classroom curricula and social skills coaching programs. In K. McCartney & D. Phillips (Eds.), *Blackwell handbook of early childhood development* (pp. 595–615). Malden, MA: Blackwell.

Bowlby, J. (2008). *A secure base: Parent–child attachment and healthy human development.* New York, NY: Basic Books.

Bowlby, R. (2007). Babies and toddlers in non-parental daycare can avoid stress and anxiety if they develop a lasting secondary attachment bond with one carer who is consistently accessible to them. *Attachment and Human Development, 9*(4), 307–319.

Boyce, L.K., Gillam, S.L., Innocenti, M.S., Cook, G.A., & Ortiz, E. (2013). An examination of language input and vocabulary development of young Latino dual language learners living in poverty. *First Language, 33*(6), 572–593.

Brackett, M.A., Rivers, S.E., & Salovey, P. (2011). Emotional intelligence: Implications for personal, social, academic, and workplace success. *Social and Personality Psychology Compass, 5*(1), 88–103.

Brooks-Gunn, J., & Duncan, G.J. (1997). The effects of poverty on children. *The Future of Children, 7*, 55–71.

Burchinal, M., Field, S., López, M.L., Howes, C., & Pianta, R. (2012). Instruction in Spanish in pre-kindergarten classrooms and child outcomes for English language learners. *Early Childhood Research Quarterly, 27*(2), 188–197.

Castro, D.C., Páez, M.M., Dickinson, D.K., & Frede, E. (2011). Promoting language and literacy in young dual language learners: Research, practice, and policy. *Child Development Perspectives, 5*(1), 15–21.

Chang, F., Crawford, G., Early, D., Bryant, D., Howes, C., Burchinal, M., . . . Pianta, R. (2007). Spanish-speaking children's social and language development in pre-kindergarten classrooms. *Early Education and Development, 18*(2), 243–269.

Chen, S.H., Zhou, Q., Uchikoshi, Y., & Bunge, S.A. (2014). Variations on the bilingual advantage? Links of Chinese and English proficiency to Chinese American children's self-regulation. *Frontiers in Psychology, 5*, 1–11.

Chesterfield, K.B., Chesterfield, R.A., & Chavez, R. (1982). Peer interaction, language proficiency, and language preference in bilingual preschool classrooms. *Hispanic Journal of Behavioral Sciences, 4*(4), 467–486.

Child Trends. (2014). *Child Trends data bank: Dual language learners.* Retrieved from https://www.childtrends.org/?indicators=dual-language-learners

Christenson, S.L., & Havsy, L.H. (2004). Family-school-peer relationships: Significance for social, emotional, and academic learning. In J.E. Zins, R.P. Weissberg, M.C. Wang, & H.J. Walberg (Eds.), *Building academic success on social and emotional learning: What does the research say?* (pp. 59–75). New York, NY: Teachers College Press.

Cole, M.W., Dunston, P., & Butler, T. (2017). Engaging English language learners through interactive read-alouds: A literature review. *English Teaching: Practice & Critique, 16*(1), 97–109.

Collins, M.F. (2005). ESL preschoolers' English vocabulary acquisition from storybook reading. *Reading Research Quarterly 40(4),* 406–408.

Commodari, E. (2013). Preschool teacher attachment, school readiness and risk of learning difficulties. *Early Childhood Research Quarterly, 28*(1), 123–133. doi: http://dx.doi.org/10.1016/j.ecresq.2012.03.004

De Feyter, J.J., & Winsler, A. (2009). The early developmental competencies and school readiness of low-income, immigrant children: Influences of generation, race/ethnicity, and national origins. *Early Childhood Research Quarterly, 24*(4), 411–431.

De Jong, E.J., & Harper, C.A. (2005). Preparing mainstream teachers for English-language learners: Is being a good teacher good enough? *Teacher Education Quarterly 32*(2), 101–124.

Dearing, E., Berry, D., & Zaslow, M. (2006). Poverty during early childhood. In K. McCartney & D. Phillips (Eds.), *Blackwell handbook of early childhood development* (pp. 399–423). Malden, MA: Blackwell.

Dearing, E., Kreider, H., & Weiss, H.B. (2008). Increased family involvement in school predicts improved child–teacher relationships and feelings about school for low-income children. *Marriage & Family Review, 43*(3–4), 226–254.

Dickinson, D.K., McCabe, A., Clark-Chiarelli, N., & Wolf, A. (2004). Cross-language transfer of phonological awareness in low-income Spanish and English bilingual preschool children. *Applied Psycholinguistics, 25*(3), 323–347.

Drake, K., Belsky, J., & Fearon, R. (2014). From early attachment to engagement with learning in school: The role of self-regulation and persistence. *Developmental Psychology, 50*(5), 1350–1361.

Durán, L.K., Roseth, C.J., & Hoffman, P. (2010). An experimental study comparing English-only and transitional bilingual education on Spanish-speaking preschoolers' early literacy development. *Early Childhood Research Quarterly, 25*(2), 207–217.

Durand, T.M. (2011). Latino parental involvement in kindergarten findings from the Early Childhood Longitudinal Study. *Hispanic Journal of Behavioral Sciences, 33*(4), 469–489.

Dweck, C. (2006). *Mindset: The new psychology of success.* New York, NY: Random House.

Espinosa, L., & López, M.L. (2007). Assessment considerations for young English language learners across different levels of accountability. *Report prepared for the National Early Childhood Accountability Task Force and First 5 LA.*

Fabes, R.A., Gaertner, B.M., & Popp, T.K. (2006). Getting along with others: Social competence in early childhood. In K. McCartney & D. Phillips (Eds.), *Blackwell handbook of early childhood development.* (pp. 297–316). Malden, MA: Blackwell.

Farver, J.A.M., Lonigan, C.J., & Eppe, S. (2009). Effective early literacy skill development for young Spanish-speaking English language learners: An experimental study of two methods. *Child Development, 80*(3), 703–719.

Fránquiz, M.E., Salazar, M.d.C., & DeNicolo, C.P. (2011). Challenging majoritarian tales: Portraits of bilingual teachers deconstructing deficit views of bilingual learners. *Bilingual Research Journal, 34*(3), 279–300.

Goldenberg, C., Hicks, J., & Lit, I. (2013). Dual language learners: Effective instruction in early childhood. *American Educator, 37*(2), 26–29.

Guerrero, A.D., Fuller, B., Chu, L., Kim, A., Franke, T., Bridges, M., & Kuo, A. (2013). Early growth of Mexican-American children: Lagging in preliteracy skills but not social development. *Maternal and Child Health Journal, 17*(9), 1701–1711.

Halgunseth, L., Jia, G., & Barbarin, O. (2013). Family engagement in early childhood programs: Serving families of dual language learners (DLLs). In F. Ong & J. McLean, *California's Best Practices for Young Dual Language Learners: Research Overview Papers.* Retrieved from http://www.cde.ca.gov/sp/cd/ce/documents/dllresearchpapers.pdf

Halgunseth, L., Peterson, A., Stark, D.R., & Moodie, S. (2009). *Family engagement, diverse families, and early childhood programs: An integrated review of the literature.* Washington, DC: National Association for the Education of Young Children.

Halle, T.G., Hair, E., Wandner, L., McNamara, M., & Chien, N. (2012). Predictors and outcomes of early versus later English language proficiency among English language learners. *Early Childhood Research Quarterly, 27*(1), 1–20.

Halle, T.G., Whittaker, J.V., Zepeda, M., Rothenberg, L., Anderson, R., Daneri, P., . . . Buysse, V. (2014). The social-emotional development of dual language learners: Looking back at existing research and moving forward with purpose. *Early Childhood Research Quarterly, 29*(4), 734–749.

Hammer, C.S., Hoff, E., Uchikoshi, Y., Gillanders, C., Castro, D.C., & Sandilos, L.E. (2014). The language and literacy development of young dual language learners: A critical review. *Early Childhood Research Quarterly, 29*(4), 715–733.

Hammer, C.S., Jia, G., & Uchikoshi, Y. (2011). Language and literacy development of dual language learners growing up in the United States: A call for research. *Child Development Perspectives, 5*(1), 4–9.

Han, H.S., & Thomas, M.S. (2010). No child misunderstood: Enhancing early childhood teachers' multicultural responsiveness to the social competence of diverse children. *Early Childhood Education Journal, 37*(6), 469–476.

Han, W.J. (2010). Bilingualism and socioemotional well-being. *Children and Youth Services Review, 32*(5), 720–731.

Harms, T., Clifford, R.M., & Cryer, D. (2014). *Early childhood environment rating scale* (rev. ed.). New York, NY: Teachers College Press.

Heath, P. (2009). *Parent-child relations: Context, research, and application* (2nd ed.). Upper Saddle River, NJ: Pearson.

Henderson, A.T., & Mapp, K.L. (2002). *A new wave of evidence: The impact of school, family, and community connections on student achievement.* Austin, TX: Southwest Educational Development Laboratory.

Hoff, E. (2006). How social contexts support and shape language development. *Developmental Review, 26*(1), 55–88.

Hoff, E., Core, C., Place, S., Rumiche, R., Señor, M., & Parra, M. (2012). Dual language exposure and early bilingual development. *Journal of Child Language, 39*(01), 1–27.

Howard, E.R., Lindholm-Leary, K.J., Sugarman, J., Christian, D., & Rogers, D. (2007). *Guiding principles for dual language education.* Washington, DC: Center for Applied Linguistics.

Howes, C. (2000). Social-emotional classroom climate in child care, child–teacher relationships and children's second grade peer relations. *Social Development, 9*(2), 191–204. doi: 10.1111/1467-9507.00119

Howes, C., Matheson, C.C., & Hamilton, C.E. (1994). Maternal, teacher, and child care history correlates of children's relationships with peers. *Child Development, 65*(1), 264–273.

Jeynes, W.H. (2005). A meta-analysis of the relation of parent involvement to urban elementary school student academic achievement. *Urban Education, 40,* 237–269.

Kratochwill, T.R., DeRoos, R., & Blair, S. (2015). *Classroom management: Teachers modules.* Retrieved from http://www.apa.org/education/k12/classroom-mgmt.aspx

Lee, L., & Lin, S.-C. (2015). The impact of music activities on foreign language, English learning for young children. *Journal of the European Teacher Education Network, 10,* 13–23.

Lobo, Y.B., & Winsler, A. (2006). The effects of a creative dance and movement program on the social competence of Head Start preschoolers. *Social Development, 15*(3), 501–519.

Magruder, E.S., Hayslip, W.W., Espinosa, L.M., & Matera, C. (2013). Many languages, one teacher: Supporting language and literacy development for preschool dual language learners. *Young Children, 68*(1), 8–12.

Mapp, K. (2002, March). *Having their say: Parents describe how and why they are involved in their children's education.* Paper presented at the Annual Meeting of the American Educational Research Association, New Orleans, LA.

Mashburn, A.J., Pianta, R.C., Hamre, B.K., Downer, J.T., Barbarin, O.A., Bryant, D., . . . Howes, C. (2008). Measures of classroom quality in prekindergarten and children's development of academic, language, and social skills. *Child Development, 79*(3), 732–749.

McAllister, G., & Irvine, J.J. (2002). The role of empathy in teaching culturally diverse students: A qualitative study of teachers' beliefs. *Journal of Teacher Education, 53*(5), 433–443.

McBride, A. (2008). Addressing achievement gaps: The language acquisition and educational achievement of English-language learners. *Policy Notes, 16*(2), 1–15.

McClelland, M.M., Ponitz, C.C., Messersmith, E., & Tominey, S.L. (2010). Self-regulation: The integration of cognition and emotion. In R. Lerner (Series Ed.) & W. Overton (Vol. Ed.), *Handbook of lifespan development* (pp. 509–555). Hoboken, NJ: Wiley and Sons.

McClelland, M.M., & Tominey, S.L. (2015). *Stop, think, act: Integrating self-regulation in the early childhood classroom.* New York, NY: Routledge.

McWayne, C., Hampton, V., Fantuzzo, J., Cohen, H.L., & Sekino, Y. (2004). A multivariate examination of parent involvement and the social and academic competencies of urban kindergarten children. *Psychology in the Schools, 41,* 363–377.

Minke, K., Sheridan, S.M., Kim, E.M., Ryoo, J.H., & Koziol, N. (2014). Congruence in parent–teacher relationships: The role of shared perceptions. *Elementary School Journal, 114,* 527–546.

Mitchell-Copeland, J., Denham, S.A., & DeMulder, E.K. (1997). Q-sort assessment of child–teacher attachment relationships and social competence in the preschool. *Early Education and Development, 8*(1), 27–39.

Morales, J., Calvo, A., & Bialystok, E. (2013). Working memory development in monolingual and bilingual children. *Journal of Experimental Child Psychology, 114*(2), 187–202.

National Association for the Education of Young Children. (1995). *Responding to linguistic and cultural diversity: Recommendations for effective early childhood education.* Retrieved from http://www.naeyc.org/files/naeyc/file/positions/PSDIV98.PDF

National Association for the Education of Young Children. (2009a). *Developmentally appropriate practice in early childhood programs serving children from birth through age 8. A position statement of the National Association for the Education of Young Children.* Retrieved from https://www.naeyc.org/files/naeyc/file/positions/PSDAP.pdf

National Association for the Education of Young Children. (2009b). *Where we stand on responding to cultural and linguistic diversity.* Retrieved from http://www.naeyc.org/files/naeyc/file/positions/diversity.pdf

National Association for the Education of Young Children. (2015). *NAEYC early childhood program standards and accreditation criteria and guidance for assessment.* Retrieved from http://www.naeyc.org/files/academy/file/AllCriteriaDocument.pdf

National Clearinghouse for English Language Acquisition. (2011). *Key demographics and practice recommendations for young English learners.* Retrieved from http://www.ncela.us/files/uploads/9/EarlyChildhoodShortReport.pdf

National Council of Teachers of English. (2008). *English language learners: A policy brief.* Retrieved from http://www.ncte.org/library/NCTEFiles/Resources/PolicyResearch/ELLResearchBrief.pdf

Nemeth, K.N. (2012). *Basics of supporting dual language learners: An introduction for educators of children from birth through age 8:* Washington, DC: National Association for the Education of Young Children.

Oades-Sese, G.V., & Li, Y. (2011). Attachment relationships as predictors of language skills for at-risk bilingual preschool children. *Psychology in the Schools, 48*(7), 707–722.

Office of English Language Acquisition. (2015). *Languages spoken by English language learners (ELs).* Retrieved from http://www.ncela.us/files/fast_facts/OELA_Fast_Facts_All_Languages_Update_508_11_5_15.pdf

Office of Head Start. (2008). *Dual language learning: What does it take? Head Start Dual Language Report.* Retrieved from http://www.buildinitiative.org/Portals/0/Uploads/Documents/Dual%20Language%20Learning%20-%20What%20Does%20It%20Take.pdf

Paquette, K.R., & Rieg, S.A. (2008). Using music to support the literacy development of young English language learners. *Early Childhood Education Journal, 36*(3), 227–232.

Patrikakou, E.N., Weissberg, R.P., Redding, S., & Walberg, H.J. (2005). School–family partnerships: Enhancing the academic, social, and emotional learning of children. In E.N. Patrikakou, R.P. Weissberg, S. Redding, & H.J. Walberg, (Eds.), *School–family partnerships for children's success* (pp. 1–17). New York, NY: Teachers College Press.

Peña, E.D., & Halle, T.G. (2011). Assessing preschool dual language learners: Traveling a multiforked road. *Child Development Perspectives, 5*(1), 28–32.

Roberts, J., Jurgens, J., & Burchinal, M. (2005). The role of home literacy practices in preschool children's language and emergent literacy skills. *Journal of Speech, Language, and Hearing Research, 48,* 345–359.

Roberts, T.A. (2008). Home storybook reading in primary or second language with preschool children: Evidence of equal effectiveness for second-language vocabulary acquisition. *Reading Research Quarterly, 43*(2), 103–130.

Rolstad, K., Mahoney, K., & Glass, G.V. (2005). The big picture: A meta-analysis of program effectiveness research on English language learners. *Educational Policy, 19*(4), 572–594.

Saft, E.W., & Pianta, R.C. (2001). Teachers' perceptions of their relationships with students: Effects of child age, gender, and ethnicity of teachers and children. *School Psychology Quarterly, 16*(2), 125.

Salovey & Mayer (1990). Emotional intelligence. *Imagination, Cognition, and Personality, 9,* 185–211. doi:0.2190/DUGG-P24E-52WK-6CDG

Souto-Manning, M., & Mitchell, C.H. (2010). The role of action research in fostering culturally-responsive practices in a preschool classroom. *Early Childhood Education Journal, 37*(4), 269–277.

Sylva, K., Siraj-Blatchford, I., & Taggart, B. (2003). *Assessing quality in the early years: Early childhood environment rating scale: Extension (ECERS-E), four curricular subscales.* London, United Kingdom: Trentham.

Tabors, P.O. (2008). *One child, two languages: A guide for early childhood educators of children learning English as a second language* (2nd ed.). Baltimore, MD: Paul H. Brookes Publishing Co.

Tabors, P.O., & Snow, C.E. (2001). Young bilingual children and early literacy development. *Handbook of Early Literacy Research, 1,* 159–178.

Tochon, F.V. (2009). The key to global understanding: World languages education—why schools need to adapt. *Review of Educational Research, 79*(2), 650–681.

Tominey, S.L., & McClelland, M.M. (2013). Factors impacting the effectiveness of a prekindergarten pilot behavioral self-regulation intervention. *NHSA Dialog, 16*(3), 21–44.

Turk-Browne, N.B., Scholl, B.J., & Chun, M.M. (2008). Babies and brains: Habituation in infant cognition and functional neuroimaging. *Frontiers in Human Neuroscience, 2,* 1–11.

U.S. Census Bureau. (2011). *Child poverty in the United States 2009 and 2010: Selected race groups and Hispanic origin. American Community Survey Briefs.* Retrieved from https://www.census.gov/prod/2011pubs/acsbr10-05.pdf

U.S. Department of Health and Human Services. (2015). Head Start program performance standards. Retrieved from https://eclkc.ohs.acf.hhs.gov/policy/45-cfr-chap-xiii

Wagner, R.K., Francis, D.J., & Morris, R.D. (2005). Identifying English language learners with learning disabilities: Key challenges and possible approaches. *Learning Disabilities Research and Practice, 20*, 6–15.

Wanless, S.B., McClelland, M.M., Tominey, S.L., & Acock, A. (2011). The influence of demographic risk factors on the development of behavioral regulation in prekindergarten and kindergarten. *Early Education and Development, 22*(3), 461–488.

Weinstein, C.S., Tomlinson-Clarke, S., & Curran, M. (2004). Toward a conception of culturally responsive classroom management. *Journal of Teacher Education, 55*(1), 25–38.

Weiss, H., Caspe, M., & Lopez, M.E. (2008). Family involvement promotes success for young children. In M.M. Cornish (Ed.), *Promising practices for partnering with families in the early years* (pp. 1–19). Charlotte, NC: Information Age.

Winsler, A., Ducenne, L., & Koury, A. (2011). Singing one's way to self-regulation: The role of early music and movement curricula and private speech. *Early Education and Development, 22*(2), 274–304.

Wisconsin Center for Education Research. (2014). *The early years: Dual language learners.* Retrieved from https://www.wida.us/resources/focus/WIDA_Focus_on_Early_Years.pdf

Wong, S.W., & Hughes, J.N. (2006). Ethnicity and language contributions to dimensions of parent involvement. *School Psychology Review, 35(4),* 645–662.

Zepeda, M.C., Castro, D.C., & Cronin, S. (2011). Preparing early childhood teachers to work with young dual language learners. *Child Development Perspectives, 5*(1), 10–14. doi: 10.1111/j.1750-8606.2010.00141.x

Zins, J.E., Bloodworth, M.R., Weissberg, R.P., & Walberg, H.J. (2004). The scientific base linking social and emotional learning to school success. In J.E. Zins, R.P. Weissberg, M.C. Wang, & H.J. Walberg (Eds.), *Building academic success on social and emotional learning: What does the research say?* (pp. 3–22). New York, NY: Teachers College Press.

Index

Abuse or neglect, *see* Mandated reporting laws and regulations
Academic skills, early, 105–107
    cross-language transfer of, 106
    drawing connections between activities and children's home language and culture and, 112–113
    embedding best practices into math and science activities for, 110–111
    embedding best practices into read-alouds for, 108–110
    engaging families in children's learning and, 113–114
    making learning activities accessible to diverse learners and, 107–108
Accommodation, mutual, 21
Activities, classroom
    Around the World With Our Classroom Community, 67
    Build Vocabulary and Language During Transitions, 84
    Calm Basket, 39
    Celebrating Our Classroom Community Through Art: Self-Portraits, 67–68
    Charting and Graphing, 117
    Family Pictures, 39–40
    Feelings Board, 95, 101
    Freeze Dancing, 138
    Learning About Diversity Through Literacy, 117
    Learning Letter Sounds Simon Says, 117–118
    Music Maps, 139
    Nature Basket, 118
    Nature Walk Scavenger Hunt, 118–119
    Number Stomp, 119
    Our Classroom Friend, 101
    Paper Plate Feeling Faces, 102
    Playground Model/Map, 84
    Reading Books with Repetition and Incorporating Home Languages, 119–120
    Roll the Dice, 85
    Rotating Sharing Day, 69
    Shape Hunt, 120
    Sing Songs in English, Spanish, and other Languages, 138–139
    Staff Show and Tell, 69–70
    Think-Pair-Share, 62, 68
    What's Missing?, 120
    What's Your Name?, 70
Around the World With Our Classroom Community activity, 67
Arts, creative, 112–113
Assessments
    conducting effective, 164–166
    involving families in decisions related to, 167–168
Attachment relationships, 56

Benefits of being a dual language learner, 1, 17–18
Best practices
    applied to classroom management, 76–77
    math and science activities, 110–111
    read-alouds, 108–110
    for supporting DLLs, 35–36
Biases and stereotypes, 63–64
Bilingual learners, 12
Block area, 112
Brainstorming, 163
Build Vocabulary and Language During Transitions activity, 84

Calm Basket activity, 39
Celebrating Our Classroom Community Through Art: Self-Portraits activity, 67–68
Census Bureau, U.S., 16
Challenges and needs of DLLs, anticipation of, 57–60
Charting and Graphing activity, 117
Classroom activities, *see* Activities, classroom
Classroom community, 53–55
    anticipating children's challenges and needs in the, 57–60
    creating a, 61–62
    framing diversity as a strength in the, 62–64
    setting the foundation for warm and trusting relationships in the, 55–57

Classroom management, 73–75
  applying best practices to, 76–77
  being a positive role model for behavior standards in, 79–80
  defined, 74
  keeping a sense of humor and being flexible in, 80–81
  narrating children's actions to promote self-regulation and language development in, 75–76
  planning and supporting transitions in, 78–79
Classroom, 27–28
  creating emotionally supportive, 89–92
  embedded best practices in, 35–36
  establishing a welcoming learning environment in, 30–33
  and getting to know the children in your class and their families, 29–30
  organized to support success, 33–34
  themes, 63
  using music in, *see* Music and movement
Cognates, 15
Communication with families, 21, 113–114, 149–150
  about mandated reporting laws and regulations, 168
Community, classroom, 53–55
  anticipating children's challenges and needs in the, 57–60
  creating a, 61–62
  framing diversity as a strength in the, 62–64
  setting the foundation for warm and trusting relationships in the, 55–57
Community bulletin boards, 31
Conference, parent-teacher, 151–153
Controlled chaos, 77
Cozy corner, 32
Creative arts, 112–113
Cross-language transfer, 106
Cultural awareness, 160–162
Cultural broker, 9, 30
Cultural responsiveness, 4, 10–11
  classroom management practices and, 77
  with families, 11
  getting comfortable with key terms and definitions and, 12–13
  implementing teaching practices that support, 20–22
Culture
  discussions and activities that help children explore their, 21
  drawing connections between activities and children's home language and, 112–113
  tourist approach to, 135
  using music and movement to learn about, 131–132

Department of Health and Human Services, U.S., 2
Developmentally appropriate strategies, 4
Discourse, 15
Diversity of dual language learners, 13–17
  classroom displays highlighting, 31
  framed as a strength, 62–64
  making learning activities accessible for, 107–108
Dramatic play, 94, 112
Dual language learners (DLLs)
  anticipating the challenges and needs of, 57–60
  benefits of being, 1, 17–18
  best practices for supporting, 35–36
  cultural responsiveness with, 4, 10–11
  defined, 1, 13
  demographics of, 14
  developmentally appropriate strategies for, 4
  diversity of, 13–17
  expanding one's knowledge of, 13–17
  families of, *see* Families
  getting to know, 29–30
  importance of supporting, 1–2
  as individuals, 56
  living in poverty, 16–17
  physiological needs of, 33–34
  recognizing and scaffolding the social and emotional needs of, 92–93
  social and emotional skills, *see* Social and emotional skills
  supporting the development of the home language and English in, 19–20, 56–57

Early childhood classroom, 1
Early childhood Environment Rating Scale-Revised Edition (ECERS-R), 28
Earned attachment, 56
Embedded best practices, 35–36, 108–110
Emotion cues, 92
Emotion regulation, 74, 90–91
  see also Social and emotional skills
Emotional intelligence theory, 60
Emotionally supportive classrooms, 89–92
Empathy and understanding in challenging conversation with families, 153–154
Engagement, family, *see* Families
English language learners, 12
External regulation, 74

Families, 145–146
  asked for feedback, 154–155
  communication with, 21, 113–114, 149–150
  cultural diversity and poverty, 16–17
  cultural responsiveness with, 11

from diverse backgrounds, engaging, 147–148
empathy and understanding in approaching challenging conversations with, 153–154
engaged in children's learning, 113–114
expanding one's knowledge of, 13–17
family engagement and, 146
getting to know, 29–30
helping children prepare for transition to school, 148–149
invited to shared music with the classroom, 132–133
involved in children's social and emotional learning, 96–97
involved in decisions related to assessments, 167–168
meeting with, 30
provided with ways to be engaged in school, 150–153
sharing classroom music with, 133–134
surveys of, 29
Family Pictures activity, 39–40
Family surveys, 29
Feedback, asking families for, 154–155
Feeling words, 94, 96–97, 104
Feelings board, 95, 101
Flexibility, 80–81
Four Curricular Subscales Extension to the Early Childhood Environment Rating Scale (ECERS-E), 28
Freeze Dancing activity, 138

Golden Rule, 20
Grammar, 15
Group meetings with families, 151
Growth mindset in teaching social and emotional skills, 97–98

Head Start, 1, 14, 28
Home language
drawing connections between activities and, 112–113
supporting development of, 19–20, 56–57
supporting social and emotional development in English and, 95–96
Humor, sense of, 80–81

Internal regulation, 74

Labeling of classroom objects, 32, 77
Language diversity, 14
Language learning diversity, 14–16
Learning About Diversity Through Literacy activity, 117

Learning Letter Sounds Simon Says activity, 117–118
Libraries, 113
Listening center, 113

Management, classroom, 73–75
applying best practices to, 76–77
being a positive role model for behavior standards in, 79–80
defined, 74
keeping a sense of humor and being flexible in, 80–81
narrating children's actions to promote self-regulation and language development in, 75–76
planning and supporting transitions in, 78–79
Mandated reporting laws and regulations, 168–169
Math and science activities, embedding best practices into, 110–111
Modeling, 64, 79–80
Monolingual children, 12
Multicultural images, displays of, 31, 63
Music and movement, 31, 113, 129–131
activities, 138–139
building children's vocabulary and early literacy skills through, 134–135
children's songs in English and Spanish, 142–143
inviting children and families to share, 132–133
learning about culture through, 131–132
shared with families, 133–134
vocabulary, 141
Music Maps activity, 139
Mutual accommodation, 21

Narration, 75–76
National Association for the Education of Young Children (NAEYC), 28, 88, 146, 164
National Head Start Association (NHSA), 88
Nature Basket activity, 118
Nature Walk Scavenger Hunt activity, 118–119
Nonverbal cues, 57
Number Stomp activity, 119

Organizing of classrooms to support success, 33–34
Our Classroom Friend activity, 101

Paper Plate Feeling Faces activity, 102
Parent-teacher conferences, 151–153
Parents, *see* Families

Partner opportunities, 62, 95–96
Phonology, 15
Physiological needs of children, 33–34
Playground Model/Map activity, 84
Poverty, 16–17
Pragmatics, 15
Professional development, 10, 159–160
   developing cultural awareness and self-reflective practices, 160–162
   expanding one's multicultural knowledge, 162–163
   on involving families in decisions related to assessment, 167–168
   learning how to effectively conduct assessments in, 164–166
   participating in, 163–164
   and teachers as lifelong learners, 169–170
   on understanding mandated reporting laws and regulations, 168–169
Prosocial behaviors, 62, 94–95

Quiet corner, 32

Read-alouds, 94, 108–110
Reading Books with Repetition and Incorporating Home Languages activity, 119–120
Recognizing and scaffolding the social and emotional needs of DLLs, 92–93
Regulation
   emotion, 74
   external, 74
   internal, 74
   self, 74–75
   sharing strategies for, 90
Roll the Dice activity, 85
Rotating Sharing Day activity, 69

Secondary attachment, 56
Secure attachment, 56
Self-esteem, 63
Self-reflective practices, 160–162
Self-regulation, 74–75
   narrating children's actions to promote, 75–76
Sensory table, 112
Sequential language development, 16
Shape Hunt activity, 120
Sign language, 77
Simultaneous language development, 16
Sing Songs in English, Spanish, and other Languages activity, 138–139

Social and emotional skills, 87–89
   creating an emotionally supportive classroom for, 89–92
   involving families in children's learning of, 96–97
   recognizing and scaffolding children's social and emotional needs and, 92–93
   supporting the development of, in English and in each child's home language, 95–96
   teaching, 93–95
   using a growth mindset in teaching, 97–98
Staff Show and Tell activity, 69–70
Stereotypes and biases, 63–64
Strategies, list of, 4–6
Strengths-based approach, 18
Surveys, family, 29

Teachers
   approaching challenging conversations with empathy and understanding, 153–154
   bilingual, 2–3
   communication with families, 21, 113–114, 149–150
   as cultural brokers, 9
   developing cultural awareness and adopting self-reflective practices, 160–162
   expanding their multicultural knowledge, 162–163
   keeping a sense of humor and being flexible, 80–81
   learning how to effectively conduct assessments, 164–166
   as lifelong learners, 169–170
   modeling a positive perspective toward diversity, 64
   monolingual English, with few tools and strategies for effectively teaching DLLs, 2
   monolingual English, with many tools and strategies for effectively teaching DLLs, 3
   own toolbox of emotion regulation strategies, 91
   as positive role models for behavior standards, 79–80
   seeking out professional development opportunities, 10, 159–160
   understanding mandated reporting laws and regulations, 168–169
   warm and trusting relationships with students, 55–57
Technology, 113
Think-Pair-Share activity, 62, 68

Tourist approach, 135
Transitions, 78–79, 93

Visual classroom schedule, 32
Visual supports, 32, 34, 77
   for read-alouds, 109–110
Vocabulary, 15
   built through music, 134–135
   feeling words, 94, 96–97, 104
   made accessible for diverse learners, 107–108
   music, 141
   read-alouds and, 110
   sending home lists and translations of, 29–30
   word list, Spanish-English, 123–125

Warm and trusting relationships, setting the foundation for, 55–57
Welcoming learning environment, 30–33
What's Missing? activity, 120
What's Your Name? activity, 70
Workshops, family, 151–152